Left, Left, Left

LEFT, LEFT, LEFT

A personal account
of six protest campaigns
1945-1965

by Peggy Duff

SPOKESMAN
Nottingham

First published in 1971
This edition published in 2019 by agreement
Spokesman Books
5 Churchill Park
Nottingham
NG4 2HF
England

Phone 0115 9708318
www.spokesmanbooks.com

A catalogue record is available from the British Library.

ISBN 978 0 85124 8813

Printed in the European Union

Front cover photo by courtesy of Euan Duff

Since it seems customary to dedicate a book
to one's nearest and dearest, this book is for

my children, Kathleen, Susan and Euan – for all the
neglect they suffered because of the campaigns;

all the chairmen and presidents, Sir Richard Acland, the late
Sir Victor Gollancz, Michael Foot, fifteen mayors of
St Pancras and Camden, Lord Gardiner, Arthur Goss, the
late Lord Russell, Canon John Collins and Olive Gibbs;

all the people who worked with me in those beastly,
bustling slum offices;

all the committees I suffered and shoved around;

the anarchists who always shouted 'Stuff Duff';

but most of all for the Aldermaston Marchers, whom I
loved – I wonder where they're gone?

Preface

This is not an autobiography.

It is a story of six campaigns for which I worked between 1945 and 1965 – small party politics (Common Wealth), hunger and famine (Save Europe Now), the Left in the Labour Party (*Tribune* and the Bevanites), the Left in local politics (St Pancras and Camden), penal reform (The National Campaign for the Abolition of Capital Punishment) and, last but not least, CND.

Inevitably it covers much of the history of what is loosely called the Left, from 1945, when many people thought the British revolution had begun, to 1965, when they began to realize it had not even started.

I write of these campaigns as I saw them and as I see them now in retrospect, as honestly as I can. In doing so I shall probably irritate many of those with whom I have worked. I find it difficult to write either about the Left in the Labour Party or about the Campaign for Nuclear Disarmament, except in the past tense. This is not to deny that both still exist but few would fail to agree that both have radically changed since Aneurin Bevan resigned in 1951 and since the unilateralist resolution was passed at Scarborough in 1960.

I am glad that I never had time to write the story earlier. The story of these failures (for most of my campaigns failed to achieve their aims) may make some contribution to a long overdue analysis of what has gone wrong with our politics and our society.

St Pancras

Contents

List of Illustrations

Thanks are due to Tribune and Sanity for the loan of back issues, and to CND for the use of their records.

Before CND

In February 1971, shortly before Left, Left, Left *was first published, Peggy Duff was interviewed by Ken Blackwell, Archivist of Bertrand Russell's papers at McMaster University in Canada. McMaster acquired Russell's Archives in 1968. Ken Blackwell catalogued the papers in Britain, including at Russell's home in North Wales, prior to their dispatch to Canada, which has become the global centre for Russell studies. This excerpt is from the opening part of the interview. Explanatory notes have been added in square brackets.*

KB: This is Ken Blackwell interviewing Mrs Peggy Duff, who has been with the British CND [Campaign for Nuclear Disarmament] movement for its entire history and who is now lecturing in North America, touring the campuses, finding out what's going on in the American peace movement. Peggy, you're looking at a book called *Mud Pie: The CND Story* by Herb Greer. What do you think of that book as a history of the CND movement?

PD: It is very hostile and in some cases, so far as I remember, inaccurate.

KB: Has there been a decent history of the CND movement?

PD: Well, the best one is Christopher Driver's.

KB: Yes, we have that one. *The Disarmers.*

PD: That's the best one so far I think. Canon Collins wrote about it a bit in a book called *Faith Under Fire* – or *Fire Under Faith*, I forget which one. Of course, there's my own that's coming out this summer.

KB: Which is called?

PD: *Left, Left, Left.*

KB: And that's to be a history of your involvement in politics?

PD: In a number of campaigns, of which CND is one.

KB: In front of me I have the earliest file of [Bertrand] Russell's, from Russell's involvement with campaigns for nuclear disarmament.

PD: 1955.

KB: Yes, 1955. There are several letters to do with his talk at the end of 1954, called 'Man's Peril from the Hydrogen Bomb'. That started things going for him. He got Einstein to join with him in a big statement in July 1955, there's a scientists conference in August 1955 and a book was published later on that year called *The Bomb: Challenge and Answer* [published] by McAllister.

PD: Of course, that was the period when Britain was agreeing to go ahead with the H-Bomb in the House [of Commons]. Aneurin Bevan opposed it, not because he was totally against nuclear weapons but he was against the first use. Massive Retaliation, in fact.

KB: He was for Massive Retaliation?

PD: No, he was against Massive Retaliation. He believed in a second-strike force: you had to have them as a deterrent. I think he was wrong, but that was his position. But he almost got expelled from the Labour Party because he refused to vote for the party resolution on the H-Bomb. That was '54-'55 and that was when Britain went ahead with building the H-Bomb. Previously, they'd been building the Atom Bomb.

KB: In 1956, not much seems to have happened with Russell except that he was busily organising the first Pugwash Conference in '57.

PD: There was a campaign in Britain called 'The H-Bomb Petition' that was run by Anthony Greenwood, Anthony Wedgwood Benn [Tony Benn], Julius Silverman. It was very inefficiently run by a man named Arthur Carr and it organised a petition and held an Albert Hall meeting which was not very successful. They had about 500 people in the Albert Hall, which looked very bad. But it's interesting that some of the people involved like Tony Wedgwood Benn later was supporting the Labour government keeping of Polaris [missiles] etc. I don't think Russell was involved in that [petition].

KB: No, I don't see any letters from him on that.

PD: After that, apart from Pugwash, there was really nothing until the National Council for the Abolition of Nuclear Weapon Tests started, which grew out of a group in Hampstead.

KB: Did Suez have anything to do with it, or Hungary – both happening in '56.

PD: I think it's possible that people switched interest from the bomb for a period and then the whole thing zoomed up again in '57 partly because of the tests at Christmas Island which, because they were British tests, caused a lot of excitement; partly because there had been a big campaign inside the Labour Party and it was expected that the 1957 conference of the Labour Party might pass a resolution for the unilateral renunciation [of nuclear weapons]. They failed to do it, partly because Aneurin Bevan opposed it. That was the famous split between Aneurin and the Left. That was one of the roots, because it was after the Labour Party failed to pass this resolution that Russell and Priestley and these people started to get together to start some organised resistance. Until then they thought that the Labour Party was going to do it.

KB: In late '57 Russell wrote an open letter to Khrushchev and Eisenhower. Khrushchev replied and [US Secretary of State] Dulles replied. Khrushchev replied again. At this time [former US

Ambassador to the Soviet Union, George F.] Kennan had given the Reith Lectures [on 'Russia, the Atom and the West'] and then CND was formed. How did …

PD: Well, it all came from different routes. There was the failure, in early October, of the Labour Party to pass this resolution and particularly the defection of Aneurin Bevan. It was the first time that the Left and Aneurin had split. The tests at Christmas Island went on through all the summer of '57 and the National Council for the Abolition of Nuclear Weapon Tests was the only organisation at that time which was providing any sort of organised resistance. There were a few local committees which set out on their own in places like Oxford and Reading which were operating without any national presence. And then there were the Russell letters to Khrushchev and Eisenhower, and the replies. And Kingsley Martin [editor of *New Statesman* magazine, got involved]. There was a lot of correspondence after that, articles by J.B. Priestley in the *New Statesman*, there were the Reith Lectures by Kennan and, as a result of that, there were two separate things that came together: the National Council decided that it should enlarge its aims to include campaigns against the weapons, not just the tests and at the same time there was this meeting in Kingsley Martin's flat in the Adelphi between Kennan, Russell, Priestley, [Nobel Prize winning physicist Patrick] Blackett and [Stephen] King-Hall, I think, at which it was agreed that some of them – like Blackett – would operate within the Establishment and that a public campaign should be mounted. The two go together. The initiative from Russell, Priestley and Kingsley was to organise a public campaign. I got in touch with them and the thing was merged.

KB: Do you think that Russell ever operated within the Establishment at that time?

PD: Not in the same way that Blackett did.

KB: Was Blackett successful at all?

PD: I think that to a certain extent they succeeded in creating some doubts and some alarm. I think that it's notable that later, by something like 1960, we had at least one General who was publicly opposing nuclear weapons.

KB: Have you read that interesting book by C.P. Snow, *The Corridors of Power*? He talks about an effort to get nuclear disarmament from within the Establishment.

PD: Yes.

KB: In front of me I have what I suppose is your first letter to Russell, 9th September 1957. Do you remember writing it?

PD: Yes, vaguely. That was an appeal for funds.

KB: This is before CND got started.

PD: It was before the Labour Party conference. It wasn't the first time I'd met him. He'd been involved in an earlier campaign I'd organised between 1945 and '49 called 'Save Europe Now', which was concerned with political campaigns against starvation in Europe but in particular for relief of both ex-allies and ex-enemies.

KB: Was that an all-party campaign?

PD: It was a Victor Gollancz campaign.

KB: What part did Russell have in it?

PD: He was one of the sponsors and he used to come to meetings.

KB: Did he speak for the movement?

PD: Yes. We held some public meetings. We raised a lot of money. We got bread rationed in order that there should be more bread for Europe. It was typical of a Gollancz campaign because Gollancz always did things you would never expect him to do. He was Jewish and he organised a campaign for help to Germany after the war. He did the same thing later for Arabs. We organised a campaign in '47 for repatriation of prisoners of war, who were still in Britain and should have been sent home. That was successful. We had a big meeting at Albert Hall, right at the beginning – it must have been about the end of '45 – and I think Russell spoke at that.

KB: Did you meet Russell in those days?

PD: Yes, I met him at meetings. He came to one meeting and I can remember him saying that if it wasn't for the Atom Bomb – because in those days there were just Atom Bombs – in the hands of the United States, that the Russians might be at the Channel Ports within a few weeks. He was very anti-Soviet at that stage.

KB: Yes. In Volume Two of his *Autobiography* he retracts that, he says he was misled.

PD: I think he was misled. He had the courage to admit it.

KB: Did you know Russell on a personal basis?

PD: A bit, yes. A bit.

KB: What was he like? Did he have all his faculties?

PD: He was very much on the ball. He would come to the meetings and, unlike a lot of people, he never said anything unless he had something to say. He was always brief and very incisive. He was always like that, you wrote him a letter and you got a brief reply which gave you everything you wanted.

KB: How was he as a 'committee man', both in those days and later on, in the Campaign.

PD: In the Campaign, he very rarely came to committees. I think this was a mistake. He was presumed to be a 'President' – sort of a 'House of Lords' – and the Executive would meet and he was very rarely invited and very rarely came. He was invited to speak at meetings. He did a lot about the European conference that we tried to hold in the summer of '58 but which was banned in Basel [Switzerland]. He spoke at the subsequent conference held in London the following January 1959. He did one or two things, like when we were banned in Basel he wrote the Swiss Confederation a very rude letter.

KB: What did he say?

PD: He said that it was not surprising that a country that even now refused the vote to women would ban a conference on nuclear weapons. He did everything he was asked. I think one of the tragedies of the subsequent split between the Committee [of 100] and CND was that he would really have been willing to do far more, but wasn't asked to.

KB: That is a pity. I'm just looking through all these folders with Russell's correspondence with you and other people in the Peace Movement. Here's a letter from you saying: 'Dear Lord Russell, Many thanks for speaking at our meeting on Monday'. What meeting do you think that was?

PD: I think it must have been at Central Hall.

KB: 'Most people seem to think it was an historic occasion', you wrote. 'Secondly, I've had a request for an article on nuclear disarmament from the Yearbook of Leeds Trades Council'. Do you remember that book at all? What we're trying to do in these archives is to trace down everything that Russell wrote, and we don't have this book.

PD: The Leeds Trades Council – they should have it.

KB: So I could write to them, then?

PD: Yes.

KB: Oh, I see, and a synopsis of his speech at the Central Hall meeting was used.

PD: Do you have that?

KB: We have that speech and it's just been re-printed in a book called *The Rhetoric of the British Peace Movement*, with some comments which aren't so good. Oh yes, here's another letter from you asking Russell if you can print his speech as a leaflet.

PD: Yes, presumably we did.

KB: The archives don't have that leaflet.

PD: I'll see if we've got it, but I'm not sure.

KB: Here's a letter from the Aldermaston March Committee.

PD: That was the first one. It was a separate *ad-hoc* committee.

KB: And that handled the first Aldermaston March?

PD: Yes.

KB: Which became part of the CND movement after?

PD: Afterwards, CND organised them ...

With grateful acknowledgements to Ken Blackwell for his permission to publish

Transcribed by Tom Unterrainer from the McMaster Digital Archive

Common Wealth: 1944-5

I started working for Common Wealth in the summer of 1944. A few months later, my husband, Bill Duff, who was assistant editor of the Forces Newspaper in the Far East, SEAC, was killed in an American bomber in which he was covering an attack on the railway along the borders of Burma and Siam (now Thailand). With three children under ten to bring up, a job, which had been a temporary war-time interlude, became a necessity. Campaigning seemed as good a way as any other of earning a living and better than most – so Common Wealth became my first campaign.

It was born during the war from a marriage between Forward March and the 1941 Committee. Forward March was a small Left, middle-class group, led by Sir Richard Acland who was what used to be known as a 'landed squire', owning large tracts of land in Devonshire. He was the Liberal MP for Barnstaple in North Devon. Converted to socialism, he left the Liberal Party, gave his estates to the nation and proceeded to found first Forward March and then Common Wealth. He remained a Member of Parliament but gave the Liberal Party an assurance that at the next General Election he would not contest it – a promise which he kept. He was and is an uncompromising socialist on ethical rather than Marxist grounds. One of Common Wealth's posters expressed his position briefly and succintly. The text ran: 'Is it expedient?' The word 'expedient' was crossed out and the word 'right' written in.

The 1941 Committee was another progressive group in which J.B. Priestley was the dominant figure. Priestley was not too happy about the merger. He was not in favour of setting up a political party. However, occasionally he spoke at Common Wealth meetings.

Common Wealth had recruited members mainly from the middle class and from left-wingers in the Labour Party unhappy about the wartime political truce. Profiting from the fact that Labour was not contesting by-elections in Tory-held seats, and vice-versa, Common Wealth put up candidates in a number of seats, and supported independent candidates in others. They backed Tom Driberg in Maldon. In January 1944 their candidate, Hugh Lawson, won Skipton in Yorkshire, a seat with a solid Tory majority where there was a local saying that if you put up a pig with a blue ribbon round its neck, it would win. Hugh Lawson's victory was, therefore, a considerable surprise. *Tribune* accurately reported on its impact:

> The supporters of the Government were sitting back complacently contemplating the favourable course of the war and reflecting that a government associated with victory has nothing to fear at the hands of the electorate ... then, the electors of Skipton reject the Government's champion and elect the champion of an insignificant party with an uncompromising programme of social change.

A little later John Loverseed won Eddisbury and with Acland already in the House, Common Wealth had three Members. They also supported Alderman White who won West Derbyshire, a seat regarded as a pocket borough of the Duke of Devonshire, whose son, Lord Hartington, unsuccessfully contested it.

The high-ups in Common Wealth were divided, like its membership in the country, between those who saw it as a permanent, small Left party and those who worked with it as a temporary substitute for the Labour Party. There was R. W. G. Mackay, an Australian tycoon type who left very early while the going was good and fought one of the Hull seats in 1945 for Labour. There were Tom Wintringham and his wife, Kitty, both of whom later went into the Labour Party. Then there was C. A. Smith, the Research Officer, who wanted to make it a permanency and carried it on later. Dick Acland himself never really made his mind up. Like so many of the campaigns with which I worked, a great deal of time was spent on arguments about the Labour Party.

Would it make a deal with Common Wealth? Would it leave it unopposed in the seats it had won? Would it allow Common

Wealth to affiliate? Would we be right to do so, if it did? The dialogue raged back and forth and got hotter as the end of the war and a general election came nearer. Mackay moved off into the Labour Party. Others tried to make friendly contacts. Transport House, as usual, remained aloof, unfriendly, lofty and unmoved. Meanwhile there were endless discussions about how many seats Common Wealth should fight, and which seats, if the Labour Party continued with its blank refusal to see that Common Wealth even existed, or had anything to offer.

Meanwhile, at the end of 1944, in the middle of these arguments, another vacancy occurred in Chelmsford. The place seemed ideal for a Common Wealth candidate. Near to London, but not a suburb. A country town, with an industrial base. A small, enthusiastic local Common Wealth Party. Then up came an ideal candidate, Wing Commander Ernest Millington, commanding a bomber squadron. (Bombers were more popular then than now!)

The Common Wealth circus moved into Chelmsford. The circus had been invented by the press who had to find some reason why this odd little party could win by-elections. So they invented a high-powered team of agents and full-time workers. This was a gross exaggeration. Common Wealth had only a small staff. They could rarely put more than two or three full-time workers into an election. At Chelmsford there were only two. The work was done largely by volunteers, loyal and devoted members of Common Wealth who came down from London, and by local people recruited during the campaign.

The Chelmsford by-election lasted a very long time. The Conservatives were reluctant to name the day. This helped Common Wealth. Through the early months of 1945 they slowly but steadily moved about the constituency. The candidate, young, handsome, with a pretty wife and two children, gradually became well known. The local Labour Party hierarchy softened up. People started to get friendly, to come into the committee rooms, to smile and greet you in the street.

The Conservative candidate was also RAF, but a staff officer in London, not operational and with none of Millington's glamour.

He was also a very bad candidate. Asked at one meeting, after a bitter attack on Communist Russia, why they had managed to fight so well if they were as dreadful as he made out, he replied: 'They organize. But the Conservative Party is going to organize too.' It was not surprising that the Tory Party fought the election on Churchill.

The nearer we got to the election, in April, the more enthusiasm grew, even though Richard Acland, speaking to a large meeting in Brentwood, promised them harder and harder times. Things will get much worse, he told them.

We held a big meeting in the main square on the eve of poll, outside the Corn Exchange, to catch the people leaving the Tory meeting there. Victor Gollancz told the crowd the whole story of Tory support for the Nazis during the thirties. I thought he was magnificent that night, but one worker complained. He was smoking a cigar, liable to offend working-class people.

I shall never forget the count at the end of that election. I have been to many counts since then ... counts which we lost, counts we won, counts when we recounted again and again, counts when some Tories tore off their rosettes because their defeated candidate made an anti-semitic speech ... but there was never a count like the one at Chelmsford. There was all the nobility of the Tory Party, county and tweedy, oligarchic and confident in the status quo. But, as the votes were counted it became clear that the status quo had had it. There was no question of a recount. A Tory majority of 16,624 was transformed into a Common Wealth majority of 6,431.

The wife of the Lord Lieutenant was in tears as he, poor chap, had to announce the result from the balcony to the waiting crowds below. Down in the street outside there was another woman in tears, a life-long socialist. Never before had her candidate won. It seemed like a miracle. Which, in a way, it was. It was a revolution, not a bloody or even a very radical revolution, but it mirrored major changes in political thinking among ordinary British people. All the miseries and mistakes, all the degradation of unemployment, the appeasement of fascism and Nazism in the thirties, had not been forgotten. Most people wanted something different from the old, something better.

The Conservatives were, of course, absolutely devastated. As usual the press was on their side. One of the agencies put out a report after the result was known, that the successful candidate, Millington, had said that the result of the election was 'not a blow against Churchill'. Denials were immediately issued by Common Wealth, but were ignored.

What was so odd, and I thought it odd at the time, was that nobody saw what Chelmsford so dearly revealed – an immense swing to the left. Skipton, Eddisbury, West Derbyshire had begun to reveal it. In Chelmsford it was crystal dear, precisely because the election was fought on Churchill's reputation.

Common Wealth, poor Common Wealth, thought it was something they had created ... that their gallant, honest, sincere and wholehearted approach to politics could win seats which had always seemed unwinnable by the Labour Party. Even the Labour Party, which had contracted out of politics for the duration of the war, letting the local parties run down, were blind to what had happened. They were still dazzled and terrified of the great war leader. So the leaders ignored the lessons of the Common Wealth victories and, uncertain of themselves, unsure of their capacity to win a majority, even played around with the notion of continuing coalition.

Common Wealth was dazzled too. But, brushed aside by Transport Honse, it had to face up to a General Election with Labour fighting almost every seat – a very different matter to uncontested by-elections. Eventually, it put up about fifteen candidates, but in only one was their man elected, in Chelmsford where Millington was adopted as the Labour/Co-op candidate. Dick Acland stood in Putney, Kitty Wintringham in Edinburgh and, believe it or not, Desmond Donnelly was the Common Wealth candidate in Evesham. He was then an eager young Eighth Army Air Force officer who used to send passionately socialist letters to *Common Wealth Review*. Mervyn Stockwood, later to be Bishop of Southwark, came up from Bristol to speak for him.

Putney was not exactly a revolutionary area. I found recently a leaflet Dick Acland used during the campaign. It sums up his and Common Wealth's approach. It is headed 'Personal Message from Richard Acland':

Before you go to vote, may I ask you a frank question?

In the long struggle against Big Business and against all kinds of privilege, am I right in thinking there is something missing now which was not missing in the early pioneering days of Kier Hardie thirty or forty years ago?

In those days there was an unlimited courage; and behind that courage there was a crusading fervour for a nobler way of life and for a cause which was held to be morally right.

Common Wealth today does not ask for 'Public Control over Big Business'; we don't believe it will work. We don't ask for the mere nationalization of three or four key industries as a matter of practical convenience; it's not enough. We insist that all our great resources – all land, mines, banks, railways, yes, and all substantial industries and factories of every sort and kind, shall be owned and run by all of us in common.

We ask this not merely in order to cure unemployment and to produce more goods. We ask it above all as a matter of high moral principle and as the basis of a nobler way of life in which fellowship and cooperation will come before self-interest and competition in the daily working lives of all citizens.

It is just because we have presented this cause in this wholehearted way that we have won sensational by-election victories in seats always regarded as Tory strongholds.

We ask electors now to send into the House of Commons an independent group of MPs to continue to preach the necessity of conducting the struggle in this courageous and thorough-going way.

His meetings were packed, and wherever he spoke, indoors or outdoors, people flocked to hear him, noted what he said ... and then went out and voted Labour. Common Wealth votes were counted in hundreds. The days of the great victories were gone for good.

I remember lying on the floor at the Common Wealth office in Gower Street listening to the results as they came over the radio.

One after another, Tory seats, Tory mandarins fell. One after another Labour victories came through. It really did seem then like a revolution. It could have been a revolution. Harold Laski said then, someone told me, that if Labour did the right things, there would never be another Tory Government. That is what it felt like then. After all the long drawn out horrors of the thirties and the war, after the culminating terror of the atomic bombs on Hiroshima and Nagasaki, here was a new world coming up.

Common Wealth in the months that followed tore itself into pieces arguing about what it should do. Should it close down and send all its members into the Labour Party? Many who had come from there had already returned. Some were reluctant to leave something which had seemed very valuable. Others talked about taking their zeal and enthusiasm, their high moral principle, into the Labour Party to keep it on the right (left) road. All the arguments came together in a conference in the summer where by a moderate majority it was agreed that Common Wealth should close and urge all its members to join the Labour Party. Reluctantly, Acland accepted the decision. A minority, led by C. A. Smith, refused to accept the verdict and carried on. So far as I know, Common Wealth still exists, still occasionally fights elections, but it is a very long time since it won one.

Richard Acland joined the Labour Party. In 1947 he fought a by-election in Gravesend and Common Wealth people turned up in droves to help him win it. Years later, in 1955, he resigned on the issue of Labour's support for the British H Bomb. He intended to fight a by-election in Gravesend on that issue, but he was unlucky. The Tories decided to go to the country and he had to fight a General Election, a very different matter. He lost, and so did Labour. Nowadays there are no parties courageous enough to risk his uncompromising honesty.

The announcement at the end of September 1945 that he was to join the Labour Party appeared at the same time as another, reporting the foundation of a new organization: Save Europe Now. This was my next campaign.

Save Europe Now: 1945-8

In the early autumn of 1945 I started work with Victor Gollancz as secretary of a new organization: Save Europe Now.

This was the first time I worked with V.G. It was an exhilarating experience. He was an expert on running campaigns and had been on the job for many years through the thirties and during the war. In the thirties there was the Left Book Club which broke the taboo on left-wing books at a time when few publishers would handle them. The Club probably did more than anything else to sow the seeds of Labour's victory in 1945. Yet the Labour Party when it came to power was scared of his individualism, recognized that there was no party line he would toe, and gave him no recognition. So while others were given honours, V.G., who would dearly have loved to have been a peer, was forgotten. Once we discussed what title he would take and agreed on 'Lord Covent Garden and Balls'. Years later, when Victor was old and mellower, they gave him a knighthood – magnificent meanness!

Most of his campaigns were against injustices, against flagrant inhumanities. In the thirties he collected large sums of money to 'buy' Jews out of Nazi Germany. Short of hard currency, Hitler was willing to release some German Jews, at a price. Here his concern arose from his race but he was frequently contrapuntal. He always had an urge to help those who had least claim on his concern. Millions of his people had died in Nazi Germany, yet he ran Save Europe Now which concerned itself largely with aid for Germans. Later, he started a campaign to help Arab refugees. This was partly because he always reacted to suffering but also because he rejected mass judgements. He would not accept that all Germans or all Arabs were wicked. He challenged the Old Testament doctrine of 'an eye for an eye'. He was not in my view a great thinker, nor yet a great writer. His books suffered from the fact that he was a publisher and nobody ever dared to cut or edit them. But he had instincts which made him react to situations passionately, often violently, but always positively. That is why so many were prepared to work with him, why so many loved him. He was very aggressively good. And he knew it.

So he commanded Rose Macaulay's 'stage army of the good'. They knew that they would have little say in what was done, that he would be the dominating figure. But they had sufficient confidence in his judgement to accept the risk, to acquiesce in his overlordship. Though many of his campaigns had wide grassroot support throughout the country, they were never democratically based. V.G. decided what was to be done. This is not to say that the executive committees were not consulted. They met regularly but if, and this happened only rarely, they decided to do something with which V.G. disagreed, it was usually conveniently forgotten. Nobody really minded because he was very good at running campaigns and if he sometimes overstated the case, or centred the campaign rather too much around himself, the hazards were not very great, for his extraordinary energy and dynamism achieved results.

He was a delightful person to work for – up to a point. He had tremendous energy and a gorgeous sense of humour (his anti-Jew jokes were the best I ever heard and he told them beautifully). He taught me most of what I know about running campaigns. The rest I got from CND, from the marchers, not the leaders. Whenever he planned a meeting he would start booking halls for overflows. When he appealed for money, the target was always way high up. He always overdid things, and while this probably wasted money, it was usually effective.

He was noisy and boisterous. There must have been some sort of intercom in that rambling old office in Covent Garden, but he never used it. He would open the door of his room on the first floor and bawl. Shortly after we moved into a top room there he told me that the reason we got on so well together was that when he shouted 'Duffy' up the stairs I ran down quicker than anyone else who had ever worked for him.

But he was often over-bearing and specialized in shouting. He used to lose his temper, temporarily and completely. Once when he was shouting at some luckless boy downstairs, the doorman from the theatre across Maiden Lane came running across, believing a riot was in progress. But his tempers were short-lived. He would scream and shout and then lie down on his easy chair in his room and sleep it off while everyone else, especially the luckless victim of his wrath, was reduced to a jelly. One of his daughters used to imitate V.G. when the bath water was cold. V.G. being cut off on the phone was a similar occasion.

Yet he never shouted at me, even when, occasionally, I made mistakes and, later, in the campaign against capital punishment, when he was really very angry with me: I never knew why. Yet it was often just as bad to listen to him bawling out others.

He could be delightful and usually was. He walked into his office one day to hear his secretary say: 'The old man is still out at lunch' to a caller on the telephone. 'Old man,' he said, 'I'll accept, but let me catch you calling me the old bugger, and you're sacked.'

He was meticulous about little things, particularly proofs and advertisements. He suffered from the delusion that unless he oversaw everything nothing would be properly done. So when he went off to the States, every letter that went out of 14 Henrietta Street had to have a carbon which was sent to him, by air mail. Here again, I was lucky. Save Europe Now grew so rapidly, got itself involved in such complicated matters, like parcels, that a great deal of autonomy was permitted for the office.

He exaggerated, of course. He could not help it but his extravagance rose from the quality of his concern, not from deliberate, cold-blooded distortions. He wrote a book about his visit to Germany in 1947, *In Darkest Germany.* Later I met in Germany one of the men he interviewed and quoted in the book. He complained that he had been misquoted but added that, since so many were minimizing conditions in Germany, Victor felt justified, no doubt, in exaggerating them. I told him that I thought he was wrong about this. V.G. had not deliberately distorted. He had convinced himself that what he wrote was the truth and this he always did. His exaggerations were emotional, not political.

Yet one could not escape loving him, difficult as he could be, megalomaniac as he so often was. Years later, when he and Arthur Koestler were at loggerheads during the capital punishment campaign, Arthur said to me: 'I wonder why, when I wanted to start a campaign against capital punishment, I had to go to him?' And he added, after a moment's thought: 'There was nobody else except him, the old patriarch.'

Save Europe Now erupted out of the situation in Europe at the end of the war, especially in Germany. It seems extraordinary now, looking back more than twenty years later, that *so* little provision had been made by the allies that widespread hunger and near-famine lingered in Europe for two years after the war ended.

It was partly due to the fact that the wheat-producing countries had been deliberately reducing their output, because consumption was limited during the war by the problem of shipping and the allied blockade of occupied Europe. It was also due to massive mismanagement and to the fact that few governments, statesmen and people cared very much if their ex-enemies starved.

The situation in Germany was aggravated by the arrival, after the war, of millions of German refugees from the East, from East Prussia and Silesia which became Polish, and from Poland. Many others came from the Balkans into Austria. They were *Volks Deutsch,* people of German origin who had lived in Rumania, Hungary and Czechoslovakia for generations. They were uprooted and sent west, under the terms of the Potsdam Agreement. Mostly they travelled in cattle trucks, steaming across Europe in conditions which worsened rapidly as winter set in.

For a time nobody noticed. Millions of Poles and Russians had died at German hands. Retribution was not questioned. Then, in September 1945, reports began to appear in British newspapers. Norman Clark wrote in the *News Chronicle* (14 September 1945):

> Faced with the prospect of disaster overwhelming a whole nation, the Allied Public Health authorities are ordering burgomasters to take measures ensuring the early burial of the dead in the winter. Graves are to be dug now which men debilitated by weeks of under-

nourishment will not have the strength to dig in a few months' time.

During the first month of the Allied occupation of Germany the death rate was as high as 61 per 1,000 and the infant mortality rate was fifty per cent.

It was to this situation in Germany and Austria and to widespread hunger in many other European countries that Victor Gollancz reacted. Save Europe Now was established. Its sponsors and executive included Eleanor Rathbone, Bertrand Russell, Lord Lindsay of Birker (Master of Balliol), the Bishop of Chichester, Dr Gilbert Murray, one or two other churchmen, and Michael Foot. One of the first activities of the new movement was a meeting at the Albert Hall which was chaired by the Archbishop of York and at which Air Vice Marshal de Crespigny, one of the five regional commissioners in the British zone of Germany, was one of the speakers. Letters were published in the press appealing for support for immediate relief schemes, on a voluntary basis, and for depots to be set up to which people could send food and clothing. It was suggested that points (coupons required for the purchase of foods in short supply, such as biscuits, tinned goods) might be sent to a central office so that their equivalent in food could be sent abroad. People were asked to send postcards to the office of Save Europe Now indicating their willingness to spare food or points from time to time.

The response was twofold. By early 1946, sixty thousand people had sent in their postcards. Before long the total reached a hundred thousand.

The Minister of Food, Sir Ben Smith, was an ex-docker. He had no sympathy whatsoever with Save Europe Now, or for the people who wished to contribute from their own rations to alleviate suffering in Europe. Britain, of course, was still rationed and, in view of the world situation, the rations tended to go down rather than up.

Save Europe Now sent a deputation to see Sir Ben Smith. All their proposals for voluntary contributions were turned down. So was a proposal that people who ate in restaurants should be obliged to give up points. The only concession they got out of Sir Ben was a promise that ninety thousand tons of surplus stocks would be sent to Europe. Later, as the situation in Europe deteriorated even further, Britain reduced her own stocks of wheat to two hundred thousand tons by diverting cargoes at sea to India. As a result, the loaf became darker and fears of bread rationing increased.

Foiled, at least for a time, in their plans for voluntary contributions, Save Europe Now issued a public appeal for funds to purchase relief through the Council of British Relief Societies Abroad, an umbrella organization covering the British Red Cross, the Save the Children Fund, the Friends Relief Service and one or two others. They wrote to all the hundred thousand who had sent postcards asking for money, since food could not be given.

By June 1946 the situation was worse, not better. The Tories were mounting bitter attacks on the Government and the press was in full cry. The Ministry of Food became a key ministry and John Strachey replaced Sir Ben Smith. This was a considerable gain for Save Europe Now for Strachey was much more sympathetic to its aims. But he was also anathema to the Tories who escalated their attacks.

He was willing to give way to Save Europe Now's demand that people should be allowed to send food parcels abroad either to individuals or for general relief. However, when bread rationing was introduced in July, the Cabinet refused to endorse his decision. Once again we were frustrated.

By the early autumn it was clear that much greater hardship faced Europe during the coming winter of 1946/7. Save Europe Now launched its own relief fund, for aid to three relief organizations, the Friends Relief Service, the Oecumenical Refugee Commission and Aid to Austria. It organized a big meeting at the Palace Theatre with an appeal for this fund and one or two other organizations, including the Catholic and Jewish Committees for Relief Abroad. Speakers included Robert Boothby, Frank Byers from the Liberal Party, Jennie Lee, Michael Foot, Dick Stokes and Bertrand Russell. By August 1947 we had collected £76,550, out of which £45,395 went to the Friends Relief Service and £11,191 to the Oecurnenical

Refugee Commission.

In the autumn of 1946 we had our first success on the parcel front. The parcel post for most European countries had reopened, but not for Germany. Save Europe Now was permitted to collect and ship parcels of clothing, shoes, linen, and some medicines from individuals in Britain to individuals in Germany.

As winter set in and conditions in Europe deteriorated, we lost patience with the Cabinet and Prime Minister who were continuing to oppose the food parcel scheme. For some time we had been using our stock of supporters, a hundred thousand strong, to pressurize the Ministry of Food. Nearly half a million letters of protest must have passed through its doors. Now, since the obstruction was elsewhere, we decided to change our target. We wrote to the hundred thousand and asked them all, during the same week, to write to the Prime Minister.

It worked. As the letters poured into Downing Street, the Prime Minister and Cabinet withdrew their opposition. People were to be allowed to send a parcel a month. They had to get a permit from a Food Office and then post their parcel off. It seemed quite simple but there were snags ahead.

There was no parcel post to Germany. It was not scheduled to open until 15 January, about six weeks ahead.

The Post Office insisted that it could not be speeded up. The Ministry of Food said that the Minister had made the announcement giving the date and that could not be altered. There was only one way out. Save Europe Now, already shipping clothing parcels to Germany, had to step into the breach and cope with food parcels as well.

I still have nightmares about parcels. It was, as the Post Office said, a complicated scheme. You had to write for, or collect, a four shilling label from Save Europe Now. Then you had to get your permit from the food office. Then you posted your parcel to the shipping agent who packed them and shipped them to Germany. There the Evangelische Hilfswerk put them in the post.

For six weeks we coped, sending out thousands of labels and thousands of leaflets explaining the scheme. Customers queued downstairs for labels and Gollancz packers did a good side trade in repacking parcels efficiently (for a consideration, of course). Even one poor chap who sent four shillings to V.G. Ltd for a book about sex got a food label sent to him.

On 15 January the parcel post to Germany re-opened and we heaved sighs of relief. We continued, of course, to collect and ship parcels for general relief in Austria, Germany, Hungary, Poland, France, Greece, Italy, Rumania and Yugoslavia, but this traffic was small compared with the inimense pile of parcels we dealt with during that hectic six weeks. By August 1947 we had sent thirty thousand parcels for general relief.

Gradually Europe became less hungry. Devaluation in Germany got rid of the black market. Slowly life returned to normal and Victor began to lose interest in Save Europe Now. But we undertook one further action before we closed it up.

Prisoners of war, both German and Italian, had remained in England long after the end of the war. They were working, mainly on the land, and useful so the Government delayed in sending them home. This was clearly a breach of the Geneva Convention. Furthermore, the prisoners were paid a mere pittance, and the remainder of the trade union rate for the job went to the Government. Dick Stokes, who employed some of them, refused to accept this and regularly banked the balance for them.

We organized a 'Memorial', a petition to the Government demanding repatriation. We had an unchallengeable case. A great many people signed the Memorial and it was duly presented to the Government. Lord Pakenham, now the Earl of Longford, was then the minister responsible for Germany. He agreed with us, so the prisoners were promptly repatriated. This was easily the quickest, most successful campaign I ever ran.

By that time, V.G. was more than a little bored with Save Europe Now. He was never a one for long campaigns. He liked to finish them off before they started to languish. 'There is nothing so depressing,' he told me once in a taxi, 'as a movement which has attained its aims.' Many of his early campaigns had eluded his efforts to close them, but with Save Europe Now he was luckier. Towards the end of 1948 we started shutting up shop. The hundred thousand postcards were packed into boxes and stored in the Henrietta Street basement. At the end of the year I moved on to *Tribune*, to what V.G. called a job for a lifetime ... though it wasn't.

Tribune and the Bevanites: 1949-55

The First Two Years

I walked into the *Tribune* offices at 222 Strand somewhere around 1 January 1949. My job was business manager and I was responsible for all the managerial side of the newspaper. The editorial staff wrote the paper; I had to sell it, which wasn't so easy.

I inhabited the east end of the offices. To the west, past the general office, there were the editorial offices (political) with Michael Foot (I am not sure whether even at that time he was nominally editor. He was the great panjandrum, the Beaverbrook of *Tribune*), with Evelyn Anderson, co-editor, and Bob Edwards, recently up from a local newspaper in deepest Berkshire, wildly enthusiastic. Beyond that there was the editorial office (literary). Tosco Fyvel was then literary editor. George Orwell had recently left. Richard Findlater, otherwise known as Bruce Bain, was dramatic critic. Later he became literary editor and like most good journalists who worked for *Tribune* moved on to higher things. Beyond the literary office was the back number store, a dark and dusty purgatory into which we had to delve every time an American academic writing a thesis on George Orwell came into the office.

It was usually a very friendly office, though there were occasional tensions. Bob Edwards used to write hard-hitting diatribes which curdled Tosco Fyvel's aesthetic sensibilities. Bob, in spite of his apparent toughness, was a sensitive plant and sulked whenever Tosco snorted.

I soon discovered that V.G.'s prophecy that this was a job for a lifetime might be an overstatement of the case. *Tribune* lived on the verge of bankruptcy and seemed to have done so for some time. Britain was never a good climate for left-wing publications. While Tribune's circulation and prestige had climbed and its deficit had dropped during the war and immediately afterwards, by 1949 it was in deep trouble. Those who had founded it and financed it and helped to build it up before and during the war were now, most of them, Ministers of the Crown: Cripps, George Strauss, and Nye himself. They could no longer write for the paper and were too involved in the day-to-day problems of their ministries and of the government to spare much time or thought for poor, old, faithful *Tribune*.

So Michael Foot carried the burden. Somehow, always, he raised the money to keep it going, often from his own pocket, and he succeeded mainly from a rooted refusal to admit defeat. Its early backers, when it was first founded, were the obvious: people like Cripps and George Strauss. But after the war there were new men, some unexpected: Jack Hilton, the Sieffs (before Israel was established and when *Tribune* was backing it), John Diamond (who certainly never shared all its politics) and, of course, Howard Samuel.

One of the life-saving plans which began shortly after I arrived was an 'arrangement' with the Labour Party. They paid us (I can't remember how much) for the regular use of two pages of *Tribune*. In addition they sent out to their mailing list a leaflet advertising the paper and appealing for sales through local parties. As a result, we built up fairly rapidly the sale of several thousand copies a week.

Apart from its effect on bulk sales, the 'arrangement' with the Labour Party did not do us much good. Its two pages were abysmally dull and *Tribune* withdrew from the bargain in 1950. This is important for some time later at the height of the Bevanite controversy we were accused by Arthur Deakin of having had a 'subsidy' from the Labour Party which had been withdrawn. He was promptly slapped down by Michael Foot who pointed out that the Labour Party had paid for space, and that we had terminated the bargain.

The one important new strategy which I embarked on during those first two years was at the Labour Party Conference. Conference had always been seen, of course, as an opportunity for the left to push its views. But it had not previously been used as a place to push the sales of *Tribune*. The 1949 conference was at Blackpool. I travelled up with a stock of *Tribunes*. On the opening day I walked into the long corridors in the Tower leading to the conference hall carrying my bundles of *Tribune*. I found a uniformed attendant who very kindly supplied me with a table and even a chair. So I set up my stall, laid out my *Tribunes* and proceeded to sell them at a rapid rate. From time to time I wandered into the tea and beer bars with a pile of *Tribunes* on my arm. I even wandered around the conference hall itself and I remember that all week, I never even had a visitor's ticket.

That year we laid on a *Tribune* tea party. Nye came, of course, George Strauss, Jennie Lee, Michael and many of the 'big names', plus several hundred delegates. That was the beginning of something which became a tradition, a keystone of *Tribune's* influence on the left of the Labour Party. Year after year, whenever Conference met, there was the annual *Tribune* meeting, always on a Wednesday, ready for the new issue of the paper arriving early on Thursday morning. Year after year, there was *Tribune* on sale inside and outside the conference (according to current relations between Transport House and *Tribune*). Others, of course, joined in and eventually it almost became impossible for delegates to get in at all, so many people were selling so many papers.

But the *Tribune* meeting was different. It became a feature of conferences, especially while Nye remained the focus. The meetings were always packed. The audience was always left, politically sophisticated and seeking the fire, this time. They were great occasions for many years – and if the fire gradually became less fierce and the occasions less momentous, that is the way with traditions.

But it was not enough. Although sales went up they did not go up enough. The enthusiasm which had waxed when Labour got in in 1945 was gradually waning, and interest in *Tribune* with it. Some drastic action had to be taken if *Tribune* was to survive. In desperation we decided to turn it into a fortnightly paper and to produce once a month a *Tribune* pamphlet.

The pamphlets had a varied success. Some sold very well. Others were very slow. Up to September 1952, when *Tribune* reverted to weekly publication, we produced nineteen under many well-known names, and some unexpected ones. Here is the list: *Set the Pubs Free* (an attack on the brewers) and *John Bull's Other Island* (an attack on Northern Ireland which was a hot bestseller across the Irish Channel), both by Geoffrey Bing. *Still at Large* (an attack on the Tories) by Michael Foot and *Full Speed Ahead* by St Just, a pseudonym for Michael Foot. *Back to the Dole* by Barbara Castle (she wouldn't write that one now!) *The Intelligent Socialist's Guide to Africa* by John Hatch. *Dirty Coal* (about the mining industry) by Robert J. Edwards. *Fair Shares for the Rich* by Roy Jenkins! *Quo Vadis* by Aneurin Bevan, Harold Wilson, John Freeman and Jennie Lee (a collection of House of Commons speeches). *It's a Mug's Game* (an attack on bookies) by Ian Mikardo. *What Happened to the Liberals* by Robert Pitman. *In Place of Dollars* by Harold Wilson (who hasn't yet found a substitute). *Job Lots for the Boys* (on the railways) by Cecil Poole. *More Red Meat* by Clifford Selly. *The Intelligent Socialist's Guide to America* by David Williams of ADA. *This Football Business* by J.P. W. Mallalieu. *The Jews at Home* by Woodrow Wyatt; and, of course, *One Way Only* and *Going Our Way*, both published during the summer following the resignations of Aneurin Bevan, Harold Wilson and John Freeman and probably by far the best known. Quite a list of titles.

Otherwise, these first two years were comparatively uneventful. The General Election of 1950 left no clear impact on my memory. But Woodrow Wyatt did. At that time he was writing a weekly column for Tribune – a fact both he and *Tribune* probably now prefer to forget. *Tribune* was not really his spiritual home, yet occasionally he got away with murder. He even wrote one column advocating the use of the atomic bomb.

We always knew when he was coming because you could smell the smoke of his cigar wafting up the lift shaft and you could hear the row he always had with the liftman on the way up. He was obviously out of place there, but I liked him. We used to have a running battle over the miserable pittance that *Tribune* paid him for his column. We were always short of money, so I always delayed paying him as long as I could. When he was desperate, he would ring and we would have a long and hilarious telephone conversation as a result of which I would pay him as little as possible. It was a form of gymnastics we both enjoyed.

I also remember very clearly a day in late March or early April 1951. Once again we were in desperate financial straits. I talked about it with Michael and for the one and only time he actually put into words the dreadful thought that was always in mind – that we might have to call it a day and close the paper down. A few days later he sent for me and took me into the far west room which was empty. He told me, in confidence, that he expected that as a result of the Budget some ministers would resign. This would give *Tribune* new opportunities, a new lease of life. A few days later, Aneurin Bevan, Harold Wilson and John Freeman resigned. That was the beginning of the Bevanite movement.

The Resignations

There were a few straws to show the way the wind was blowing. It was, of course, well known that Aneurin Bevan had threatened to resign a number of times, when timidity was showing itself in the Cabinet, notably on the issue of the nationalization of steel.

On 9 February 1951 *Tribune* carried an outspoken leader revealing increasing alarm at the trend of American policy in the Far East:

> Several months ago, say, at the time of the North Korean aggression, most people in the Labour Party would have been prepared to accept the view that the paramount cause of the world tension was the policies pursued by the Soviet dictatorship .... It is equally necessary, however, to recognize that a new situation has arisen. The danger of world war no longer arises solely from Soviet policy. It arises also from the temper which has been roused in the United States and the foolhardy policies on which the erstwhile more progressive Government in Washington has been launched at the bidding of an ever more raucous and hysterical reaction.

Tough words. It was also notable that, although Aneurin Bevan was put up to reply to the Tory vote of censure in the Defence Debate, he stressed in his speech very strongly that Britain was making a greater contribution to defence, in relation to her size, than any other country. Nevertheless, at that time he accepted the need for rearmament: 'We shall carry it out,' he said. 'We shall fulfil our obligations to our friends and Allies, and at the same time we shall try to prevent such an exacerbation of the world atmosphere as makes it impossible for nations to come together in peace and harmony.'

A more significant pointer came in a speech he made in the East End of London in which he strenuously attacked any attempt to cut the social services and, in particular, the Health Service.

Hugh Gaitskell accepted the challenge. To meet the Defence Estimates (£4,700 million in three years, £1,500 million that year) he put fifty per cent charges on teeth and spectacles, robbed the National Insurance Fund of £100 million and restricted increases in old age pensions to certain groups.

Tribune's response was immediate and inflamed the situation. In a caustic leader, it compared the 1951 budget to Philip Snowden's in 1931. Since the 1931 budget was regarded in the Labour Movement as a sell out of all socialist principles, it could hardly have been ruder:

> At the moment of crisis he [Snowden] deserted his socialism and the powers of reaction were able to swarm to victory through the breach he had made. We had to wait twenty years for a Labour Chancellor to win such warm approval in Conservative quarters .... Mr Gaitskell has made the grade .... Now, as then, the majority of Labour MPs are proud of their Chancellor, impressed by his mastery of intricate financial matters and lulled into a false sense of security by their certainty that he is a good man who would not willingly do them wrong. The parallel might be too close for comfort. In that wretched 1929 Parliament, whose record no socialist now defends, most Labour Members were blind to Snowden' s shortcomings. They allowed themselves to be led like lambs to the slaughter.

Its main attack, of course, was on the Health Service charges:

> He has not resisted the temptation to attack the National Health Service in a manner which has caused more rejoicing in the Tory heaven than all his delicacy in rejecting socialist measures. There is no case whatsoever for this proposal on grounds of merit .... He has opened a breach in the Health Service which can be made wider and wider each year by some future Tory Chancellor 'resisting socialist temptations'. ... It is hard to resist the conclusion that Mr Gaitskell shares the detestation of the Treasury officials for the principle of a free service.

'Resisting socialist temptations' was a quotation from a laudatory leader in *The Times*. Anticipating accusations of disloyalty, *Tribune* threw this one straight back at Gaitskell and his supporters: 'The responsibility for disunity ... rests with those, and Mr Gaitskell is only one of them, who are seeking to force a timid and squalidly inadequate policy down our throats.'

It did not help Mr Gaitskell and his friends very much that the Stock Exchange and practically all the British press differed from *Tribune*. The *Financial Times* reported almost boom conditions on the Stock Exchange. The financial editor of the *Manchester Guardian* noted that the 'Budget was remarkably well received on the Stock Exchange'. *The Times* purred with pleasure: 'This charge on spectacles and dentures – on that part of the Health Service where waste is suspected to be worst – has been widely accepted as the least harmful way that could be found of curbing extravagance' – as if people were getting themselves dentures for the fun of having their teeth extracted. But the *Daily Express* must have been the most embarrassing: 'Mr Gaitskell introduces a Tory Budget. He puts a fifty per cent charge on teeth and spectacles. That is what the Tories would have done. Now the job is done for them.'

As Michael Foot had forecast, three ministers resigned: Aneurin Bevan (then Minister of Labour), Harold Wilson (President of the Board of Trade) and John Freeman (at the Ministry of Supply). In his resignation speech in the House of Commons Bevan widened the issue from the charges to the question of defence expenditure. He attacked the size of this, not merely the means that had been used to raise the money. He prophesied that too rapid rearmament could get out of hand and produce 'a campaign of hate in a campaign of hysteria, which may make it very difficult to control that machine when it has been created'. He went on:

The lurchings of the American economy, the extravagant and unpredictable behaviour of the production machine, the failure on the part of the American Government to inject the arms programme into the economy slowly enough, have already caused a vast inflation of prices all over the world, have disturbed the economy of the Western world to such an extent that if it goes on more damage will be done by this unrestrained behaviour than by the behaviour of the nation the arms are intended to restrain.

His main attack had two prongs: that the arms programme could not be realized, and that the cuts in the social services were unnecessary. The £4,700 million arms programme, he said, 'is already dead'. On the Health Service charges he was bitterly ironic:

> If he finds it necessary to mutilate, or begin to mutilate the Health Service for £13 million out of a total of £4,000 million, what will he do next year? Or are you next year going to take your stand on the upper denture? The lower half, apparently, does not matter, but the top half is sacrosanct.

He also attacked the 'theft' of £100 million from the National Insurance Fund. Referring to Mr Gaitskell's budget speech, he said:

> There was a passage towards the end in which he said that he was now coming to a complicated and technical matter and if Members wished to they could go to sleep. They did. Whilst they were sleeping he stole £100 million from the National Insurance Fund − so the rearmament of Britain is financed out of the contributions that the workers have paid into the fund in order to protect themselves. [Hon. Members: 'Oh.'] Certainly, that is the meaning of it.

Harold Wilson, who followed him, was, of course, less provocative. He also claimed that the £1,500 million could not be spent, but he emphasized that he supported an effective defence programme and expressed his deep sense of privilege to his colleagues for the opportunity of serving with them and 'in however modest a way' to have played a part in the real and concrete achievements of the Government.

John Freeman, whose comments were sent in a letter to Attlee, also spread the argument. He wrote of 'a world which is torn between the brutalities of Soviet communism and the chaos of unrestrained capitalism in the United States' and of 'a serious and far-reaching crisis ... in Anglo-American relations'. Later, of course, he became the British Ambassador in Washington.

Two speeches in the House of Commons, one letter to the Prime Minister plus the columns of *Tribune* were clearly not sufficient to ventilate a matter of such importance. The resignations were not to be the end of the matter. It was decided, almost immediately, that the issues on which the three had resigned should be elaborated in a *Tribune* pamphlet. This was produced at high speed. It was called: *One Way Only: A Socialist Analysis of the Present World Crisis*. Twenty-five un-named MPs were consulted on its contents and subscribed to it. This was the beginning of the Bevanites. So far as I remember, Michael Foot wrote most of it, though Dick Crossman was responsible for the foreword, signed by the three ministers. A meeting at *Tribune's* office agreed the final text. There Dick Crossman was luckier than Michael. Since most people thought Nye had written the foreword, it was left undisturbed.

In fact, *One Way Only* did not widen the argument very much. It merely enlarged on it. After emphasizing in the foreword that they would 'account it frivolous and barren to do anything which might in the least impair the unity and strength of the Labour Movement' they made a passionate appeal for serious consideration of their arguments:

> From time to time the affairs of mankind converge towards a climax where a few simple decisions determine the pattern of man's fate for decades, if not for ever. We are at such a point now. Silence at such a time would be cowardice. No one who presumes to influence, or who by the accident of circumstances is in a position to influence, the minds of his fellows is entitled to stand aside and let the streams of human endeavour meet and leap towards catastrophe without doing his utmost to avert the tragedy.

The first chapter or section of the pamphlet was obviously aimed at the October Conference of the Labour Party which would be the first occasion when the Labour Movement would have an opportunity to reveal its views. It laid down five principles: 1. That war was not inevitable and a settlement must be sought with the Soviet Union; 2. That the under-developed countries had a right to complete their social revolution and must be helped to do so; 3. That Mutual Aid must have priority over military rearmament; 4. That what rearmament was necessary must be financed under socialist controls, not at the cost of inflation and the social services; and 5. That there must be more rapid progress towards socialism.

The pamphlet also made it clear that the Bevanites did not hold the view that Britain should deprive itself of the 'means to effective defence – for if we did, fear would supervene. But it is our view that the vast war machine to which the Western world is fast committing itself will obstruct and not open the paths to peace and freedom.' Neither was there any intention to advocate withdrawal from the Atlantic Alliance: 'We do not, of course, suggest that the Alliance should be broken. We do propose a series of British initiatives to rectify the top-sided nature of the Alliance and to secure certain specific purposes.'

Among the purposes cited was an armistice leading to a negotiated peace in the Far East, a refusal to restart the civil war in China, and opposition to German rearmament and any truck with Franco. There were no hints then of a call for withdrawal from NATO which did not arise until much later, in the CND campaign. All the Bevanites asked at that stage was that the British Labour Government should seek to 'restrain the Americans' and 'deter the Russians'.

It is, therefore, a little surprising that *One Way Only* caused such a furore. Practically every newspaper in the country attacked it in news stories or reviews, and in leaders. Naturally this was very good for sales, but there were difficulties. In the days and weeks before publication we had tried desperately to convince wholesalers that there would be a big demand for it, but with very little success. W. H. Smith, having seen our early press cuttings, before publication, reluctantly raised their order from four thousand to five thousand. Wyman's remained unimpressed and added only seventy-eight.

The consequence was that while the pamphlet was being asked

for at practically every bookstall and bookshop in the country, it was almost unobtainable. In London, the really eager purchasers came up to the office and, on the day of publication, we took £20 (800 copies). We had heated arguments on the telephone with W. H. Smith and even more vitriolic conversations with Jennie Lee who wanted to know why it couldn't be had. Eventually I had a brainwave and brought the two together. I suggested to Jennie that she telephone W. H. Smith and told her whom to contact. The effect was instantaneous. A very aggrieved manager rang up; asked me who she was, complained that she had accused him, quite rightly, of political prejudice, and proceeded to add 15,000 to their order, and on the days that followed 25,000, then another 10,000, then 7,500 for current orders. Wyman's, which runs all the bookstalls on Western and Midland Region stations, was still unimpressed. They added a thousand and sold less over the whole of that area than one bookstall in Fleet Street.

We flooded them out in London, of course, where we could supply them, directly, on sale or return, to bookshops and bookstalls. We sent thousands to Labour party and trade union branches. We took them around to meetings. Reg Davis-Poynter, who was always willing to help *Tribune* in any way, and I even took them to the Durham Miners' Gala, where we sold very few, for the gala is not an occasion for reading. We did not need to advertise. Every newspaper in the country was having a go. Finally, when we eventually got to Scarborough for the Labour Party Conference we found that the streets around the hotel where the NEC were staying were also advertising it. 'One Way Only' all the signs announced. Altogether we sold over 100,000. We could have sold double that if the trade had cooperated.

The press really enjoyed themselves. The pamphlet was an even better target than the resignations. Here is a selection from their diatribes:

Daily Telegraph:
If the Government and the Socialist Party policy makers imagined that the Bevan storm had spent its fury, they have suffered a rude

shock. Mr Bevan, Mr Wilson and Mr Freeman have given their benediction with some unspecified and apparently minor reservations to a *Tribune* pamphlet of inordinate length, woolliness and verbosity and of not inconsiderable disingenuousness.

Daily Mail:

Its comparative mildness, nevertheless, came as a distinct relief to socialist leaders. There is none of the fire and fury they anticipated.

Birmingham Post:

Forcefully and bitingly phrased, the programme of socialism sponsored by Mr Bevan, Mr Harold Wilson and Mr Freeman is a massive attack on Government policy .... Astute tactician as he is, Mr Bevan is attempting to ensure for himself and his colleagues the best of both worlds – to introduce a new dynamic leadership while disclaiming all intention of dividing the Labour Party.

Yorkshire Post:

Another long step towards a general levelling of incomes and towards the destruction of private property. It means, in other words, a step towards the Communist system .... Those who allow themselves to be taken in will be sorry for it later.

News Chronicle (10 July):

... in the Bevanite analysis of the impact of rearmament on our economy, there is much that is accurate. In his vision of the aid that can and should be given to the under-developed countries there is much that is sensible and just.

A. J. CUMMINGS, in the *News Chronicle* (17 July):

It is to be doubted whether any political document has ever received a more hostile press than Mr Aneurin Bevan's *One Way Only*. The *Daily Worker* and the *New Statesman* are apparently the only two British journals to say a good word for it.

Glasgow Herald:

Whatever one may think of *Tribune*, there is no denying that the people behind it are in a class by themselves in the art and practice of pamphleteering. Technically *One Way Only* is one of their best efforts.

Statist:

And what is Bevanism? The true mind behind the fat façade of Mr Bevan is the Robespierre mind of that sea-green, incorruptible, febrile, class-conscious agitator, Mr Michael Foot.

And so on, and so on .... Meanwhile the Trade Union Congress in early September gave Hugh Gaitskell a great ovation, but they also embarrassed him by passing unanimously a resolution demanding that National Insurance benefits be increased and maintained at the same level, in real money terms, as at the beginning of the scheme. That is, they cheered him, but rejected solidly a part of his famous budget.

One Way Only continued to sell and the tide in the Labour Movement seemed to be running our way. The October Conference was the mecca of our hopes. What was important was to keep the argument open and alive. So it was decided to produce another pamphlet, a sequel to *One Way Only*, called *Going Our Way*. It was in many ways tougher than its predecessor, more polemical and cheeky. There was an introduction by Aneurin Bevan who claimed that the resignations and *One Way Only* had provoked world-wide argument on the issues: 'Second thoughts are occurring to the minds of those who thought they were so sure. Already changes of policy are taking place and more have been announced ... the duty of the Labour Movement is clear. It is to resolve the argument and at the same time maintain unity.'

It then proceeded to reiterate the arguments in *One Way Only* but with considerable evidence to show how right they had been in predicting the impact of rearmament on the economy. But it also launched a very impertinent attack on the TU members of the National Executive Committee of the Labour Party, who had voted for an NEC resolution supporting the budget, in defiance, said Ian

▲ 1a   Victor Gollancz   ▼ 1b   Aneurin Bevan

▲ 2a   Labour Party Conference at Morcombe, 1952.

▼ 2b   Arthur Deakin declaring war on the Bevanites at Morcombe, 1952.

Mikardo (for it was he who wrote this section), of the views of their unions. The men indicted of this crime were heavyweights from the top unions in the country; the NUR, the National Union of Agricultural Workers, the T & GWU, USDAW, the M & GWU, the Miners, TSSA and the ETU. Such a direct attack on the hierarchies further goaded the right wing. The backlash came later.

The pamphlet also contained pro-Bevanite cartoons by Vicky, Low and Searle and was peppered with a series of quotations. One of these, headed: *There's nothing like keeping Personalities out of Politics*, was a selection of virulent attacks on the Bevanites. The quotations included Hartley Shawcross ('Extreme Left-wingers ... some with outlooks soured and warped by disappointment of personal ambitions, some highbrows educated beyond their capacity'), Stanley Evans, MP ('Leading an uneasy coalition of well-meaning emotionalists, rejects, frustrates, crackpots and fellow travellers'). and Lord Winster ('The sponsors of this pamphlet and the authors have put their heads in the sand, so exposing their thinking parts').

We sat up very late one night in my flat in St Pancras pasting up the pages. This, some of us felt, would be a milestone on the road to victory at Scarborough. It was published a week or so before the conference. We had less difficulty this time in getting the wholesalers to take copies. We held a press conference at the House of Commons which went well. As I walked down the stairs afterwards with Michael I said: 'There's only one snag which could upset everything – if Attlee calls a General Election.'

This, of course, is exactly what he did. Labour had been returned with a small majority in 1950. He saw, apparently, an opportunity to increase it and called an election for 25 October. Conference was demoted to a two-day affair for elections to the Executive and for rabble-rousing.

It was devastating news. A hard-hitting pamphlet shortly before a Labour Party Conference was nothing outrageous, but a pamphlet like *Going Our Way* shortly before a General Election was something quite different. It was too late to stop it. Copies had been delivered to the wholesalers. The press had it. After hurried conferings and heart searchings it was agreed to lay low. We decided to go to Scarborough with our *Tribunes* and our two pamphlets and to sell them quietly and not too ostentatiously.

So off we went. Bob Edwards, who had been working for the *People* since *Tribune* became a fortnightly, working one day a week for *Tribune*, Reg Davis-Poynter and I and, of course, most of the Bevanite team.

It was a very odd conference – the most alcoholic I can remember. I suppose people put five days' drinking in two days. In spite of all the problems there was still a Bevanite victory. Manny Shinwell, one of *Tribune's* most virulent critics, was knocked off the Executive and Barbara Castle went on, as one of the seven CLP members, and not as before as one of the five women members. Manny took it badly. One of the political pitfalls for members of the NEC is that if you lose your seat you still have to sit there on the platform and smile, because the new EC doesn't take over until after the conference. But not Manny. He went off home as quickly as he could, sulking.

Going Our Way, and *One Way Only* as well, were forgotten for the duration of the election. It was only afterwards, when the Tories were in power again, that the backlash came.

Looking back now at the events of 1951, recollected not in tranquillity but in continuing controversy, there are two questions which come to my mind.

1. Were the Health Charges, a direct affront to Aneurin Bevan, really necessary? It was clear, and even Gaitskell had to admit it later, that the possibility of spending £1,500 million that year was very dicey. The charges saved only £13 million. There were other ways in which this comparatively small sum could have been found. Why did he do it? There is some evidence that, taking advantage of the fact that Attlee was sick in St Mary's Hospital, Paddington, Morrison and Gaitskell deliberately forced a confrontation with Bevan. This is certainly in line with Gaitskell's behaviour, years later, on the Bomb. When the unilateralist resolution was passed,

he scorned all possible compromises and himself made it an issue of his leadership. He deliberately risked disunity and disruption in the party and insisted on asserting his own authority.

2. Why was the left in the Party so slow in beginning to question American policy? There had, of course, been running criticism of Ernie Bevin's cold war, during the late forties. But legitimate fears of Soviet totalitarianism and brutality seemed to have blinded them far too long to the equally acute dangers of American policy, especially in the Far East. They never questioned, for instance, the Korean war. Only James Cameron, later, reviewing I. F. Stone's book *The Hidden History of the Korean War* in *Tribune*, went so far as that. 'This repellent business has now reached a point,' he wrote, 'where it is possible to protest without, as has been customary hitherto, being denounced as an idealist, a Communist, or an imbecile.'

He went on to question the whole basis of the war – which *Tribune* and the Labour left seemed to have accepted until then. He asked the '64 dollar question: whether on 25 June 1950 North Korea did indeed attack without provocation or whether, as seems hard to deny, the attack was encouraged politically by the bellicose Syngman and provoked militarily by three feints across the border. The UN Commission on the spot – it is worth recalling now – has never even yet committed itself.'

From the time of the resignations on, *Tribune*, Bevan and the Bevanites became more and more critical of America. But it was not until 1954 when there was a real danger that Britain might be dragged into a further war in the Far East – in Vietnam – that Nye went so far as to propose that Britain should threaten to withdraw from the Alliance. By that time, of course, the Conservative Foreign Minister, Anthony Eden, was also conscious of the danger. What was galling, and Nye certainly must have found it so, was that 'the British initiative to rectify the lopsided nature of the Alliance' urged in *One Way Only*, came briefly, in 1954, from a Conservative Government. Later, when Nye was dead, and Labour came to power again, his comrade in resigning, Harold Wilson, reverted to a sycophancy towards the United States unrivalled by Hugh Gaitskell himself.

The Bevanites

Who were they? What did they do? Why did they cause such a
storm among the powers that were then in the Labour Party?

At the beginning they were just a group of Members of
Parliament who supported Aneurin Bevan and *Tribune*. They
numbered around fifty but their allegiance varied greatly. The hard
core could be identified usually by the fact that they took part in
Tribune brains trusts. Youngsters who were still at school or in the
prams at that time will be surprised to learn that Desmond Donnelly
was one of them. He left them in a typically highly-publicized
manner during the 1954 Conference when he 'stabbed Nye in the
back' from the rostrum. They might also find it strange that Anthony
Greenwood was not. He remained very much on the fringe until the
mid fifties when he became a left nominee for the National
Executive Committee.

Harold Wilson was there, of course, as one of the original
resigning ministers. He became chairman of the meetings in the
House. He spoke at *Tribune* meetings, both at Conference and
around the country and took part in occasional brains trusts. I
remember that during or after one meeting at the *Tribune* office he
proposed that when the left had won, right-wingers who wanted to
earn their passages back into favour should be asked to sell *Tribune*
on the street for three months. It would be interesting to know how
many of his late Government performed that particular chore.

Some of the names were listed in *Tribune* in early 1953 in a
column advertisement of meetings and brains trusts in about twenty-
five towns around Britain. There was Sir Richard Acland, John
Baird, Geoffrey Bing, and, of course, Fenner Brockway. Then there
was Barbara, George Craddock from Bradford, Dick Crossman and
Harold Davies who went back to Hanoi in 1965 and wondered why
he was no longer welcome. Then came John Freeman, Will Griffiths

(Will, not James), Leslie Hale, Aithur Irvine, and Jennie Lee. Marcus Lipton and J. P. W. (Curly) Mallalieu, Archie Manuel, Ian Mikardo, Walter Monslow, Maurice Orbach, Cecil Poole, Barnett Stross, and Stephen Swingler. Add to these Michael Foot, Hugh Delargy, Emrys Hughes, Zilly, Sydney and Julius Silverman and Lord Faringdon, who drove brains trust teams around in his Rolls, and you have the hard core of them. But this list is not exhaustive and I apologize to any who would like to be remembered. Today, it seems an odd heterogeneous group, but the left has always come and gone with the wind and today's revolutionaries tend to be tomorrow's potentates – not all of them, of course. Some, like Fenner and one or two others, have not moved or changed.

In the early days they met weekly at the House of Commons, taking over from the old Keep Left group. They discussed various political issues, according to the state of the House and the Movement, and papers provided by members of the group or by academics who occasionally attended. When these meetings came under heavy fire, they moved out of the House to hold luncheon meetings at Dick Crossman's house in Vincent Square. At the same time, of course, Hugh Gaitskell and his buddies were also meeting over lunch, but their meetings were not regarded as dangerous or illegitimate.

Unfortunately, they had very little support from trade union leaders. Bryn Roberts, of NUPE, was one of the few and NUPE is not a very big union. This was the major difference between the Bevanites and CND. By the end of the 1950s CND had top trade union leaders like Frank Cousins and John Horner, as well as rank and file support bringing unions like the AEU to their side against the virulent opposition of their leaders.

The Bevanites were the apostles. They went out into the country and told the gospel. From 1951 to 1955 when I left *Tribune*, and beyond that, they tramped the country, putting the case. There were big public meetings, for which the big names were used, especially Nye, but also Barbara Castle, Harold Wilson, Dick Crossman and Michael Foot. But the brains trusts were the core of their campaign. There had been brains trusts organized by the Keep Left group and they were, I think, the brain child of Ian Mikardo, who remained the best chairman of a brains trust ever known. In his book, *The Politics of Harold Wilson*, Paul Foot refers to 'prodigious propaganda work outside Parliament': 'A massive apparatus of *Tribune* brains trusts, held at the rate of four or five a week, and supplemented by numerous weekend schools, reached into almost every constituency in the land.' He is right about the brains trusts, though I can remember no weekend schools. There were, of course, many weekends spent on four or five brains trusts in a particular area of the country. They were different and exciting. The resignations and the pamphlets had provoked tremendous interest in Labour parties. Most of them, as elections to the NEC showed, were firmly behind Nye. They were only too anxious to lay on meetings for him. The brains trusts were popular because they brought not one good speaker but three, four, or five and they allowed for audience participation. The chaps on the floor joined in and could argue in a series of supplementary questions with the team on the platform.

They were organized by Elizabeth Thomas, then Michael Foot's secretary, now literary editor of *Tribune*. The MPs operated as a team, or a number of teams, for the membership varied from place to place. Weekend after weekend, we would set off from London with the team and the usual bundles of Tribune, covering a number of towns over the two to three days. One who often took part was Lord Faringdon and he certainly gave the team an air which it lacked when he was absent. He owned a beautiful, rather ancient, pale green Rolls Royce, with the Faringdon arms on the doors, very small and dignified. The team would pack itself into its affluent seats and set off along the A1, the A5, the A6, the A4, whatever the weekend's bookings required, at a steady thirty-five miles an hour. His Lordship would never drive faster than that, and would not allow anyone else to drive it. Later, when we had the Tribune van, the little red Ford for which we launched an appeal in May 1953, we would set off in cars and the van.

It was a massive apparatus. In January 1953 *Tribune* advertised a long series of the trusts, and the demand seemed insatiable. We must, eventually, have covered nearly every constituency in the country, except the far north of Scotland. One summer we went to Cornwall and did a tour there lasting a week or more. There was one ghastly mistake there. We booked the team into a temperance hotel. But even that wasn't too bad for it turned out that it was only temperance because the landlord had lost his licence for drinking out of licensing hours with his friends, and there were always crates of beer around, if you knew where to look for them. After that, with cars and the little red van, we set off for Brecon and Radnor and toured around the upper Wye valley and the Breconshire villages with Tudor Watkins, the MP.

Then there were the meetings. Nye could have done seven a week, but he sensibly rationed himself, for they were a considerable strain. During those years I travelled throughout the length and breadth of the land in the little *Tribune* van to his meetings. I heard him speak so often that many parts of his speeches became very familiar, but I never tired of them. The best speeches I ever heard him make were at the *Tribune* meetings at Party Conferences. There was no question there of stringing together a number of parts of different speeches. Here was a highly politically educated audience – for Nye, the best audience in the world. There he really excelled himself. There was '52 in Morecambe, '53 Margate, '54 Scarborough, '55, after I had gone, Margate again. At Morecambe, we were unable to get the main hall in the Winter Gardens for the meeting and had to use the ballroom which took only one thousand seated but plenty over that standing. That year we had hired a small ancient blue van to take up all the *Tribunes* and we drove along the front in it a good hour before the meeting was due to begin. As we neared the Winter Gardens, there was an enormous queue along the front, about twenty to thirty deep, just like an Aldermaston March on Easter Monday, waiting to get in. They recognized the van and some of them chased us into the car park, frantic for tickets which were all sold. Somehow, we got them all in.

Occasionally we also laid on big meetings in London. We held two in the Prince's Theatre, now the Shaftesbury, of which Jack Hilton, who was also a Bevan fan, held the lease, and one in

Seymour Hall. All we had to do was to advertise them in *Tribune*. They were always packed. The first meeting at the Prince's raised the money to buy the little red Tribune van.

The fifty or so MPs, more or less, who manned the brains trusts, worked as a group in the House and met regularly at least for a time, were the front line, the upper strata of the Bevanite Movement, the First XI. But there was also a lower strata, people outside the House, who were either parliamentary candidates or aimed to become so. This was the Second XI. In the beginning it was an informal group but it gradually became more formal and more important as the heat on the First XI increased. After the famous resolution was passed by the Parliamentary Labour Party banning all group organizations other than those officially recognized, the Second XI was promoted. From 1954 on, certainly, it met regularly once a month, kept minutes of its proceedings, established sub-committees and took in a few MPs to provide a link with the House. It even organized occasional social gatherings, usually at Lord Faringdon's house at Buscot Park. A proposal to hold an annual dinner in the House of Commons was shelved. They thought the venue 'too dangerous'.

The Second XI set up four sub-committees: on Elections, to compile lists of constituencies and possible candidates; on Contacts, to discover like-minded people; on Policy and Propaganda; and on Conferences, to plan and prepare activity from a very early stage on.

Who were these people who were so very carefully selected? The MP members included Ian Mikardo, Michael Foot, Barbara Castle, John Freeman, Geoffrey Bing, Stephen Swingler and Harold Davies. There was also Gavin Faringdon. Members who subsequently made the grade and got themselves into the House were Hugh Jenkins, Renee Short. Stan Orme, Arnold Gregory and Albert Booth were suggested as members just before it closed. Other members were Ted Castle, then looking for a safe seat so he could join Barbara at Westminster, Jo Richardson who was its secretary, Lyn Mostyn, Ralph Miliband, and Geoffrey Drain of NALGO. Russ Kerr was a member in its first days but went back to Australia at an early stage. Many of the names now mean nothing. They have emigrated or faded out of politics. There was certainly no quick and ready route from the Second to the First XI. Indeed, on the whole they seem to have suffered from a shortage of adequate candidates, especially, of course, for hopeless Conservative seats in the country.

They differed occasionally on the relative merits of short-term empiricism and long-term utopias. Their list of resolutions for Conference one year reveals this dichotomy. On the one hand they wanted to abolish the Lords, to reaffirm their fundamental belief in common ownership and in equality. On the other, they were concerned with insurance contributions, municipalization of housing, housing subsidies. They had trouble with Hugh Jenkins who wanted his constituency, Westminster, to table a resolution calling for a vote of no confidence in the leadership. Reluctantly he was persuaded not to do so. Eventually they decided that they ought to produce two programmes: one for the period 1960 to 1965, one for 1965 to 1970. History does not record what happened to them.

It was at that stage that word came from Harold Wilson, who had then moved back in with the party hierarchy, that the existence of the Second XI had been observed. He told Barbara Castle, who told Ted, that the NEC was proposing to take action against them. Silently, they folded up their tents and departed. That was in midsummer 1956, when Bevanism was beginning to decline.

Yet the Second XI was not entirely ineffective. It never made the headlines, like the First XI, but that was not its aim; rather the contrary. Since the main obstacle to left-wing policies lay in the right-wing majority in the Parliamentary Labour Party, an effective tactic, then as now, was to get more left-wingers into the House. Many constituencies which had long been 'pocket boroughs', for whom candidates were nominated and subsidized by one of the big trade unions, had started to be choosy. Indeed, as early as November 1952, *The Times* reported that some union leaders had been 'looking at the donations they made to the Labour Party and pondering over the fact that these funds are used to help Parliamentary candidates whether such candidates are Bevanites or in other ways undesirable'. It suggested that they were considering a plan to overcome the difficulty whereby 'constituencies are showing an increasing tendency to prefer lively young Bevanites to worthy but dull trade unionists who are approaching the retiring age.'

The First and Second XIs *Tribune* articles and pamphlets were not the only source of the Bevanite gospel, but undoubtedly they were the most important. *Tribune* was accepted as the spokesman, the mouthpiece of the movement. Certainly, after the resignations, its circulation (as Michael Foot had foretold) and its prestige increased rapidly. It also began to change in character.

During the summer of 1952, we started to talk about the possibility of reverting to weekly publication, and of changing the style and format of the paper. Until then, *Tribune* had a magazine format, similar to the *New Statesman* and *Spectator*, but rather less orthodox. It was certainly not, in design, exciting. Indeed it was pretty ghastly. What was now suggested was that it should be larger, newspaper size, like the *Standard*, a weekly, and cheaper. These were pretty revolutionary proposals for a paper nearly always flat broke, but there was logic behind them.

I was convinced that, if *Tribune* was to become a weekly newspaper, it was absolutely essential that it should have a newspaper-type-journalist as editor. Bob Edwards must be persuaded to leave the *People* and come back, full-time, to *Tribune*. Bob Edwards was only too willing to oblige and this was soon agreed. After that we spent ecstatic weeks planning the new paper.

The new *Tribune* made a great impression. The first issue was produced for the Labour Party Conference and the second issue arrived, mid week, to be sold there. The system we had built up for selling *Tribunes* around Conference paid off. Thousands of copies were sold. *Tribune*, more than ever before, was the voice of the Bevanites.

But it was also useful in other ways. While the First and Second XIs busied themselves locally pushing suitable resolutions for Conference, or for the NEC, *Tribune* supplemented their efforts. It was easy to see that from July on, it had its eye on the Annual Conference to come. It was especially valuable for the promotion of the seven to be elected by constituency parties for the Executive Committee. Every year you would see the left aspirants featured in

Tribune. One year, as in 1954, they would jointly sign a *Tribune* pamphlet against German rearmament. Another year, you would find their names, together with flattering photographs, under a series of articles, during August and September. Anthony Greenwood's success was preceded by just such a build up. Indeed, since he was a newcomer, he got two articles. *Tribune,* after he was elected, innocently congratulated him on his fine showing. Later, of course, they were trying to get him off. Some of us once discussed the possibility of charging a fee for this service.

That was the Bevanites. There was nothing underhand or wicked about them. In a free society they had every right to behave as they did. They were just as legitimate as the Campaign for Democratic Socialism launched in 1960 by Hugh Gaitskell. What was so extraordinary was the reaction of their opponents within the party. This was revealed, after the General Election of 1951, in a series of major battles between the National Executive and the Parliamentary Party, and the Bevanites: the backlash.

The Backlash

The backlash started slowly as1951 moved into 1952. There had been a truce during the General Election. 'My friends and I,' said Nye, speaking at the party rally on the eve of the brief Scarborough Conference, 'have made up our minds that every single resource we have at our disposal and that all the might we could summons up, must be devoted to destroying the Tory challenge and to get a Labour majority back to the House of Commons. When that has been done we might resume our discussion.'

It did not help matters that Labour failed to win. Worse still, as the year rolled on to its end, it became clear that Bevan, Wilson, and Freeman had been right about the rearmament programme. The first signs of distress were visible in November. 'It is now obvious,' said the *Observer*, 'that we shall not be able to carry through our rearmament programme and maintain our external balances without some form of American aid.' Even the Tory *Telegraph* started moaning: 'Without such aid, it is becoming increasingly evident that our economy cannot bear the full strain.' *The New York Herald Tribune* reported that Plowden was expected to appeal to NATO that Britain's arms burden was too heavy.

Worse followed. In December, Winston Churchill announced in the House, not without some malice aforethought: 'We shall not succeed in spending the £1,250 million this year and some of the late Government's programme must necessarily roll forward into a future year .... Mr Bevan, by accident, perhaps not for the best of motives, happened to be right.'

Michael Foot went rapidly on to the offensive in *Tribune*:

For the sake of saving £13 million of expenditure the Chancellor pushed through these charges on the Health Service against the obvious wishes of the Parliamentary Labour Party. That decision almost involved the defeat of the General Council of the TUC at the last Congress. For the sake of saving a few millions, the Chancellor abrogated a principle underlying the National Insurance Act and introduced discrimination against the chronic sick, the unemployed and certain categories of old age pensioners ... and now we learn that all this grief and dissension was provoked to make possible a provision of military estimates which could not be fulfilled.

Tribune was always generous at times like these. Mr Gaitskell was invited to defend himself and could hardly refuse. He provided a long and turgid article attempting to excuse hiniself. 'We also held,' he wrote, 'that any sign of weakening in the will of Britain to play her proper part in NATO would have very bad international consequences, especially in Europe.' Even then, he was firmly wedded to NATO. Michael Foot returned to the attack:

> Meantime it is proved as irrefragably as anything can be proved in politics that the charges on the Health Service and the disruption of a main principle underlying the National Insurance Act were pushed through the House of Commons and down the throats of the Labour Party, last April, on the basis of figures about which Mr Gaitskell happened to be wrong as surely as Aneurin Bevan, in Churchill's phrase, 'happened to be right'.

The list of Bevanite crimes piled up. First, the resignations, then *One Way Only*, then *Going Our Way* on the eve of the election and with its attacks on trade union leaders, then Manny knocked off the NEC, then, worst of all, the 'happening to be right'.

But next there was the wicked and irresponsible behaviour of as many as fifty-seven MPs during the Defence Debate in March 1952. The Tories were aiming to increase the Defence Estimates by bet/ween £200 and £300 million. The opposition decided to put down an amendment approving the White Paper but doubting the capacity of Tory ministers to carry it out – which was a bit cool from Mr Gaitskell and a bit too much for the fifty-seven MPs. A considerable number abstained on the opposition amendment and the fifty-seven were wicked enough to vote against the Tories.

Immediately, the question of discipline was raised in the Parliamentary Labour Party and there were threats to withdraw the whip. Fifty-seven whips are an awful lot to withdraw, and since it was obviously impossible to withdraw the whip from so many, nothing was done. But in the next issue of *Tribune* Mr Arthur Deakin, of the T&GWU, responded to an invitation to express his complaints about *Tribune*. In a speech at Bristol he had accused the Tribune group of seeking a short cut to the leadership of the party. He set out to justify himself:

> I would say quite clearly that the *Tribune* group of politicians I had in mind goes beyond the joint editors and contributors writing in its pages. The people who have attached themselves to the 'bandwagon' are well-known. They are people who have continuously sought to discredit the policies determined by Labour in Government, and the general policies of the Movement reached by majority decision, when they were in the minority .... Why is it necessary to establish the *Tribune* or to gather together that dissident element? Is there not sufficient scope within our Movement, using the official agencies, to provide for an effective expression of opinion, without certain factions seeking to operate as a 'pressure group' within the party? ... The charges I make ... that the *Tribune* group of politicians have continually flouted party decisions. That they have sought to discredit the policies of Labour in Government and have done great disservice to the party. This leads me to the conclusion that the chief object they have in mind is to secure the advancement of the political fortunes of persons in that group.

Small fires continued to burn in the field during the spring and early summer. With the circulation rising rapidly, *Tribune* then announced its plans to become a weekly again and a newspaper. As the next Party Conference hove in sight, the opposition brought up its heavy artillery. Mr Patrick Gordon Walker made a statement in Dorking:

'One of the great difficulties in discussing within the Labour Party such matters as German rearmament is that we cannot consider the merits properly. We have to take into account that there is a deliberately organized party within a party – this endangers the proper democratic working of the Parliamentary Party.'

This new cliché – a party within a party – caught on immediately. Mr A. J. Cummings went into the attack in the *News Chronicle*. He claimed that the Bevanites were a tightly organized group, with their own private meetings and their own whips. He claimed that Ted Castle was the 'manager'. This was certainly untrue. Ted was an ardent Bevanite but had little to do with organizing either the brains trusts or the parliamentary group of Bevanites. If anybody managed, it was *Tribune* and Ian Mikardo. Meanwhile floods of resolutions on rearmament flooded in to Transport House and the Morecambe Conference loomed nearer. No hope or fear, this time, that a General Election would intervene. In early August, generous as usual, *Tribune* allowed Lork Pakenham to expatiate on the subject of 'a party within a party':

> It has been widely stated without denial that they hold regular meetings of their own group before the meetings of the Parliamentary Labour Party, that they concert their own line and choose their own spokesmen for the purpose both of these discussions and of Debates in the House itself. In Parliament, these spokesmen put the Bevanite as opposed to the official Labour standpoint and show scant respect to the official leadership in doing so.

Accusations rocketed to and fro as Morecambe became more and more imminent. Reg Davis-Poynter and I set off in the little, blue, hired van, stopped overnight in deepest Derbyshire, and stopped early next morning in Macclesfield to buy the Sunday papers. There was the *Sunday Pictorial*, with Hugh Cudlipp also having a go! 'END THE BEVAN MYTH' it shouted in huge caps on the front page. 'A Frank Attack on the Man who has forfeited his Claim to the Loyalty of the Labour Party.'

It was the one and only time that the Labour Party conferred in Morecambe. The Winter Gardens were cramped and very hot. The hot air was even hotter. Daily, while the tide disappeared miles out into the Irish Channel, Arthur Deakin, General Secretary of the T&GWU, plodded his weary way to the rostrum. 'Shut your gob,' shouted Will Lawther, Secretary of the Mineworkers, to a delegate who dared to interrupt him. The big victory, of course, was not in the resolutions passed but, as usual, in the elections to the NEC. Both Harold Wilson and Dick Crossman went on, and Morrison came off.

But even that had a backlash, for a day later Dick, sometimes known as 'double-dick', went to the rostrum aud said: 'Yesterday I prepared a number of fine things to say, but delegates will understand why today I am not going to say them ...' The cheers that had greeted him changed to boos. They thought he was ready to sell them out, now he had a seat on the NEC. Maybe, in the long run, they were right. But why don't they boo now!

The Conference itself, these two victories in the elections for the NEC, the remarkable *Tribune* meeting that year in the ballroom: all these enhanced the position of the rebels. But it was Gaitskell himself who really raised the temperature to fever point. Furious at the defeat of Herbert Morrison (unlike Manny he took it very well and sat there all week on the platform, 'smiling at grief') Gaitskell went off as soon as the Conference was over to speak at a meeting in Stalybridge. There he really let down his hair. He talked of 'mob rule' and made the same sort of mistake as in 1960 when he spoke of 'pacifists, neutralists and communists'. 'I have been told,' he said, 'by some observers that about one-sixth of the Constituency Party delegates appear to be communist, or communist-inspired .... This figure may well be too high. But if it should be one-tenth or one-twentieth it is a most shocking state of affairs to which the National Executive should give immediate attention.'

Tribune, which never lost its sense of humour (which particularly infuriated its enemies), produced a little rhyme:

▲ 3a   A *Tribune* Conference Meeting: Michael Foot, Claude Bourdet (Parti Socialiste
Unifie), Ian Mikardo and Aneurin Bevan.

▼ 3b   End of an era: Aneurin Bevan and Hugh Gaitskell united on the plinth of Trafalgar
Square in opposing H-Bomb Tests, 1959.

◀ 4a Kennistoun House in September 1960 when bailiffs finally took possession of Don Cook's barricaded flat.

▼ 4b Tom Barker, St Pancras Mayor who travelled by 68 bus, and his wife with Peggy Duff and Charles Ratchford (who succeeded John Lawrence as leader of the Council).

> Twinkle, twinkle, little Hugh,
> How I wonder how you knew
> Who was red and who was not –
> Mass observation on the spot.

The Times was almost as annoyed as Gaitskell, but more restrained. 'The seven representatives of the local parties on the Executive,' it proclaimed, 'are elected by the half-informed and politically active workers in the constituencies.'

The old stories about secret meetings and party managers were trotted out again. As soon as Parliament reassembled, the battle began. A resolution was proposed at a meeting of the Parliamentary Labour Party, calling for 'the immediate abandonment of all group organizations within the Party other than those officially recognized' – and calling on 'all members to refrain from attacks on one another, either in the House, the press or the platform'. While this might, in the circumstances, have been seen as an attack on Hugh Gaitskell, it was passed. The *Manchester Guardian*, of course, approved and accused the Bevanites of being 'masters of invective and malignant vituperation'. Hugh Gaitskell accepted a further invitation to write in *Tribune* and naively invited the paper, instead of being the organ of a group, 'to represent the whole of the Movement with an editorial board selected accordingly'. Faint hope and harsh prospect! In reply, Michael Foot cited the natives of Papua – 'a fierce and intractable race of savages who when fired upon had no scruple in retaliating'. J. P. W. Mallalieu, as usual, fanned the flames of controversy by his wit. His Westminster Commentary was headed with an official stamp:

PASSED FOR PUBLICATION
Parliamentary Labour Party
Censorship Division.

Lord Stansgate, father of Anthony Wedgwood Benn, expressed the growing concern of many liberals within the party. 'The resolution,' he said, was 'too much like emergency regulations in a tropical colony in revolt. ... The symbol of victory is a torch, not a jackboot.'

Came the New Year, and there in the new style *Tribune* was a whole column advertisement of three big meetings: Coventry, Sheffield and Liverpool and twenty-two brains trusts, some over a weekend involving four to five different towns. The effect was rather like a molotov cocktail. Once again, the Parliamentary Party went on the offensive. Another resolution was passed, early in February, demanding an 'investigation' into Tribune brains trusts. They were, of course, terribly stupid. There was no surer way of filling our halls than by publicly calling for such an investigation.

A sub-committee of the NEC, mad keen to get at the enemy, went ahead and denounced the brains trusts. 'Those taking part in these brains trusts,' they declared, 'do form a separate group, within the Labour Party.' Naturally, the NEC agreed. J. P. W. Mallalieu, undeterred, wrote a couple of hilarious columns in *Tribune*, reporting a Sherlock Holmes investigation of a brains trust in Manningtree. (Actually, I think that one never took place. So far as I remember, deep fog fell on Essex and nobody got there.)

John Strachey also reacted, less hilariously:

> I see reports in the press of proposed moves to ban this or that form of public meeting or one particular independent journal. I cannot for one moment believe that these moves will be pressed. What country is this, anyway – the birthplace of liberty or some totalitarian state?

Kingsley Martin also protested in the *New Statesman* and the *News Chronicle* congratulated him on coming to the defence of his commercial rival.

The Labour Party, nevertheless, proceeded to press on. But what was done to carry out this investigation we never knew. We just used to wonder which was the Transport House nark sitting in the audience. Transport House then threatened to launch its own weekly paper. Mallalieu was funny again about this, suggesting a number of ribald titles.

After this things quietened down a bit and the year rolled on. *Tribune* held its meeting at the Prince's Theatre in May and purchased the *Tribune* van. The summer moved on again and the next Labour Party Conference started to loom on the horizon. The six Bevanite candidates for the NEC set up their banners in articles in *Tribune*. Nye, in fact, wrote a series. *Tribune* also hoisted a banner: an advertisement for the usual *Tribune* meeting at the Dome, Margate, followed by a meeting at the Seymour Hall in London immediately after Conference, plus five more big meetings around the country and twenty brains trusts. Whether or not it was a machine, it was working well.

The Margate Conference, when it came, seemed somehow an anti-climax. While the six, of course, were safely re-elected to the NEC, the conference itself was depressing. Maybe it was because even six members of the NEC were always in a minority while the big unions dictated the decisions. Maybe because we never got any real victories on the conference floor because the big bloc votes were always against us. I remember that year Harold Davies made an impassioned appeal to Conference, moving a resolution on East/West Trade. 'Comrades,' he said, 'I've been moving resolutions, year after year, and I never got one through. Comrades,' he pleaded, his face purple with emotion, his white hair blowing in the wind of his Welsh oratory, 'please, just this once' ... or words to that effect. Maybe the comrades were willing, but the bloc vote was not, and he was defeated. A year or two later it became platform policy. It was also, I think, that the movement was a bit tired of all the bickering, tired of being in opposition.

Once again there was trouble after the Conference. It was J.P. W. Mallalieu who sparked it off this time by a comment on the discrepancy between votes at Conference and for the Parliamentary Committee. He reported a conversation with a constituent, who asked him to explain why Nye got so many votes at Margate but so few in the House of Commons. 'What goes on?' he asked. Mallalieu explained in his *Tribune* column:

> The only explanation I could give my constituent was that there is a substantial difference of view on policy between the Constituency Parties and a majority of Labour MPs. I said it was not only that the

constituencies preferred men who demanded cuts in arms expenditure and the removal of charges on the Health Service, while a majority of Labour MPs preferred to select men who supported the maintenance of arms expenditure and the imposition of Health Service charges.

Far more important, I said, was that the Constituency Parties as a whole supported a more aggressive socialist policy, while the Parliamentary Party as a whole supported consolidation.

To this my constituent objected that he personally had never heard any Labour MP speaking in the country in favour of consolidation. MPs, he said, vied with each other on public platforms in demanding further steps to socialism.

It looks, he said, as though some of these chaps say one thing in public in the country and another thing behind closed doors in the party meetings.

Mikardo, about the same time, had a go at the General Council of the TUC for issuing a statement supporting the Tory Government line on British Guiana, completely ignoring the position taken by Labour official spokesmen in the House. Again, the usual accusations of personal attacks were raised to which *Tribune* replied with a spirited defence of freedom of speech.

On this occasion, the Parliamentary Party climbed down. Neither Mallalieu nor Mikardo retracted. Attlee issued a mild rebuke. It is interesting to note how small a part Attlee played in the goings on between 1951 until he resigned the leadership. He rarely became personally involved – yet he failed to stop it. As 1954 dawned, *Tribune* announced that it had held its 150th brains trust and that forty parties were still waiting. 1954, however, was a year in which issues became more important than personalities. The rows that occurred were almost entirely concerned with foreign policy: on the H Bomb, on Indo-China, the Vietnam War and SEATO, and on German rearmament.

Concern over the H Bomb erupted partly because of the *Lucky Dragon* incident (members of its crew were irradiated by fallout from a US H Bomb test in the Pacific), and because Britain was clearly moving towards the manufacture of British H Bombs.

Following the fate of the crew of the *Lucky Dragon*, *Tribune* published a front-page article which reads like a statement by Strachey or some other 'middle of the roader' during the CND campaign. It called for a constructive and imaginative plan for relieving world tensions, for rooting out the pressures and animosities and fears which have persuaded the leaders of the nations to devote so large a part of their resources to arms. Still, the agitation promoted a campaign against a British H Bomb. This was led by Fenner Brockway, Anthony Greenwood, Sydney Silverman, Anthony Wedgwood Benn and a number of others. It was basically Labour Party rather than pacifist. It launched a petition against the Bomb. It was not very well organized by Arthur Carr who had been Youth Organizer of Common Wealth, and who suffered from the illusion that any organizer who spends twenty-four hours in the office is doing a first-class job. The opposite is almost always the case. The petition finished with a rather depressing meeting at the Albert Hall, which was nothing like full.

It was a pretty dismal affair and *Tribune* did not even report it. It concentrated on the row over the Atomic Energy Authority Bill. Sixty-three MPs, quite a lot in those days, voted for an unofficial amendment that no H Bombs should be made by Britain without Parliamentary agreement. This was done against the advice of the Labour spokesman, George Strauss, incidentally one of *Tribune's* founders.

Please note: they did not oppose British manufacture of the H Bomb. They merely asked that nothing should be done without discussion and approval in Parliament. They remembered, no doubt, that Attlee had proceeded with the manufacture of the A Bomb without any discussion in the House at all. Labour had set the Tories an unfortunate example.

On this occasion, the rebels included three of the whips, one of whom was my own MP at that time, Kenneth Robinson. Since we have so often disagreed, I must record that on this occasion I was proud of him. He lost his whipship.

The second issue was Indo-China and the SEATO Alliance planned by John Foster Dulles. The Vietnam war was dragging slowly but inevitably to its close. The French had clearly lost it. The Vietnamese had, then as now, clearly won it. It was at this stage that, in an attempt to stave off defeat, the United States tried desperately to involve her Western allies and even, when the defeat at Dien Bien Phu loomed up, to get agreement to the use of the atomic bomb. The danger of world war in the Far East was clear and unmistakable.

As the Geneva Conference began, John Foster Dulles stumped around the allied capitals in search of support. Aneurin Bevan came out with a frank statement of his position in *Tribune* (14 April 1954): 'The only card we can play at Geneva is recognition of China in return for peace in Indo-China. And that means on a basis of independence for the Indo-Chinese. ... There are no qualifications to this. If the Indo-Chinese elect to go Communist, they should be allowed to do so.'

He went on to comment on the proposals for a new, SEATO, alliance:

> The demand that we should join an alliance for the containment of communism in South-East Asia is not sought as an instrument for the prevention of war but rather as an extension into the international field, of the defence of American social, political and economic values. The military threat is a cover for counter-revolutionary measures. We are being asked to join not an alliance for the preservation of peace, but a bulwark against political and social progress. ... This new move by the United States, therefore, brings us up against the old dilemma. Should we agree in the end, or should we carry our opposition to the point where it might mean a break? The answer is, quite simply, that we shall never be able to make America understand our attitude or adjust herself to it until we are prepared to break with her unless she does. ... We should tell America in the plainest possible terms. If, after that, she persists, then she must do so alone.

This was Nye at his best and he followed words with action. A week later *Tribune* reported the debate in the House on the Pacific alliance. When Eden agreed to examine the proposals and Attlee offered only a few mild observations, Nye sprang up and resigned his seat on the Parliamentary Committee. Even *Tribune* was shaken ... but how right Nye was, for British and French cooperation in the SEATO Alliance left the way open for the United States to ignore and sabotage the Geneva Agreements which Britain and France with Russian and Chinese support had forced through. If Eden and Mendes-France had been forced to take a stronger line on SEATO the history of the past fifteen years in South-East Asia might have been very different. Years later, when Labour came to power, Wilson lacked both the acumen of Bevan and the limited courage of Eden.

The third argument that year was about German rearmament. While a few who took part in the campaign against German rearmament were emotionally anti-German, the vast majority recognized that to agree to it was to accept a hardening and intensification of the cold war in Europe. Soviet and Eastern European fears of Germany were legitimate and understandable. Nevertheless, the right-wing majority on the National Executive Committee of the Labour Party and on the Parliamentary Labour Party were determined to push it through.

Tribune, as usual, led the campaign against it. It lambasted an official Labour Party pamphlet: '*In Defence of Europe*', published in June. When the BBC put on a programme, *Tribune* complained bitterly that only the official Labour Party view had been put, and *Truth* revealed that the BBC had intended to invite Bevan, but Morrison had refused to appear with him. Desperately, the powers-that-be tried to sell their case around the Labour movement. Private conferences were arranged for Labour Party and TU members. They did not go very well. At some, not a single vote or voice defended the official position. Then, with one eye on the Trade Union Congress in early September and the other on the Labour Party Conference a month later, *Tribune* produced its own pamphlet. It was, of course, signed by *Tribune's* six nominees for the Constituency Party section of the National Executive. But there were developments in this. Arthur Greenwood, father of Anthony and greatly respected treasurer of the party, died, and Gaitskell was nominated for the post, and for the seat on the NEC, by the T&GWU, the M&GWU and the AEU. Enough to get any man on! Gaitskell, of course, had always failed to get elected for the constituency section. He was anything but popular there. But the treasurer was elected by both unions and parties. The Bevanites decided that the challenge must be met and Nye was promptly also nominated for the treasurership. This left a vacancy on the constituency section, for Nye could hardly stand for both. Anthony Greenwood was hurriedly groomed for the vacant place. Hence his two articles in *Tribune*.

The TUC met in early September and passed a resolution in favour of German rearmament – but by so small a majority that it was pretty clear that the Labour Party Conference, with the Constituency Party votes, would reject it.

The Scarborough Conference of 1954 was undoubtedly one of the milestones in the history of the decline of the authority of Conference – and of the Labour Party. It showed, as 1960 showed also later on, that the notion that Conference decided policy, even with Labour in opposition, was a myth. All the expectations of a defeat for the NEC on the issue of German reannament came to nought because the powers-that-be in the Amalgamated Society of Woodworkers agreed to switch their votes and to defy the decision of their own conference. 129,000 votes moved from left to right and that was enough to save the platform. Needless to say, there was a tremendous huffle buffle afterwards. Hundreds of resolutions from branches of the ASW poured into their office, but it was too late.

This was also the conference at which Desmond Donnelly, as publicly as possible, quit the Bevanites. There was another enormous *Tribune* meeting in the Floral Hall where Nye made an impassioned and bitter attack on the *Manchester Guardian* which, with *The Times*, hailed the victory for German rearmament as 'the end of the Bevanites'.

Nye, of course, was defeated easily for the post of treasurer and Gaitskell got himself on to the NEC. So did the remaining *Tribune* five, plus Tony Greenwood. The right held only one seat in that section, with good old beat-your-breast-with-a-strong-Welsh-accent James Griffiths.

After that the scene of battle moved. Undeterred by all it had lost at Scarborough, *Tribune* set off on a real challenge to the Poohbahs of the right. It got itself involved in the dock strike, in support for the 'Blue Union' against the monster T&GWU, in a confrontation with Arthur Deakin himself.

The Docks

Ian Aitken, who had been research officer of the Confederation of Shipbuilding and Engineering Unions, came to *Tribune* as industrial correspondent just about this time. As a result *Tribune* began to carry a great deal more stories about unions and union affairs. This is how, towards the end of 1954, it got itself involved in a row between the Transport and General Workers' Union and the NASD, the National Amalgamated Stevedore and Dockers, generally known as the 'Blue Union'. It had considerable membership in four ports, London, Birkenhead, Liverpool and Hull, and the attitude of the T&GWU to it was anything but friendly. Naturally the fact that *Tribune* became the chief protector and protagonist of NASD further inflamed its relations with the right.

In October, the dockers in London went on strike against compulsory overtime, opposition to which had, at one time, been the policy of the T&GWU. But they now appeared to have changed their tune. From early 1954 there had been a ban on overtime which had hardened into a strike. On 12 October, 12,000 dockers marched to Victoria Park, Hackney. Certainly not all of them were members of NASD. Dockers, generally, were opposed to compulsory overtime. Immediately, they were attacked by Arthur Deakin, General Secretary of the T&GWU, who charged that the NASD was 'the spearhead of the communist drive for the control of the ports in this country'. *Tribune* joined in the battle on 22 October. Mr Deakin, said Ian Aitken, did not know what the strike was about and had no interest in finding out. *Tribune* pointed out that, not long ago, the opening of an NASD office in Hull had been denounced by the *Daily Worker*:

These then are the plain facts. Mr Deakin may think he has the right to try and crush a little union out of existence by branding it as communist. But few people are likely to agree with him.

A week later, the Court of Inquiry on the strike produced a report which made no attempt at reconciliation and NASD was chucked out of the TUC for failing to produce satisfactory explanations for their enrolling of T&GWU members in Hull and Birkenhead.

The heavy artillery opened up on *Tribune*. Percy Cudlipp first of all reported in the *News Chronicle* that 'certain powerful leaders of the TUC want to see disciplinary action taken against *Tribune* and the leaders of the hard core of Bevanites expelled.' The General Council of the TUC passed a resolution censoring *Tribune* for the article. The National Executive Committee of the Labour Party followed my leader. The article was, they said, 'an unwarranted, irresponsible, and scurrilous attack on the leadership of the Transport and General Workers' Union', and they added that 'the article be strongly deprecated as calculated to impede an honourable and orderly settlement of the dispute and as a breach of the injunction that members of the Labour Movement should not indulge in personal attacks on one another'. A letter was sent to Michael Foot, Jennie Lee, and J. P. W. Mallalieu, directors of Tribune Publications, Ltd., by Morgan Phillips, secretary of the Labour Party, inviting them to state how they reconciled the attack on the T&GWU with their membership of the party. They were further invited to state their future policy in the light of the NEC's resolution. This was a foolish action. The three indicated were only too capable of defending themselves.

Meanwhile, the docks dispute was settled after twenty-eight days on strike. It was agreed that an immediate attempt to reach agreement on overtime should be made and that no docker would be disciplined for refusing overtime. Also, they were informed by the Ministry of Labour that, following a statement by Arthur Deakin that overtime was voluntary, the question so far as provincial ports were concerned would be raised by them through the normal negotiating machinery. The T&GWU had capitulated. The action of the 'Blue Union', the dockers, and the support of *Tribune*, had forced the T&GWU to revert to its previous position on overtime. But there remained the question of NASD recruiting in the northern ports – and the NEC's resolution re *Tribune*.

In the meantime, however, throughout the docks dispute and a long time after it ended, we took advantage of the fact that *Tribune* was one of the very few papers putting the dockers' case. Week after week, as each new *Tribune* came off the press, I would set out for the docks early in the morning, on Thursdays, Fridays and Saturdays, and even sometimes on Mondays. It meant getting up very early in the morning, for dockers go into work sharp at 8 a.m. For about an hour before, they hang around in thousands outside the dock gates. So I used to leave home about 6.30 a.m. and drive through the quiet London streets down to the Royal Docks on Thursday, to Surrey Docks on Friday, to Millwall on Saturday and to the London docks on Monday. The Royal Docks were always the best.

While *Tribune* sales were mounting steadily at the docks, not only in London but also in the north, the directors of Tribune Publications, Ltd., drafted their reply to Mr Morgan Phillips. It was published as a special supplement, *The Case for Freedom*. It was quite a document, too long to quote extensively, but here are some extracts from it:

> At the outset we flatly repudiate the suggestion that the article was scurrilous or that it constituted a personal attack on Mr Arthur Deakin, the individual concerned. The whole article was a criticism of Mr Deakin in his public capacity as a trade union leader. We concentrated on his own public statements and the consequences which we considered they implied ...
>
> Criticize a man's case or policy, name him as the author of it, and the cry of personal attack is invoked. If the injunction is thus interpreted, it becomes a wholesale ban on all forms of controversy ...
>
> In reply to the Executive's invitation to explain how we reconcile the attack on the leaders of the Transport and General Workers' Union with our membership of the Labour Party, we ask: has a similar letter

been sent to Mr Arthur Deakin asking him how he reconciles his attack on the leadership of the Stevedores' Union with his membership of the Party? If not, it appears that there is one law for the leaders of large trade unions and another for the leaders of small trade unions, one law for those who command large voting powers and another for the rank and file members of the party ...

A Party which aspires to expand the empire of liberty must practise it within its own territory. British Labour would quickly cease to be a liberating movement if it permitted totalitarian practices within its own ranks. The most melancholy feature of the National Executive's letter to us is that it might lay the Executive open to the charge of asserting a totalitarian doctrine.

The Labour Party NEC climbed down. Morgan Phillips sent a letter in which he said that the NEC had no desire to limit the established bounds of freedom within the party. (Of course, they clearly had, but they wouldn't admit it!) 'At the same time it is important to distinguish between freedom and licence,' etc. etc.

The row among the dockers and their unions continued. More than 8,000 dockers out of 14,000 in Liverpool signed a petition asking the NASD to accept them into the union. Dick Barrett, secretary of NASD, proposed a plebiscite, under TUC auspices. It was turned down by Sir Vincent Tewson. A T&GWU spokesman said that dockers who transferred would be sacked – though it was certainly not clear that the Dock Labour Scheme permitted that. On 23 May 1955 20,000 dockers struck in Liverpool, Birkenhead and Hull and stayed out for six weeks in support of their right to join the Stevedores' Union. They only went back to work when Dick Barrett accepted the TUC ruling. As *Tribune* said:

The Government opposed them. The employers opposed them. The Transport and General Workers' Union opposed them. The Communist Party opposed them. Even this powerful alliance could not end the strike. Only when the TUC denounced the dispute and the men's own union executive decided to accept the rebuke was the strike finally crushed.

I sometimes wonder where Frank Cousins and Jack Jones were in those days, when *Tribune*, with the 'Blue Union', was fighting the T&GWU. Whose side were they on then?

The Bomb and the Bombshell

During the final six months of my time with *Tribune* there was one more row between the Bevanites and the leadership of the Labour Party. It was about the bomb and was, in a way, a test run for CND. The Conservative Party in their Defence White Paper published early in 1955 included a proposal to go ahead with the manufacture of thermonuclear weapons. Earlier, in *Tribune* (28 January), Aneurin Bevan had reminded the Labour Movement of an official Labour Party resolution moved by Clem Attlee himself, in the House on 5 April 1954. The motion, recognizing the immense range and power of the hydrogen bomb, called for a summit meeting to consider the reduction and control of armaments. The Bevanites were, in fact, divided on the issue, but they united with some others in support of a resolution along the same lines as Attlee's in 1954: 108 signed it.

The issue that raised all the furore during the defence debate, however, was the question of the first use of the bomb. Aneurin Bevan queried the meaning of a paragraph in the Defence White Paper (Paragraph 19, Page 6): 'This deterrent must rest primarily on the air power of the West armed with nuclear weapons. The knowledge that aggression will be met by overwhelming nuclear retaliation is the surest guarantee that it will not take place.' He also questioned the meaning of a sentence in the official Labour Party amendment: '... It is necessary as a deterrent to aggression to rely on the threat of using thermonuclear weapons.'

He went on to ask both the Government and the Leader of the Opposition whether they meant that nuclear weapons should be used against 'aggression' even if nuclear weapons had not been used by the aggressor: 'Do they mean that nuclear weapons will be used with the support of the British Labour Movement against any sort of aggression? I want to know the answer.'

At the end of Attlee's closing speech, Bevan interrupted to ask the question again. He quoted the American General Grünther's statement that he had no choice but to use atomic weapons whether or not the enemy does so. 'What we want to know,' said Bevan, 'is whether or not the use of the words to which I have referred in our amendment associates us with the statement that we would use thermonuclear weapons in circumstances of hostilities although they were not used against us?'

Attlee was evasive, and not very communicative: 'I am using this in the most general terms. I am not referring to anything in the White Paper but to the general thesis, with which I think my Right Hon. Friend agrees, that deterrence by the possession of thermonuclear weapons is the best way of preventing another war.'

Nye was not satisfied. Together with sixty MPs he refrained from voting for the amendment.

Before I move on to the consequence of these abstentions, I must emphasize several important aspects of Bevan's position on that occasion. He did not oppose the manufacture of the H Bomb. He objected to its first use by Britain against an attack with conventional arms. He supported a second strike nuclear force. He believed in that as a deterrent.

The irrationality of this position became clearer in the early sixties, after Nye was dead. For the V Bomber force which was built to carry Britain's nuclear bombs never was a credible second strike force. Even with the Ballistic Missiles Early Warning Station on Fylingdales Moor, it was futile to expect that the British Bombers could survive an attack on Britain. The USSR, which had intercontinental ballistic missiles deep hidden in silos, had a credible second strike force. Britain never had and as the Soviet Union obviously knew it, the British deterrent was useless as a deterrent. The Polaris submarine, maybe, but the V Bomber, never.

But it is also important to stress here that Nye never was a unilateralist. Presumably he accepted during the life of the first post-war Labour Government the decision to manufacture A Bombs. In 1955 he accepted the decision to manufacture H Bombs. Attlee made this clear and obviously thought Nye was equivocating on the question of a second use. So, in 1957, when he opposed the resolution calling for the unilateral rejection by Britain of nuclear arms, he was not reneging on the left. He merely stayed where he was, and maintained what had always been his position. Yet, in another sense, he deserted them, because, for the first time, the left in the Labour Party moved beyond him, leaving him behind.

Back to 1955. Furious, the Parliamentary Labour Party, as usual, decided to show its displeasure in no uncertain way. It distinguished itself by passing two contradictory resolutions. The first, as Nye had asked, censored the Government for failing to press for high level talks. The second proposed the withdrawal of the whip from Aneurin Bevan and also to refer the matter to the National Executive Committee – they wanted him expelled from the Party. No action was taken about the other sixty MPs who had sinned. However, the vote in the Parliamentary Party was uncomfortably close – 141 to 112, and the majority vote was less than half of the party.

The NEC faced a dilemma. The expulsion of Nye Bevan would obviously create extreme tension in the Movement, and an election was expected in the early summer. The NEC met on 23 March and a vote to expel was defeated by one. Gaitskell, Morrison and eleven others favoured expulsion, come what may. They were the hard, hatchet men. Attlee was not. It was then agreed to ask a sub-committee of the Executive Committee to interview Aneurin Bevan and report back a week later.

Bevan's massive following in the Movement rallied to his support. Even the Executives of the NUR and the AEU came out against expulsion. The consequence was that at its second meeting the NEC decided to endorse the decision of the Parliamentary Party to withdraw the whip and to warn that drastic action would follow if he offended again. The proposal to expel was dropped.

Meanwhile, almost unnoticed in the excitement over Nye, Sir Richard Acland resigned on the issue of the bomb. His action got very little publicity compared with Nye's. *Tribune* gave him a small mention in very small type. I suppose that with Nye threatened with expulsion, they felt they had to be careful. But they were never in favour of people leaving the party.

Dick Acland intended to fight a by-election in Gravesend on the issue of the bomb. He was unlucky. Labour delayed, understandably, in moving the writ and a General Election was announced for May. There is all the difference in the world between fighting a by-election on a single issue, and fighting a General Election where people choose a Government. Dick lost the seat, and so did Labour. A rather liberal Tory, Peter Kirk, got in.

Tribune tried to make the H Bomb the main issue of that General Election campaign. Donald Soper wrote articles attacking the Archbishop of York for supporting manufacture of the bomb. He was certainly a wholehearted unilateralist. Maurice Edelman, writing in *Tribune* on 20 May, reported that he belonged to a considerable minority within the party who opposed manufacture of H Bombs in any circumstances. The party united on the issue of tests. This was irrational as there was no point in having the bombs if you did not test them. However, that did them little good. Britain, at that time, seemed unconcerned about the dangers of tests or of the bomb. Labour lost the election. Shortly afterwards I lost *Tribune*.

For some time there had been occasional clashes between Robert J. Edwards and I. I was always capable of being difficult. So was Bob, and he was in an embarrassing position. For the press and most political people, Michael Foot was *Tribune's* editor. But he was not. Michael was the Beaverbrook of *Tribune*, and chairman of the editorial board. Bob was the editor. It must have been galling for as good a journalist as he was to be ignored so often. I suppose it is not surprising in the circumstances that he sometimes tried to behave like a tycoon.

Then there was Howard Samuel, the property tycoon. He came to *Tribune* as a director, not for love of the paper, but for love of Nye, whom he worshipped. He helped to keep the paper going because it was the voice of Nye. He raised considerable sums for it and, in the end, even bought himself a large holding of *New Statesman* shares, going on to the board there too. He saw this as an insurance. He wanted to be sure that at least one weekly supported Bevan. Oddly enough, when he first joined the board of *Tribune*, the existing directors had some doubts. They safeguarded their position by giving Michael Foot a hundred *Tribune* shares so that he could always outvote the rest. So in spite of Howard's money, Michael held the block vote.

I was never very good with millionaires (except with Laurie Kershaw, who was treasurer of CND for many years and whom I loved and admired – but he wasn't a millionaire at that time). Howard was nominally put in control of the administrative side of *Tribune*. There must be a deal of difference between running large properties and running a permanently bankrupt newspaper. In the end, Michael Foot acted with a ruthlessness which others discovered – some before, like Jon Kimche, others afterwards, like Roy Shaw. I, like them, was fired on the spot, out on the street that day. So some seven years after starting what Victor Gollancz had called 'a job for a lifetime' I found myself one afternoon walking down Fleet Street, out for good, unemployed.

A day or two later, Ian Aitken came up to my flat in St Pancras and collected the little red van and drove it away to be sold. Before the year was out, both he and Bob Edwards had left *Tribune* for the *Daily Express*. 1955 was the beginning of the end of that period of the Bevanites. Meantime I found that what I missed most was the little red van, even though it never would start on a wet morning.

Sixteen years later, looking back, I know I would hate to have missed it. It was the one time after 1945 when the Left in the Labour Party might have won, might have swung the party from compromise towards socialism, because they had then a real alternative leadership. Later, in 1960, though they then had many of the union block votes, they lacked that alternative leadership, and since Gaitskell himself made that the issue, they were bound to lose.

Nye was an alternative – not to Attlee, but to Gaitskell. If opinion inside the unions at that stage had been less docile, less ready to accept the dictates of the Deakins and their friends, he might have succeeded Attlee instead of Gaitskell.

It is not altogether pointless to estimate now what difference that might have made to Labour in opposition, to Labour in power. For Nye believed in power. Social justice and socialism could only be achieved by scaling the 'commanding heights of power' and for him the only instrument to achieve power was the Labour Party. When he saw his fellow Welshmen in the twenties and thirties, workless and hopeless, at the mercy of the Tories, the mine- and steel-owners, he saw the only remedy in a Labour Government. And it was because of this, I believe, that he finally compromised with Gaitskell and the right wing in the party. The possibilities of swinging the party behind himself and the Bevanites had faded by 1957. He thought there could be no progress at all if Labour remained in opposition. So he accepted, at last, the leadership of the man he disliked so bitterly in the interests of the party he loved. He parted with the left and his defence of the bomb at the 1957 conference sealed the new coalition. I think he was wrong. The party and the left in the party has never recovered from that decision.

In the early days of CND, I went to the 1958 Conference of the Labour Party and heard him speak for the last time to the Conference he had dominated for so long in passion if not in votes for motions. I think he knew then that he was dying. He made a speech which for many had all the old fire but which was gall and brimstone to the backwoodsmen of the Bevanites. As we came back on the special conference train from Blackpool he came down the train and sat and talked with Ian Mikardo whom, I was told, he had shunned since the break with the left in 1957. If he knew then that he was to die soon, did he also realize that while the Labour Party might, under his own disciples, win the power he coveted for it, it would then sacrifice most of what he sought through power. It is, perhaps, just as well that he never knew that Harold Wilson who had resigned with him in 1951 in protest against charges on the Health Service would himself nearly ten years later put them back, that he would commit himself more completely than Attlee ever did to the Atlantic Alliance they had together called into question.

What seems particularly odd now is that Aneurin roused so much anger and fury within the party, within the establishments, and even within the so-called liberal press. Vituperation and abuse of the

Bevanites was to be expected from the Tory press, but the *Manchester Guardian*, the so-called bastion of liberalism, hated him, pursued him relentlessly, and then wept crocodile tears when he died.

Of course, he was flamboyant, rumbustious, bitter and mordant. He called Gaitskell a 'desiccated calculating machine' which wasn't even true, for Hugh could be and frequently was highly emotional. He reacted sharply to criticism and was irritated and impatient with timidity and stupidity. But he was a first-class administrator. (Nowadays, when organizing skill is damned as 'bureaucracy', that would do him no good!) He had enormous charm – what would be called today 'charisma'. He put hot, red blood into the cold veins of the Labour Party. Maybe that was partly the reason, for those who hated and feared him, Gaitskell, Deakin, and even Attlee, had little charm and even less fire in their bellies.

Yet how stupid they were, how inept. They never attempted to contain Nye within the Party centre. They wanted to exclude him, to expel him and his friends, to shut the hated *Tribune* down, whatever the results might be for the Labour Party. So they ignored his large following among the rank and file and their own inability to win the support of the grass roots. And every time they reacted with hue and cry to Nye's latest misdemeanour they inevitably brought out the centre in his support – the solid, the respectable, the liberals, the more tolerant, like Stansgate, Strachey, Kingsley Martin and Francis Williams. Their excesses were far worse than those of the Bevanites. In support of their leadership and control of the party, they were willing to sacrifice democracy, freedom of speech, much of the liberalism which is supposed to distinguish social democracy from communism.

A little more tolerance, a little less sensitivity to criticism, a little more socialism in the highest echelons of the party and of the TUC could have perpetuated the alliance of the early years of the 1945 government, which broke down, essentially, because the right moved further right, not because the left moved further to the left.

It did them no good either. They failed to expel Nye and his friends. They failed to win elections. When victory came at last in

1964 the bulls that had chased Nye around the arena were either dead, like Gaitskell, or out to grass.

Of course, they did *Tribune* a lot of good. Michael Foot was quite right when he said in 1951 that the resignations would 'save' *Tribune*. And it was not only that Nye and the Bevanites sent its circulation soaring up; it was most of all those constant attacks from the NEC and the union leaders, those frequent attempts to muzzle it and close it down. They provided us with an advertising campaign we could never afford. Every time they came out with a new set of hammer blows, up went our circulation. Every time one of them lost his temper, we increased our print order. Power corrupts, as Lord Acton told us ... but that power should be wielded by people so incredibly stupid is a sobering thought.

Idolatry does not usually flourish in back rooms, at least never in mine. So my respect for Aneurin Bevan was always this side of idolatry. He was often autocratic. He was neither a great innovator, nor, I think, a great thinker. He did nothing to enlarge the boundaries of socialism. He made no major contribution to socialist thought. He spoke better than he wrote. I found his book, *In Place of Fear*, disappointing. He was agitator more than prophet or philosopher. But his rhetoric was important because it highlighted, in the context of a social democratic government which had won power in 1945 and seemed capable of winning it again, an emphasis on radical change, an assault on the structures of power, on rejection of capitalism, the lack of which had doomed social democratic parties in Europe by the late 1960s. He sought much the same goals as Dubcek and his colleagues in 1968 – social justice with liberty for the individual, a socialized economy without the repression which the Soviets called democratic centralism. It is significant that by the late 1960s the hope of achieving that lay much more in a reformation of communism than in a radicalization of social democracy. In international affairs, he saw a socialist Britain not as a part of an independent third force between the harsh alternatives of rampant capitalism in the West and Soviet imperialism in the East (he did not go as far as that) but at least as a check on the two hegemonies.

The Gaitskells, those who opposed Nye and, later, many of those who stood with him, saw Labour achieving power and retaining it only through a more efficient, technological management of a capitalist society. A little more gentle to the poor, a little less racist to the coloured people, a little more compliant to the United States, a little more capable of raising the GNP. No fire this time or next time. Fire died with Aneurin.

St Pancras and Camden:
1945-67

In the early autumn of 1945 I started work with Victor Gollancz as secretary of a new organization: Save Europe Now.

From 1945 to 1967, the Labour Party in St Pancras was a sort of spare time background, busman's holidaying, to my campaigning activities. Contrarywise, the campaigns often seemed like one long by-election. In the party, and later on the Council, there was the same sort of feverish activity, the same passionate arguments, the same dilemmas, the same limitations, the occasional victories, the all too frequent defeats.

I joined the Labour Party in St Pancras in 1945 when I left Common Wealth. For four years I did very little, rarely attended meetings, and was only marginally involved. Maybe it was partly because by then, by 1949, I was working for *Tribune* and closer in touch with Labour Party affairs. Also, in 1949 there was a by-election in North St Pancras which helped to turn me into an active party member.

At that time there were three constituencies in St Pancras, all held by Labour MPs – George House, Santo Jeger, and Hadyn Davies. The three were to be reduced to two for the next General Election. George House was a sick man and would not stand again. Hadyn Davies, whose seat was to disappear, hoped to inherit the North. He was unlucky. George House died too soon and St Pancras was faced with a by-election which Hadyn Davies was not free to contest.

The London Labour Party organizer, Jim Raisin, running true to form, rang up the secretary of the North Party, Reg Davis Poynter, told him to call a meeting of the Executive Committee for the following Wednesday, but to take no other action. He, Jim, would bring down candidates for the committee to consider. But the North Party had a mind of its own. They feared, and rightly, that Jim's proffered candidates might not be to their taste. So they called an earlier meeting of the Executive Committee the day before to consider whether the party wished to put forward its own nominee. There were three local men on the Transport House B List. The committee decided to put up Kenneth Robinson, left-wing then and a Councillor elected while he was still serving in the navy in the Far East.

On the following night, the Executive Committee met again. Jim Raisin was there, accompanied by Len Williams, then the National Agent, and two candidates for selection. One was George Darling, who later became one of the Nottingham MPs, and later still a peer. He was not notably left-wing. The other was Jack Cooper, later General Secretary of the Municipal and General Workers' Union, and also, later still, a peer of the realm. The M&GWU had a habit of putting its budding executives into the House of Commons for a year or two – for the experience. Hence Jack Cooper's interest. Needless to say, the union would have contributed generously to his campaign. Needless to say, Jack would never have got so far with that union if he had ever shown any tendencies towards the left.

The two candidates were presented to the committee. They were invited to choose between them – Hobson's choice, indeed. But the Chairman then objected. The North Party also had a candidate to field, he told Jim. Nonsense, said Jim, no other candidate can be considered. He was told that the committee had met and had agreed to put Kenneth Robinson up. Jim refused to accept him. Finally, in order to prevent a riot, Len Williams intervened and Kenneth was added to the list. Inevitably he was chosen though he had no union backing, no money. St Pancras never cared about things like that. Triumph for democracy – triumph for the left – at least for a time.

But, as the years passed, North St Pancras's MP became steadily less left, increasingly alienated from the party. One of the first problems was the Bevanites whom he carefully shunned. Later there were other issues, like the Bomb in the late fifties and early sixties. On social issues he was always excellent. Safe with his large majority, he was willing to stick his neck out on dangerous issues like abortion, capital punishment, homosexuality – and on these he showed great courage and stood up to local reactionary opinion. But on political issues, and especially after he became shadow Minister of Health, he moved from the left to the middle of the road and stayed there. He lost touch with many of his old friends in the party. He showed no interest in local council affairs. 'Chasing the shadow,' we once said, 'not the substance.'

One crisis occurred after the unilateralist resolution was accepted by Conference in 1960. First, Tony Greenwood was nominated for the leadership, on the issue of acceptance of Conference decisions. Then Harold Wilson agreed to stand, on the same issue, and Tony withdrew in his favour. Tony rang me up and warned me that Kenneth intended to vote for Gaitskell and asked me to try and do something about it. I arranged a meeting with Kenneth at the House, which we somehow both missed. Then I went up to his house in Grove Terrace, late one Friday evening.

The miserable shadow minister prowled up and down the room. 'I could not bring myself,' he said, 'to vote for Harold.' 'Would you have voted for Tony?' I asked him, for Tony was an old friend. He did not reply. Since then he has been voting for Harold when I wish he hadn't.

The situation has not changed much. A few months ago he was once more in trouble with the local party. This time, on the issue of Health Service Charges, which he had agreed to accept. Roundabout and roundabout and roundabout we go ... and roundabout he's gone now out to pasture.

It was not until 1953 that I went on to the council. It was all Reg Davis-Poynter's fault. 'Let's stand in Ward 1,' he said. Ward 1 was the most northerly and most Tory end of the Borough. 'We shan't get in, but it will be fun.' So we stood though I had to assure Michael Foot, who thought all one's time ought to be devoted to *Tribune,* that there was no danger of getting in.

It was a gross miscalculation. We both got in, and Michael was furious. It was not so bad for Reg because he escaped to Crawley shortly after. I stayed on for fifteen years.

At that time, St Pancras Council was abysmally dull. Since the end of the war the Council had swung with each election, first Labour, then Tory, then Labour again, and there was not all that much difference between them. Certainly there was much more cooperation between the very orthodox Labour leader, Fred Powe, and the Tories than between Fred and his back benchers. Council meetings were brief. Occasionally we were treated to a measured speech, usually on libraries, and, once a year, on the rate. Backbenchers slept on the backbenches. In 1956, we went to the polls again. Very reluctantly I agreed to stand again, though there seemed little point. Not much campaigning spirit those days in the council chamber. But we broke the usual pattern of one term in, one term out. Labour was re-elected. There were a number of new faces, but little expectation of radical change. No one expected the revolution to come.

It all started over the aldermanic seats. Most Labour Parties think aldermen are undemocratic, but no Labour Government has yet eliminated them. Some Labour councils, in order to live up to their democratic principles, appoint sitting councillors to aldermanic seats, and then fight by-elections – so everyone, including aldermen, is elected. St Pancras never had enough money for that, so it just selected suitable people. That was not the trouble in St Pancras in 1956. At the first statutory meeting of the Labour Group, Fred Powe was swiftly re-elected as leader. A mayor was appointed. Next came the question of the five aldermanic seats. It soon became clear that Fred had an agreement with the Tories on their allocation. It was this that caused the trouble. Somebody moved that we take all the seats, not so much because they wanted to deprive the Tories, but because they objected to Fred making agreements behind their backs. Fred made a very unwise move. 'If you pass this resolution,' said he, 'I will resign as leader.' They passed it. He resigned. So did the newly-elected Chief Whip. There was a horrible silence. Then someone nominated John Lawrence from the South Party. There were no further nominations. Fred was out and John was in. St Pancras was also in for five years of turbulence.

John Lawrence was a curious but likeable man. A native of Staffordshire, he had been for a long time a leading figure in the Trotskyist group, the Socialist Labour League and editor, or co-editor, of its journal, *Socialist Outlook.* He left after a bitter row with Gerry Healy, that formidable agitator who continues to organize and activate Labour Leagues of Youth and Young Socialists, year after year, as fast as the Labour Party disaffiliates them. The row between John Lawrence and Gerry Healy was ideological. Gerry complained that John was no longer a Trotskyist. There was some justice in this complaint. John certainly supported the Soviet line on many issues, on Hungary and on the Bomb. Like the Communist Party until 1960, he was not a unilateralist. Yet, in spite of his support for such unpopular causes as the Soviet invasion of Hungary, he continued to dominate the South Party and the Council for many years.

John was really a rather old-fashioned type of agitator. He was born too late. In the nineteenth century, or even in the twenties and thirties, he might have been a great national leader. But he tried to preach revolution, a rather simple, naive type of revolution, in very non-revolutionary times, and on a small Borough Council hardly ripe for radical change and with none of the powers required for it.

It was his personality which won him friends and followers. His excesses had a charm of their own, a sort of slap-happy, up and punch 'em approach which enlivened the council chamber and even delighted the Tories. When he got up to speak, they would settle down in their seats to enjoy the show. He would call the Tory ladies 'gals' and oddly enough they liked it. They enjoyed the excitement and the way in which St Pancras was getting the headlines. It was never boring and in the end it paid off. They came back in strength in 1959.

Yet the causes he espoused, the issues he highlighted, were a very odd collection. There was the mayor's allowance, the red flag, civil defence, and rents.

Long ago, in the twenties and thirties, Labour councillors had fought to raise the mayor's allowance, so that Labour members with little money could afford to take on the job. But not for John. He thought the allowance, the mayor's reception, the mayoral car, a wicked waste of money – and I suspect that many local citizens agreed with him. So we found a mayor, a grand old man called Tom Barker, with a lifetime of socialist activity all over the world behind him. He was willing to abandon the allowance, the reception and the car – and to travel on a 68 bus. (Goodness knows why they picked on the 68 bus. True enough, it goes through the borough, but it was and is just about the worst service in London.) Tom got far more publicity than earlier more orthodox mayors. He was a charming old man and good at the job. But orthodox Labour councillors in the borough and all through the country were furious. For them, this sort of bumbledom made life on the council worth while.

Civil defence was different. This was a real political issue. The trouble here was that St Pancras was too late. If it had come out earlier in support of the Coventry council's action, there might have been some hope of a significant group of councils jointly refusing to operate the civil defence services. Such a thought had never entered the heads of Fred Powe and his friends. By the time that John Lawrence persuaded the council to opt out on civil defence, Coventry had been beaten into the ground, largely because the Act, passed by the 1945/50 Labour Government, had been carefully drafted to rob councils of any autonomy on the question of civil defence. If a council refused to cooperate, the Home Office put in a commissioner to run the service and, in addition, the council lost its large grant from the government. So in St Pancras as in Coventry the service continued and the councillors found themselves facing the possibility of a surcharge through the loss of the grant.

Since St Pancras under Lawrence frequently faced the threat of surcharge and in the end was twice surcharged, I had better explain here and now the procedure which prevents councils and councillors getting out of hand and defying the central government. The Metropolitan Borough Councils, and a great many through the country though not all, had their accounts annually audited by the District Auditor. The District Auditor had the power to surcharge councillors if they undertook expenditure or got themselves involved in expenditure not covered by statute or in defiance of statutes. Councillors are surcharged jointly and severally. The auditor could act on his own initiative, but any complaint about expenditure formally made by a group of ratepayers to the auditor on the opening of the audit had to be investigated by him. In the case of a surcharge under £500, an appeal could be made either to the minister, usually the Minister of Housing and Local Government, or to the High Court. If the surcharge is over £500, the appeal has to go to the High Court. Councillors on whom a surcharge is upheld have to pay the money themselves and can be debarred from remaining councillors. If they fail or refuse to pay, the penalties are not imprisonment, but distraint on the goods or property of any of the surcharged councillors who happen to have goods or property.

This is where John Lawrence was unlucky. His great hero was George Lansbury who had gone to prison in the thirties for paying unemployed men in Poplar more than the law allowed. But in the 1950s there was no question of going to prison. The bailiff was a poor alternative to the gaoler.

So far as civil defence was concerned, St Pancras avoided a surcharge. Eventually it had to accept the inevitable and resume its duties. The minister, the Home Secretary, I think, in this case, kindly reinstated the grant and, anxious to avoid further trouble, dropped the question of surcharge.

But the most entertaining incident of this rather abortive campaign was the occasion when John Lawrence chained himself to the gates of the civil defence headquarters in Camden High Street. I remember this well, because I was ill at the time with jaundice and was dragged out of bed by a telephone call asking me to lay on the press. So I arrived in the High Street to find a small group of John's supporters, including several councillors, parading up and down outside the CD HQ with suitable banners: 'Ban the Bomb', 'Destroy the Bomb or it will Destroy You', 'Stop the Tests'. It was, of course, 1957 and the British tests at Christmas Island were imminent.

After some time a policeman arrived and plodded up and down the street beside the paraders. Now and again a very disapproving member of the WVS, who shared the building with CD, pushed her way through to the gate. Then, when the copper was standing, half asleep, some way up the road, John produced a rather large and ostentatious padlock and chain and attached himself to the bars of the gate.

For a time nothing happened. Nobody noticed. Shoppers hurried by and never turned to look. The policeman went on plodding up and down. Buses passed to and fro. No press arrived. There was the leader of the council chained to the CD gates – and nobody had even turned to look. I had a horrible feeling that nobody ever would.

Then at last the policeman as he passed saw that something was amiss. He stopped. He stared. 'Why, sir,' he said, 'who did that to you?' 'Nobody,' said John. 'I did it myself.' 'But why did you do that, sir?' the simple copper asked. 'I did it as a protest against nuclear weapons,' John simply replied.

The policeman hurried off to telephone a higher authority. Shoppers continued to pass by, unconcerned. Then, at last, a press photographer. Then another. Then a police car with more important, peak-capped coppers. Then gradually a crowd, at last. The police brought out of their car an enormous pair of clippers with which they cut the chain of the padlock. They took John off in their car, carrying on its rear number plate one of our placards proclaiming 'Ban the Bomb'. On this occasion I don't think they charged John with any offence. But the chaining of the leader to the gates of the Civil Defence Headquarters did more to publicize the confrontation with the Home Office than anything else, even the threat of surcharge.

The red flag incident was different. Unlike civil defence in the nuclear age, it was a rather old-fashioned campaign. It could hardly be called a basic, ideological issue. May Day was widely celebrated on the continent as a public holiday, but not in Britain. So when St Pancras decided to give all staff a holiday on that day and, in addition, to fly the red flag from the Town Hall, the emotional impact, especially on the Tories, was instantaneous and large. You would have thought that a communist take-over of the borough was imminent. Needless to say, the Council did not have a red flag in stock. It had to buy one. John solemnly raised it himself at 7 a.m. on the morning of May Day.

Later, at midday, there was an open-air meeting at the corner of Euston Road and Ossulston Street near to the Town Hall. Several councillors attended and Lena Jeger, the MP in the south of the borough. Some Empire Loyalists also turned up. It is not surprising that there was trouble, and the meeting ended with John Lawrence and one or two other councillors being carted off in a black maria. This time, three councillors were charged with breaches of the peace and fined.

The consequence was that St Pancras became nationally known as the red flag borough. Goodness knows, the red flag has little political significance these days, yet it was used by the Tories to inflame feeling against the local council. When they fought the next election in 1959, the red flag over the Town Hall was one of their main attacks on Labour.

So much for the red flag. The real battle, the political battle, was over rents. Maybe this was because housing development was one of the few real powers held by the old London Metropolitan Boroughs and certainly bad housing was the greatest social evil in St Pancras. I was more interested in this than all the rest of the hullabaloos put together.

Immediately after the war it had not been difficult to build new housing at low cost. Under Hugh Dalton as Chancellor of the Exchequer, conncils could borrow money from the Public Works Loan Board at two per cent. The main problem was shortage of materials.

But gradually the cost of borrowing money rose, the Public Works Loan Board became no longer available and money had to be raised on the open market at rates three times as high, and more.

Through the fifties, rents of uncontrolled private accommodation soared, especially in Central London, together with the price of houses for sale. There were two consequences in St Pancras. More and more ordinary working people were moved out of the central areas, especially from Holborn, and possibilities of council developments there were limited by the high cost of the land. Many areas which had once been residential, like those beautiful Holborn terraces – John Street, Doughty Street, Milman Street, Great James Street – had been converted for office use. And in Bloomsbury, the University swallowed up everything it could get.

As the cost of housing, and especially the cost of borrowing money, soared, rents could only be kept down through larger and larger additional subsidies from the local rates.

The Tory Council elected in 1949 met the difficulty by grading flats. There were high-rented flats, reserved for the better off and the more respectable. There were medium-rented flats for the middle range. Then there were the older, pre-war estates with low rents kept for the poor. This was, in fact, an acceptance by the council of the age-old Housing Department practice of grading estates socially rather than financially. The two usually coincide.

The Labour Council elected in 1953 faced a dilemma. It had bitterly opposed the Tory scheme and it had to provide an alternative. It did, but it was a very poor alternative. A new scheme was introduced for the new, horrible barrack-type structures then being completed on the Regent's Park Estate, west of Hampstead Road. The principle was the higher the flat, the higher the rent. The rent went up by two shillings for each floor. So, in an eleven-storied block, the tenants on the top floor paid £1 more than those on the ground floor. Now that tall blocks are so unpopular, it seems a ludicrous scheme. Nevertheless, in desperation, because they had to do something, the scheme was agreed, though there was considerable opposition to it.

When John Lawrence took over as leader, I became chairman of the Housing Committee and this was my first problem. The first thing I did was to get rid of the differentials, so tenants on the top floor had a rent reduction of eighteen shillings, and so on, arithmetically. This was a momentous occasion. It was probably the last time a council in Britain actually lowered rents. Naturally, the Tories were furious. They opposed the reductions in council to no effect. So they tried a new tactic. They produced a local citizen, a ratepayer, who objected to the reductions at the opening of the audit. He was supposed to be a neutral citizen of the borough, though a member of the Tory party.

This was the first time we were in trouble with the District Auditor. But we were lucky. I was able to persuade the District Auditor that the differentials were unreasonable, that it had become more and more difficult to let the higher flats, that tenants had had to be transferred to fill them, and that too few tenants or tenants-to-be were willing to pay extra for the privilege of a view.

Encouraged by this success, we proceeded on our way refusing, in spite of pressure from the Tories and the Labour right, to increase rents. Once again, a year later, a group of Tories thinly disguised as ratepayers challenged us on the opening of the audit – this time on three counts: the general level of rents, civil defence, and on our refusal to raise the rents of tenants of derequisitioned houses.

On the first count, the general level of rents, we were lucky again. But we were warned that a general review of council rents was overdue and we had come to learn by then that 'a general review' of rents meant increases. We also evaded the worst on the civil defence count.

The real problem arose on something that seemed a minor issue: this question of the rents of tenants in derequisitioned houses. Labour in St Pancras was not in favour of derequisitioning in any case. With the housing problem still as enormous as it was there seemed no justice at all in handing back these houses to their owners together with the tenants who would lose their security after a number of years. We would have preferred additional powers to requisition empty houses – a fine hope even with a Labour Government, much less with the Tories in power. But the law is the law and reluctantly, at the last possible moment, we handed back the houses we held. It was the 1957 Rent Act which caused the trouble. Under this, rents of derequisitioned properties could be raised in accordance with the act, unless there was a certificate of disrepair on the property. It was bad enough to have had to hand the houses back, but now we were asked to raise the rents of these tenants (who still paid rent to the council, who paid the owners) while all our other secure tenants were left as they were. The position was that the council could pay the extra itself, but only if it could justify each individual case.

The Town Clerk warned us that if we refused to pass on the increases, *en bloc*, we were in for trouble. Each case must be examined on its merits. This we did. Innumerable forms giving details of the property and the tenant came to committee and in each case we decided not to pass on the increase. This is what caused the trouble, the totality of it. If we had exempted only half a dozen, we might have avoided a surcharge.

The amount involved on the first audit for the year ending 31 March 1958 amounted to £799 6s. We had to appear several times before the District Auditor. While he was always civil and, at times, even generous, he was a lawyer and accountant and what mattered for him was the law, not the social issues involved. By that time too, John Lawrence had been expelled from the Labour Party, had ceased to be leader. The consequence was that the accused were now two groups: John Lawrence and the councillors who had left with him now acting as an independent group on the council, and fourteen councillors still in the Labour Party. On this occasion we were surcharged too. The independent group appealed to the High Court and lost. The fourteen appealed to the minister who waived the surcharge. So far so good, but although the council as soon as the Auditor announced the decision to surcharge immediately raised the rents in question, we were still in trouble because in the meantime another year had passed and for the year ending 31 March 1959 the amount involved was £1,400. We went through the whole procedure again, more and more difficult because the independent group were only too anxious to plead guilty – they wanted to be surcharged – while the others genuinely did not realize what they had risked.

This time the surcharge was £1,400. No option of appealing to the minister, only to the High Court, where John Lawrence had already been rejected once. The High Court confirmed the surcharge and kindly waived the rule that councillors surcharged more than £500 were disbarred as councillors. Some of us would have preferred it the other way round!

There was, of course, no Poplar situation. Nobody went to prison. We went through the slow and painful process of raising the money, partly through a public appeal, partly by comparatively small payments over a long period. Revolution did not follow and rents continued to rise. The citizens of St Pancras, including many council tenants, unmoved by all our efforts on their behalf, voted us out in 1959.

The battle of the rents went on. The new Tory Council introduced a differential rent scheme. Many of the tenants who had refused to listen to our warnings sprang into action against the new scheme though they had given little active support to the attempts of the old Labour Council to keep rents down. Now Tenants Associations were set up on every estate. They organized. They marched. They filled the Town Hall gallery. They flung leaflets into the Chamber. They were frequently evicted from the gallery and on one occasion John Lawrence, no longer a councillor, chained himself once again, but this time to a seat in the gallery. The final debate on the scheme went on until 4 a.m. while tenants milled and shouted in the streets outside singing 'We will overcome', 'We will not be moved'.

A United Tenants Movement was set up, led by a very shrewd operator, Don Cook. When the first increases came into force there were massive rent strikes. Many tenants refused to pay the increases. Some even refused to pay any rent at all. Notices to quit followed and then eviction notices. The Movement decided to fight two cases and their protagonists were Don Cook himself with a flat in Kennistoun House in Kentish Town and a boisterous character called Arthur Rowe who lived in one of the big blocks on the Regent's Park Estate, Silverdale. They barricaded themselves into their flats and night and day tenants and their friends guarded the approaches. The Tories refused to give way, to meet the tenants, or to consider any changes in the scheme. It became a personal battle between the Tory Leader, Councillor Prior, and Don Cook.

One day, in the autumn of 1960, when the Edinburgh to London CND March was coming up through the suburbs of London to its finale in Trafalgar Square, the battle in St Pancras reached its climax. Early one Friday morning the police with the bailiffs broke into the flats at Kennistoun House and Silverdale and took possession. All day, outside Kennistoun House, the crowds gathered and the dispossessed cried for action. In the evening, three thousand set off for the Town Hall. Not all of them were tenants; sympathizers and toughs had joined in from all over London. At the Town Hall the demonstration turned into a near-riot. Banner poles were used as staves. John Lawrence and many others were arrested. Violence spread and trolley bus windows were broken far from the Town Hall.

Michael Wall of the *Guardian* told me later that he was outside Kennistoun House all day. From the time the police broke in, speaker after speaker called for violence. 'If there had only been one or two moderating voices,' he said, 'it might have made all the difference.' At that time I was with the march moving down towards Watford. I drove into London that night for a CND meeting and did not hear about the riot until early the next morning. I rang Charlie Ratchford, the Labour leader, and at last we managed to get some sense out of the Tories. Prior agreed to meet us at noon with the Town Clerk. I drove out to Watford and put the march on the road and then drove rapidly back to the Town Hall. By then, the Government had banned all marches and demonstrations in the borough. Prior agreed to meet the tenants, to consider some amendments to the scheme. Slowly the tension lessened.

That weekend, when the Edinburgh to London March had ended with the Scottish pipers leading it into the Square to be greeted by Lord Russell, still President of CND but only just, there was a party for the hard-core marchers at the Party Rooms in North St Pancras. I left it to attend a meeting in the tenants' hall at Silverdale to discuss plans.

John Lawrence was there. He wanted, as usual, to challenge the state, to defy the ban on demonstrations. This was, he thought, the beginning of a revolution. The Communist Party was also there, cautious and much more careful. They did not, at that time, use the word 'adventurism', but that is what they meant. No precise decision was taken, but gradually the situation deflated, the temperature dropped. Some tenants went on refusing to pay the increases. Some paid up gradually, some never did, I suspect.

The circumstances in which John Lawrence was expelled from the Labour Party were cumulative. He was never quite as popular in the South Party as on the Council and his increasing friendliness with the local communists did not help. The last straw, the final nail in his coffin, was a meeting at the old Holborn Hall, now demolished, on the occasion of the adoption of a new Tory candidate for the South, Mr Geoffrey Johnston Smith. The meeting was intended to introduce him to the Tory faithful and the electorate. I was warned of trouble and went along with Giles Taylor, A.J.P.'s elder son.

The Holborn Hall was a very dreary hall. It had only one

entrance, at the back. Behind the platform there was a small room for speakers but the only exit from this was onto the platform, and into the hall. When I arrived the hall was fairly full of the oddest collection of people. There were the Tory faithful, come to hear the word. There were John and his friends, well to the front and ready for action. There were also the fascists who were wandering up and down the aisles selling *Action*. After a while the Tory hierarchy moved out of the back room and took their places at the platform table. Trouble started almost immediately. Before long there was uproar. John Lawrence had taken over the meeting and the platform party had withdrawn to the back room.

Yet, surprisingly, nobody got hurt. I remember at one moment looking across the hall and seeing one of John's supporters, a Covent Garden porter, with a chair held over his head ready to fall. Yet, somehow, everyone got out of the hall without any injuries and without any arrests. The police, near at hand, for their station was then across the road, behaved with restraint. When everything was over and everyone had gone, the platform party escaped from their retreat. John Lawrence went round the corner and spoke at an open-air meeting in the Bourne Estate together with Jock Nicholson, Communist candidate for North St Pancras, which was one of the sins that finished him.

So, John Lawrence was expelled and a number of councillors and party members went with him, including my daughter and son-in-law (though we never allowed such political differences to become important and we remained good friends).

The North Party certainly regretted their departure and refused to supply Transport House with a list of members that had gone with him. In 1960 we challenged the decision at the Party Conference and as I was the party delegate that year I moved the suspension of standing orders, so that John might be heard in his own defence, and opposed the decision of the NEC. As usual on these occasions I lost even though my motion was seconded by Frank Cousins, not because he had any particular interest in that particular case, but because he felt strongly that there ought to be some proper machinery for appeals against expulsion.

There is one particular aspect of the long battle over rents which is disquieting and which arises from the powers of the District Auditor. In the 1962 elections, Labour won again in St Pancras with the biggest swing in the country. During the election campaign and in their election address they undertook to remove the hated differential rent scheme. The citizens of the borough were well aware of this when they voted them back on with a very large majority.

Yet we found that it was not possible to carry out our promise. It soon became clear that the abolition of the scheme and the substitution of a standard rents scheme would involve very con· siderable reductions in rent, and an increase in the deficit on the housing revenue account, unless the new standard rents were fixed so high that only a small proportion of tenants could afford to pay them. A differential scheme once adopted could be modified in small ways. It could not be abandoned without further surcharge on the councillors responsible. The District Auditor, in fact, dictated the level of council rents, not the councillors, nor the citizens who elected them. Later on, we got to the point where the District Auditor informed us at the end of the financial year how large a deficit on the Housing Revenue Account he was prepared to accept. Within those very narrow confines we were free to act as we pleased. This meant that the citizens of a borough were free to vote, as they had, to get rid of a scheme, but the council had no power to carry out their wishes, except at the risk, indeed the certainty, of surcharge. Government by District Auditor, an official appointed by the ministry, unelected, unmoved by local opinion. We tried to raise this issue both with the National Labour Party and with the Ministry of Housing and Local Government, but we never got a spark of response.

St Pancras changed into Camden. The borough was bigger and had far wider powers. We were now responsible for many social services, children, welfare and others. New and large departments were established. Inevitably the question of rents ceased to be the hub and centre of our socialist faith. Gradually we came to see that the level of council rents was not the only criterion – the quality of our developments was as important.

During my last years in the Labour Party and on the council, I was chairman of the Planning and Development Committee and this was my main preoccupation. How could we pull down and rebuild large areas of the borough in such a way that new communities could be created in the difficult car-ridden circumstances of inner city life? How to get away from the old concept of the Council House Estate, with its communal balconies and asphalt surrounds, separate and distinct enclaves within the borough? How to involve the people in the areas to be developed in the long, complex process of rebuilding?

The part I enjoyed most and helped to put into action was this process of consultation with the people living in an area to be developed. In the north of the borough a very large redevelopment had been proceeding for many years. Some areas were already built and occupied, but about half of it was still to be done. We ran into trouble locally over an area known as Oak Village in Gospel Oak. Here there were a number of small streets, with small, semi-detached houses with gardens. Architecturally they had no particular merit, but the streets were quiet and pleasant.

The trouble began when a developer moved in and started buying up houses. As soon as the existing tenants could be moved out, and usually they were offered sums of money to go, the houses were gutted completely inside and reconstructed at high cost. They were then sold at very high prices. Other houses in these streets, Oak Village, Elaine Grove and one or two others, had been bought by individuals who had improved them and brought them up to standard at their own expense but with a council grant. Naturally these new owner-occupiers were alarmed and horrified when they learned that the area was to be redeveloped. Naturally too, the private developer was not very pleased. But also the area had been originally very working class, in fact the houses had been built for the workers in a brick kiln nearby, long disused. The working-class people in the area whose houses were badly substandard were only too anxious for the development to proceed. They resented these newcomers in their midst who were making such a hullabaloo.

We called a meeting in the only available hall in the neighbourhood, in a fairly new modern school. We took along the architect for the scheme, the Deputy Town Clerk who did the purchasing, the Planning Officer, the Borough Architect and the Housing Manager. When we got there we found that the hall was overflowing. Every seat was full, they were standing up and down the aisles, they were out in the corridors, they were hanging through the windows. Unfortunately we had not arranged for a loudspeaker.

As soon as I opened the meeting I found that the owner occupiers were solidly entrenched in the front rows. For a time, there was utter chaos. Everyone shouted as loud as they could. Half the people, even of those who had seats, were standing on their feet, waving their arms or shaking their fists. The council officers, unused to political occasions, paled and fidgeted in their seats.

For a time, I let chaos ride. Gradually they calmed down. Gradually they sat down. Then I put on the Scheme Architect who had brought plans and slides. 'Be kind to him,' I said. 'He's just an architect, not a politician.' They were kind, not because they particularly cared for architects but because they were interested.

After that we took the Planning Officer, then the Deputy Town Clerk who told them exactly what their rights were if they wanted to sell now, or later after the compulsory purchase order. Then we took the Housing Manager who told those that were tenants what would happen to them. Eventually, after a long session of questions and answers, we managed to close the meeting just before the pub across the road closed its doors. The following week we held a further meeting for those who had failed to get in the week before.

What followed was even more important. We put up the plans on display in an empty shop in the neighbourhood and we had long meetings with the residents' association established in Oak Village. As a result we produced a compromise scheme which left Oak Village and a lot of Elaine Grove untouched and the genuine owner-occupiers undisturbed. But it was proposed to turn the street into a pedestrian precinct and they were asked to agree to this and to a common standard of decoration for the area. They were only too happy to do so. The developer, however, was out. Houses not yet improved would still be purchased by the council which would do the job.

This was a great triumph and I was really very happy about it. After I had left the party in May 1967, over Vietnam and Greece, I heard that the Minister, Tony Greenwood, had turned down the scheme and exempted the area from the development. I was very, very angry. I very nearly joined the party again, in order to resign again, on that issue.

I left the Labour Party in May 1967 when the Labour Government's support for the United States in Vietnam and its failure to condemn the Junta in Greece together added up to more than I could stomach. For a year I remained as an independent councillor, for the party, having just lost all seats on the GLC, was only too anxious to avoid a by-election. I don't really miss it very much. It was not a clean, quick break; the process of disengagement lasted a year. Yet I still have a strong affection for the borough and would hate to live anywhere else. When I come back from abroad, as I frequently do these days, and cross the boundaries of Camden in my taxi, and see the bright orange dustcarts, I know I am home again.

Capital Punishment: 1945-7

After a brief post-*Tribune* period of what they call in the theatre resting, I went back to work for Victor Gollancz on a new campaign: the National Campaign for the Abolition of Capital Punishment.

There were a number of reasons why the time seemed ripe for a new, big push to get rid of hanging. The Labour Government of 1945 included a great many members who strongly supported abolition and there now seemed a real chance of getting rid of it. A clause was included in the Criminal Justice Bill of 1948 proposing abolition for a trial period of five years. It was passed on a free vote. But the Lords, of course, threw it out. At that stage there had been little change of mind among the judges, the bishops and the nobility.

There it died, for many reasons. The Government was nearing the end of its term and notably losing courage on many issues. The clause was a part of a long and important bill and to send it all back to the Commons would delay the whole bill. The Home Secretary of that day, Mr Chuter Ede, was opposed to it, though he later changed his mind. So the bill was dropped and a common device was used to delay matters. A Royal Commission was established under the chairmanship of Sir Ernest Gowers. But its terms of reference specifically excluded consideration of the issue of abolition. The Commission was only permitted to examine and suggest changes in the existing capital law.

When the report of the Commission was finally issued it was clear that if it could, the Commission, or at least a majority of it, would have proposed abolition. Their general conclusion was that there was no way to limit capital punishment, except by leaving the jury to decide – an intolerable burden for them. 'Its disadvantages,' said the report, 'may be thought to outweigh its merits.' It went on ...

If this view were to prevail, the conclusion to our mind would be inescapable, that in this country a stage has been reached where little more can be done effectively to limit the liability to suffer the death penalty, and that the real issue is now whether capital punishment should be retained or abolished.

Sir Ernest Gowers then wrote a book, *A Life for a Life,* which was published at the height of our campaign in early 1956. He explained in it how in the course of considering all the evidence presented to the Royal Commission he himself changed his mind and became an abolitionist.

In 1955, of course, there was a Conservative Government and for this reason a new attempt to change the law might have seemed inappropriate. Yet there were a number of murder cases and developments in the early 1950s which roused opinion as never before against hanging.

There was the case of Derek Bentley, a nineteen-year-old boy who was hanged for a murder committed by Christopher Craig fifteen minutes after Bentley had been arrested. There is little doubt in this case that because a policeman was killed, and because Craig was too young to hang, Bentley paid the penalty to satisfy the police.

Derek Bentley could write his name and no more. They taught him to read while he waited in prison to be hanged – a curiously profitless occupation. He had never shown any tendencies towards violence. He had only one conviction for petty crime. He went out one night with Christopher Craig – a dominating, violent, maladjusted boy whose hostility to society had been deepened by his loyalty to his older brother, serving a long sentence in prison. Bentley was arrested. There was a cosh in his pocket but he never took it out. When his captor was wounded, he waited patiently to be re-arrested. He allowed the police to use his body as a shield. He told the police what arms Craig had. It was alleged that he cried out 'Let him have it, Craig', but it was never clear whether he meant that Craig should hand over the gun or use it. They hanged him all the same.

There was the case of Timothy Evans. He had been hanged for the murder of his child. He confessed in fact to the murder of his wife and child in that later to be notorious house in North Kensington, 10 Rillington Place. There were many inconsistencies in his confessions and many doubts about it. He claimed, for instance, to have left the bodies of his wife and child in a wash house for several days. During that time the wash house was used by workmen who saw no bodies there. He claimed he locked the shed. There was no lock. He said he left the baby in the flat all day, after killing his wife. Yet nobody heard crying.

He was hanged, and there was little concern about it until Christie, who had been a major witness at Evans's trial, was arrested for the murder of six women in the same house. He was clearly guilty. This was too much of a coincidence. People simply could not believe that there were two murderers in the same house. More and more it was claimed that Evans must have been innocent and that Christie had killed the wife and child. Responding to the public outcry, the Government appointed Scott Henderson, QC, to conduct an inquiry – but it was private, not public. Nobody was really surprised when Scott Henderson confirmed Evans's guilt, but few were convinced.

There was no doubt that Ruth Ellis was guilty. She shot her lover in Hampstead and never attempted to deny it. She was drunk. She was distracted. She had recently had a miscarriage. He had been notably unfaithful. What roused public feeling on this occasion was that she was young, beautiful and unhappy. When the Home Secretary refused to reprieve her, feeling against capital punishment intensified greatly.

Nevertheless, in a debate on capital punishment on 10 February 1955, the Home Secretary, Major Gwilym Lloyd-George, rejected on behalf of the government all appeals to consider abolition. They still held that it was a uniquely effective deterrent and that there was no alternative. The detention of some murderers for long periods, possibly for life, would give rise to much more serious difficulties than the Commission expected. They rejected all the conclusions, evidence, and judgement of the Royal Commission.

The National Campaign for the Abolition of Capital Punishment began when Arthur Koestler approached Victor Gollancz with the suggestion that what was needed was a short, brisk campaign. Naturally, Victor was entirely in favour. The next recruit was Gerald Gardiner, QC, who had been a lifelong opponent of hanging. They were quite a powerful trinity. Arthur Koestler's objections to hanging had been strongly reinforced during the Spanish Civil War when he was imprisoned for three months as a suspected spy, witnessing the execution of his fellow prisoners, and daily expecting his own. To Victor, the hanging of a man, and, even more, of a woman, was an abomination. Gerald Gardiner rejected it on all counts, moral, rational, legal – he covered the whole spectrum.

It was a very different sort of campaign. Penal reform had never been a matter for mass movements. Reforms had got through always against majority opinion, opinion among working people, among top people. The most virulent opponents of abolition were the affluent, beautifully-hatted, tweedy, Tory women who screamed for the rope and the cat at Tory Party Conferences. But this was a campaign that cut across parties, across classes, across professions, and across left and right. There were forty to fifty Conservative MPs who supported abolition. There were six Labour MPs who opposed it. Many who worked with the campaign to abolish hanging had hated the Bevanites and later scorned the Ban the Bomb movement. The Tories included Montgomery Hyde, who was a member of our Committee, spoke around the country, and worked hard in the House of Commons. He paid the highest price, for his constituency in Northern Ireland refused to select him again as their candidate for his abolitionist sins. There was Reggie Paget, QC, MP, who hated the Bevanites and loved the bomb. There was Lord Shawcross, one of the most virulent haters of *Tribune*. There was Michael Foot. An extraordinary mixture. No wonder it was so successful.

Victor Gollancz was the first chairman and our first office was at 14 Henrietta Street. Later Gerald Gardiner took over, and we moved the office to the top storey of the *New Statesman*. There was Canon Collins, Reggie Paget, C. H. Rolph, a psychiatrist – Jack Hobson – who specialized in murder cases. Oddly enough, the initial committee did not include Sydney Silverman. They decided that he was difficult. Certainly they had plenty of personalities without him. But they looked pretty silly without him in 1956 when he was moving his bill through the House with magnificent proficiency. They hurriedly changed their minds and invited him in. Sydney was magnanimous and accepted.

The Committee spent the first few months of its existence publicizing itself and recruiting support. Articles were placed in newspapers; books and public meetings were planned. A mailing list of ten thousand was accumulated. Quite a good total for such a campaign.

Its first large public activity was a meeting at the Central Hall, Westminster (a traditional opening for campaigns). This took place on 10 November 1955 and presented what is commonly known as 'a broad based platform'. There was Canon Collins, Gerald Gardiner, who was the main speaker, Gilbert Harding, Christopher Hollis, Montgomery Hyde, Commander Sir Stephen King-Hall, Frank Owen, Reggie Paget, Lord Pakenham, J. B. Priestley, Frank Byers, who took the collection, and Victor Gollancz. Quite a gathering. Gerald Gardiner put the case magnificently for abolition in an hour long speech. The others got a few minutes each, except Victor.

A series of meetings were also planned in the provinces and small committees were set up to run them. I remember that the meeting in Birmingham Town Hall took place on the foggiest night known this century in Birmingham. In spite of that several hundreds turned up.

Meantime the Campaign was sponsoring or promoting a number of books. Gerald Gardiner dealt with two crucial arguments: does hanging deter? is there an alternative? in *Capital Punishment as a Deterrent, and the Alternative*. Arthur Koestler in *Reflections on Hanging* produced a more complex, colourful indictment combining historical scholarship, sardonic comment and moral passion. Victor Gollancz himself put the absolute case in a pamphlet. In addition to these books, the issue was very widely covered in the press.

Meetings were planned for February in Glasgow and Edinburgh, to be followed in March with meetings in Liverpool and Manchester. But on these meetings we ran into trouble. A debate in the House of Commons was announced for the same night as the Edinburgh meeting. Obviously, it was important that our greatest expert, Gerald Gardiner, should be around and available in Westminster that night, so Christopher Hollis stepped into his place. Montgomery Hyde also spoke but carefully paired himself with a retentionist.

The meeting was packed. Sir Compton Mackenzie did not speak but sent a message. It was a rule of his to stay in bed throughout February, not exactly a pleasant month in Scotland. After the meeting we went back to the North British Hotel and feverishly phoned London for news of the debate. I had to catch the night train back to London. The debate was still proceeding and the vote had not yet been taken, and, at last, I had to leave the hotel and make my way down to the train to find my sleeper. At the last moment, just as the train was preparing to leave, Montgomery Hyde came running down the platform with the good news. We had won. It was a great moment for me, but not for the sleeping car attendant who turned out to be a convinced retentionist!

But in spite of the victory all was not well in London. Thirty-five Tories had voted for abolition. Six Labour MPs had opposed it. More important, Anthony Eden had been asked after the vote 'Whether we may take it that the Government will take steps to implement the decision of the House?' He replied: 'The Right Hon. Gentleman can be assured that the Government will give full weight at once to a decision taken by this House on a free vote.'

It was this that caused the trouble. Outside the House, Victor Gollancz, Gerald Gardiner and Arthur Koestler conferred together. Victor was convinced that the Campaign had won, that all that was necessary now was to wait for the Government to introduce a bill. He proposed to cancel all the meetings immediately. Arthur Koestler was not so sure. He did not trust the Government. He thought that the pressure ought to be maintained and increased until a bill had gone through both Houses. Gerald, as usual, was tactful. There was no consensus. They parted and went home.

The next morning, when I reached the office from my train, Victor acted, as usual, unilaterally and cancelled the meetings. Both Liverpool and Manchester were annoyed, after all the work that had gone into them. It was, of course, a colossal mistake.

Arthur was quite right. The Government did not accept the verdict of the House. All they did was to allow time for Sydney Silverman (who had been kept off the Committee) to move a Private Bill. Unfortunately, I was brave enough to tell Victor I thought he had been wrong, which did not improve matters, especially as Victor must have realized how foolish he had been.

After that, there continued to be difficulties between Victor and Arthur Koestler, with me, uncomfortably, in the middle. There were, of course, already certain rivalries between them. Both had written biographies and I think Victor had a sneaking suspicion that Arthur's was better and, worse still, had sold more copies. However, in spite of this and especially because Gerald Gardiner was always there, cool, calm and dispassionate, the Campaign went on. We picked it up in the country as best we could. We spent enormous time and trouble on the passage of Sydney's bill through the House. This was magnificently organized. The abolitionists had their own whips, Labour (Kenneth Robinson was one of them), Liberal and Tory. Detailed and erudite memoranda were produced on every important aspect, on every amendment moved, and circulated to all MPs. It was finally passed with little damage done but then came the final hurdle on which previous attempts to end hanging had fallen – the House of Lords.

In the summer of 1956, when we began to realize that hope of surviving the Lords was pretty thin and that final success might well depend on the willingness of the Government to allow time for the bill to go through the Commons again in order to defeat the veto of the Lords, we organized an enormous Memorial to the Prime Minister in favour of abolition. This was a huge undertaking. Earlier, on the issue of the release of prisoners of war, Victor and I had produced a similar Memorial, but this was tiny compared to the 1956 effort. We circularized the leading members of every profession in the country. Thousands of copies went out with postcards for return and an envelope as well. Day and night we addressed envelopes, folded memorials, filled envelopes and sent them off. Here I must pay a tribute to Gerald Gardiner. Very often, in the evening, he would come into the office with a large suitcase. He would fill it with the memorials and envelopes, take it off home, and late into the night he and his wife would fold and fill. Early the next morning, on his way to his Chambers, he would call in again and leave the results of his night's work with us. I have had many chairmen over the years, whom I loved, admired, occasionally hated, often argued with, but there never was any other chairman who did that.

Meanwhile we worked on the Lords. This was difficult because there were so many of them and it was difficult to know which of them were likely to turn up. A vote on the rope was always an occasion for backwoodsmen. I went down to the House of Lords for the debate – the one and only time I penetrated that fastness. There they were, the blind, the halt and the lame, tottering into the Chamber to ensure that hanging by the neck until you are dead remained a bulwark of British justice for evermore. But there were changes. The bishops, those with a seat in the Lords, had a group meeting beforehand and there was actually a majority for abolition. So those who favoured it, including the Bishop of Manchester who was magnificent, spoke and the rest kept silent. But even that was not enough and the bill got thrown out.

The big question then was: would the Government provide time for the bill to go through the Commons again. It was too much to hope. The Government was slowly moving towards the end of its term of office; it had all those old harridans at its heels. So the bill died, but instead the Government introduced a Homicide Bill which accepted the principle of degrees of murder, abolishing hanging for some forms of murder, retaining it for others, notably for shooting, for killing a warder or policeman, for a second killing. The fact that this had been exhaustively considered by the Royal Commission and rejected did not seem to matter.

There was clearly no possibility of getting back to early 1956 when complete victory had seemed so near. All we could do was to fight the Homicide Bill, clause by clause, amendment by amendment, to make it as good as possible. In the meantime, we ran one more meeting at the Festival Hall, mainly, I think, because Victor wanted to run a meeting at the Festival Hall.

Then with admirable logic we decided that there was nothing

more to do except wait for another election, another Government. So we closed the campaign down. This was typical of Victor. He was always for getting rid of things when they had served their term. But first we wrote to everybody on our mailing list asking them to send a little money which could be banked, so that when times changed and new possibilities arose, the campaign could be resurrected quickly, with money there for the purpose.

So after spending many weeks sending out those last letters and banking the money, we packed up the records and closed the office. In a little less than two years we had at least saved the lives of ten or more people each year. Something had been achieved. As for me, I went off to get involved in a very different kind of campaign against something that threatened the lives of millions – the H Bomb.

Sometime later, during early 1964, I heard that Gerald Gardiner was to become Lord Chancellor of the next Labour Government. Then I knew that the job would be finished and hanging abolished for good and for all – for Gerald would never have accepted that post without a cast-iron assurance that capital punishment would be abolished at last.

CND: 1958-65

The CND Symbol

It was Gerald Holtom who designed it. He came to the first meeting of what was to be London Region CND in the small hall at St Pancras Town Hall a few weeks before the first Aldermaston March.

He unrolled at the back of the hall a long strip of black cloth. He attached a bamboo pole to each end and requisitioned two people to hold them. The strip was about six yards long and it was designed to be carried sideways along the side of a march by two people on foot or on bicycles.

On the black cloth were the words 'Nuclear Disarmament' in white and at each end the strange symbol in white against the black: the broken cross inside the circle.

He told us what the symbol meant. First, the semaphore for the initials, ND. Second, the broken cross meant the death of man, the circle the unborn child. It represented the threat of nuclear weapons to all mankind, and, because this was new, the threat to the unborn child.

He 'sold' us the symbol that night – and not only the symbol, but also, for a long time, the colours too, the white on black or the black on white, which was a part of the symbolism. Stark and funereal.

Then he went back to Twickenham where he lived and made the Aldermaston March banners. MARCH FROM LONDON TO ALDERMASTON, they declaimed in white letters on the black cloth, and there was the symbol too. In 1959, when we turned the march round, we crossed out the 'from' before London and changed it to 'to', and crossed out the 'to' before Aldermaston and changed it to 'from', and went on using the same banners, year after year. And every year we tied to the top of them a bunch of daffodils, a symbol of life and the spring.

It was Eric Austin of Kensington CND who made the first symbol badges. They were pottery badges, made from clay and baked in an oven, white, with the circle and cross in black. Later we made them in plastic and in metal, but the pottery badges were the first and the most to the point for, said Eric, if nuclear war came and we all went up in nuclear fire, the badges would survive and remain as our memorial, to be found maybe centuries later by whatever race managed to survive the holocaust.

So we put it on badges, on leaflets, on posters, on notepaper, on flags and on banners. And most of all we put it on walls, for it was ideal for graffiti – so easy to draw, so quick to paint on a wall, I have found it all over the world, on Glasgow bus shelters, on tiny villages in East Anglia and the Isle of Wight, far afield in the United States, in Greece, in Japan. I found it on bridges with FREE GEORGE CLARK; on bridges with BAN THE B and a long trail of white paint left by the painters as they fled from the police. For years it remained on a bridge near Parliament Hill Fields with the slogan: BAN THE BOMB MEETING NEXT SUNDAY ST PANCRAS TOWN HALL. I often wondered how many Sundays people turned up for that meeting.

For a long time it stayed black and white, as Gerald wanted it. Later on, though I still went on fighting his battle, it turned up in pinks, greens, blue, golds and orange and in every colour of the spectrum. But it was never so good as black and white, stark and simple. And for many years we kept the colours for our leaflets and banners and posters, so that the style, the symbol and the colours became the hallmark of the campaign.

Designers loved it. They took it and played with it, made it tiny and enormous, twisted it, cut pieces off it, but always it was unmistakable. I remember one year when Ken Garland had designed a double crown poster for us with a large symbol, cut off on the left. We wanted a larger one, a quad crown, for display on the last few weeks before the march. So he took a dozen of the smaller posters and laid them underneath each other, so that gradually the circle of the symbol faded to a small ellipse, a small crescent moon. And the line of symbols disappearing looked like the line of a march disappearing down the road.

It defeated the powers-that-be of London Transport. They would never accept political slogans on posters. Yet the symbol said nothing overtly, though everyone knew what it meant. Year after year it passed their censors and politicized the posters, put the message across.

It was free for all, because while there were some who would like to have patented it, restricted its use to the respectable and acceptable people, this was never possible because it wasn't ours. It was first produced for that ad hoc committee which organized the first Aldermaston March. It was used by CND, by the Direct Action Committee, the Committee of 100, the Independent Nuclear Disarmament Election Committee, by all the ad hoc groups, and by Richard Gott fighting his election on the war in Vietnam in Hull. It was used by Canon Collins, Bertrand Russell, Pat Arrowsmith, George Clark, Michael Randle, Ralph Schoenman, old uncle Tom Cobleigh and all.

It outgrew the campaign and outlived many campaigners as it travelled around the world. It became a symbol of protest, of defiance, of resistance. There is still one on a wall of St Pancras Station with the slogan 'Against Tyranny' dating from the demonstrations against Queen Frederica of Greece. It was used by the civil rights movement in the States, by the movements against the war in Vietnam. When Grigoris Lambrakis, the MP who led the peace movement, was killed, the million or so who marched behind his coffin carried the symbols. The marble stone on his grave still has, cut out in the stone, the CND symbol.

In Chicago, in August 1968, after all the violence, the attacks on demonstrators, the blood, the tear gas, late through the night into the early morning and the dawn, Bishop Crowther, formerly the Bishop of Kimberley, led three hundred of the demonstrators in prayers under the trees in Grant Park. They prayed for Bobby Kennedy, for Martin Luther King, for Dick Gregory in gaol in Chicago; they prayed for their brothers in Prague, and as the sun came up they prayed for the line of guardsmen standing silently watching them. And the bishop wore on his scarlet cassock something *The Times* correspondent called 'the device of the new Christianity', the cross above the CND symbol.

Ten days earlier, when the Russian troops moved in their tanks into Czechoslovakia, they found it, defiant, scrawled on the walls of Prague. More than two years later, the Veterans, a million marchers, and the May Tribe (7,000 arrested in one day) proudly bore it on their banners in Washington. The symbol, like Che and Ho, still lives.

The Beginning

Since atomic weapons were first used in 1945 it is odd that there was no big campaign against them until 1957. There had been one earlier attempt at a campaign, in 1954, when Britain was proceeding to make her own H Bombs. Fourteen years later, Anthony Wedgwood Benn, who was one who led the Anti H Bomb Petition then, was refusing the CND Aldermaston marchers permission to stop and hold a meeting on ministry land, outside the factory near Burghfield, Berks, making warheads for Polaris submarine missiles. *Autres temps, autres moeurs.*

There were two reasons why it suddenly zoomed up in 1957. The first stimulus was the H Bomb tests at Christmas Island in the Pacific. It was these that translated the committee formed in Hampstead in North London into a national campaign, and which brought into being a number of local committees around Britain which pre-dated CND itself – in Oxford, in Reading, in Kings Lynn and a number of other places. Tests were a constant and very present reminder of the menace of nuclear weapons, affecting especially the health of children, and of babies yet unborn. Fall-out seemed something uncanny, unseen and frightening. The Christmas Island tests, because they were British tests, at last roused opinion in Britain.

The second reason was the failure of the Labour Party in the autumn of 1957 to pass, as expected, a resolution in favour of unilateral abandonment of nuclear weapons by Britain. Then, and for many years after, a great many people saw the Labour Party as the only road to ban the British bomb. First, you had to change Labour Party policy. Then you had to get Labour elected. It sounded quite simple, but even in 1957 something went wrong.

The resolution, composited from sixty-six calling for unilateral renunciation of H weapons by Britain, was moved by Harold Davies and seconded by Vivienne Mendelsohn from Norwood

Labour Party. The story goes that Harold came out of the compositing meeting and told his waiting friends that a nice little blonde girl from South London was to second the motion. They asked her name. Then they told him gently that the nice little blonde girl was the most militant Trotskyist in the Labour Party.

But that was not why the resolution was defeated. Basically, the reason was Nye Bevan. He was then shadow foreign minister and he called, on behalf of the NEC, for the rejection of Harold's resolution. It is said that he tried, before the debate, to persuade the movers to moderate it, probably to opposition to a first use of nuclear weapons which remained his position. He failed. So, on behalf of the powers-that-be, he defended the British bomb and pleaded with delegates not to send him naked into the conference chamber. Since at that stage the communist-dominated unions (represented, of course, by Labour Party members, but putting the CP point of view) opposed unilateral action on the bomb, Nye was bound to win. He did – by 5,836,000 to 781,000. Quite a victory.

The effect on the left was devastating. Nevertheless, in spite of the size of his victory, perhaps because of it, opposition to the British bomb soared steadily.

By that time I was working for the National Council for the Abolition of Nuclear Weapon Tests, as organizer. The chairman was a Quaker, Arthur Goss, owner of the *Hampstead and Highgate Express*, an excellent newspaper known locally as the *Ham and Hi*. He was a committed pacifist and persistently maintained throughout that summer and autumn that a movement so important ought to be run by important, national figures. He was modest and did not rank himself as such but, in their absence, he and his committee did everything they could. The secretary was Sheila Jones and other members included a number of Quakers, Gertrude Fishwick, Peggy Darvell, Rex Phillips from Orpington, also Nell McGregor, a Labour Party member from Hampstead Garden Suburb, and Sidney Hilton, a scientist, and Ianthe Carswell. One observer at their meetings was a certain Mr David Ennals, then working for UNA, who afterwards became a junior minister at the War Office.

When I first started working for the National Campaign it was operated from a long trestle table in Sheila Jones's sitting room in Well Road in Hampstead. Daily, I plodded up East Heath Road and there we organized meetings and marches, sent out names of MPs to be written to, collected names of sponsors and money, while her children played around the room and practised the piano. It looked very amateur, but wasn't.

Then we moved to a small office at 29 Great James Street, lent by the National Peace Council. There, when the series of tests at Christmas Island was over, we started to discuss whether the objects of the committee should be widened to include not only the tests but the weapons as well. It seemed illogical to oppose the tests and not the weapons. So, during the early winter, we wrote off to all the sponsors and to the committees which existed asking if they would approve this extension. They all did, except one. Lord Russell had doubts.

During these months, spurred on by the debacle at the Labour Party Conference, a number of intellectuals began to take action. Lord Russell and J. B. Priestley wrote articles in the *New Statesman*, edited then by Kingsley Martin. George Kennan, in the 1957 Reith Lectures, 'Russia, the Atom and the West', questioned the whole basis of nuclear strategy, and raised the temperature still higher.

Just as the National Committee was getting ready to extend itself and was moving to larger offices at 146 Fleet Street, there was a meeting at Kingsley Martin's flat in the Adelphi. Those who attended included Lord Russell, J. B. Priestley and his wife, Jacquetta Hawkes, George Kennan, Professor P. M. S. Blackett and Commander Sir Stephen King-Hall.

The meeting decided on two courses of action. Blackett, as always, saw his role behind the scenes, in 'the corridors of power'; so, to a certain extent, did King-Hall. But in addition it was agreed that a mass movement was required. Kingsley Martin, J. B. Priestley and Russell were detailed to this.

During the days that followed Kingsley contacted the offices of the National Committee and heard of their plans to extend their objectives. After a lot of toing and froing it was agreed to invite all the sponsors of the National Committee, plus a number of others known or expected to be interested, to a meeting at Canon Collins's house near St Paul's on 16 January. I remember I spent almost all of the Christmas holiday typing out the letters of invitation which were all top copies. From this meeting it was hoped to launch a new national campaign against nuclear weapons. The National Committee, with a compliance extremely rare in peace movements, was willing to hand over its office, its funds, its files, its organizer, and the meeting it had planned for 17 February at the Central Hall. Arthur Goss, who had said for so long that what was needed was national figures, really meant what he said.

I cannot remember now everybody who attended that famous meeting. It included a very good selection of what Rose Macaulay once called 'the stage army of the good', including Rose Macaulay herself, Dr Bell, the Bishop of Chichester, Lord Russell, Michael Foot, James Cameron, Sir Julian Huxley, Sir Richard Acland, Ritchie Calder, General Adam of UNA, and most of those who afterwards served as sponsors or executive committee members.

It was not a difficult meeting. There was no dissension. Everyone agreed that a campaign was needed. The main disagreement was about the name and after some arguing Campaign for Nuclear Disarmament was chosen because it was brief and to the point. But finally some sort of a committee had to be set up. Nothing had been preplanned. Kingsley Martin was in the chair and together, as people talked, we jotted down a list of names and then put them to the meeting. One or two refused for various reasons. One or two others were added. Lord Russell agreed to be president. The question of a chairman was left for the first meeting of the committee. The committee finally consisted of Canon John Collins, Ritchie Calder, James Cameron, Howard Davies (of UNA), Michael Foot, Arthur Goss, Sheila Jones, Kingsley Martin, J. B. Priestley and Professor Joseph Rotblat.

The National Committee was thanked for its noble self-sacrifice. Up to that point everything had gone swimmingly. There followed, however, a few death pangs from the old committee. Arthur Goss and Sheila Jones were not very happy about the way in which the committee had been chosen though the meeting had seemed happy enough about that. They were also unhappy about the chairman. After some consultation between Kingsley Martin, J. B. Priestley and me, Canon Collins was suggested and I took him down to the Albany to meet J. B. Priestley whom he did not know. That was the beginning of a beautiful friendship between them which has outlasted their association with the campaign. Arthur Goss and Sheila Jones would have preferred Ritchie Calder, but Ritchie, both then and later, was not willing. The consequence was that the chairman was not elected at the first meeting. At the second meeting, on 28 January, a formal resolution was passed constituting the campaign and its officers. Lord Russell was formally confirmed as president, but the committee also agreed that 'a good churchman' be enrolled as president with him. Russell was no doubt good, but certainly no churchman. Nothing was ever done about this and Lord Russell remained the one and only president CND ever had. I was formally appointed as organizing secretary. Years later, in 1963, I was 'elevated' to 'general secretary'.

But some members of the old National Committee were also not very happy that Sheila Jones and Arthur Goss should be the only members of the old committee to transfer to the new. The Executive Committee met this problem by agreeing to accept two people, and leaving it to the old committee to decide who they should be. So the final meeting of the old committee, in the Fleet Street offices, lasted long into the night, mainly because Arthur Goss, a good Quaker, disliked taking votes and wanted a consensus which simply wasn't there. Finally they had to vote. They put Arthur and Sheila on, but asked the new committee to consider adding Nell MacGregor and Sydney Hilton, as co-opted members. The new committee finally lost that proposal having done nothing about it.

Policy was the first problem that faced the new campaign. It was not difficult to select short-term objectives: tests, missile bases, overflights of planes loaded with nuclear weapons. The main problem was that the committee was anxious to keep UNA with them and UNA was scared of too radical a programme. In an effort to woo UNA, the first policy statement approved and issued for the Central Hall meeting was certainly ambiguous. It was not entirely unilateralist. It was far less tough than the resolution moved by Harold Davies. This is what it said:

> The purpose of the campaign is to demand a British initiative to reduce the nuclear peril and to stop the armaments race, if need be by unilateral action by Great Britain. As a first step towards a general disarmament convention, Britain should press for negotiations, at top level, on the following issues:
> 1. The stopping of all further tests of nuclear weapons;
> 2. The stopping of the establishment of new missile bases;
> 3. The securing of the establishment of neutral and nuclear free zones;
> 4. The securing of the abolition of the manufacture and stockpiling of all nuclear weapons;
> 5. The prevention of the acquisition of nuclear weapons by other nations.

In order to underline the sincerity of her own initiative, Britain should be prepared to announce that, pending negotiations:

> a. She will suspend patrol flights of aeroplanes equipped with nuclear weapons;
> b. She will make no further tests of hydrogen bombs;
> c. She will not proceed with the establishment of missile bases on her territory;
> d. She will not provide nuclear weapons for any country.

This ghastly hotchpotch of English prose was obviously the work of a committee, and might well have been accepted by Aneurin Bevan. Indeed, until the Central Hall meeting on 17 February, there was nothing very different about the policy of the new Campaign for Nuclear Disarmament.

The first storm signals were seen in the response to the advertisements for the Central Hall meeting. The speakers were to be Michael Foot, Cdr Sir Stephen King-Hall, J. B. Priestley, Lord

Russell and A. J. P. Taylor, with Canon Collins in the chair. The new campaign held a press conference in St Bride's Hall off Fleet Street and got practically no attention at all from the press. But applications for sixpenny tickets for the Central Hall flooded in so fast that with an enthusiasm I had learned from my years with Victor Gollancz, we hired hall after hall for overflow meetings. We finished up with an overflow in Church House, two in Caxton Hall, one other somewhere else nearby which I cannot remember, and the small hall at Central Hall for recordings of the speeches upstairs.

Hurriedly we lined up extra chairmen and speakers. I produced a complicated roster of speakers, moving from one hall to another and a number of guides for the speakers to make sure they got to the right place. Large numbers of stewards and collectors were laid on. Speakers were threatened with excommunication if they spoke over their time – that would have caused chaos in every hall. In fact, they were very well behaved and not one of them sinned.

The size of the response had its effect on the speakers. Faced with mass audiences in five halls, they lost their inhibitions about UNA. One and all came out with a militant denunciation of nuclear weapons, and Britain's in particular. One and all they called for unilateral action by Britain. A. J. P. Taylor got the wildest applause when he said that MPs supporting nuclear weapons should be hailed as 'murderers' wherever they appeared in public. From that moment, the campaign was unilateralist. A meeting the following evening for national organizations supporting the new campaign unanimously demanded that unilateral action by Britain in renouncing nuclear weapons be written into the campaign's policy statement.

The Executive Committee, unaccustomed to such rough treatment, accepted the inevitable, but stalled a little. A 'clarification' of the policy statement would replace the old one, but they refused to send it to the press. It was just as well that they were amenable because refusal would, by then, have caused an enormous hullabaloo in the new campaign and, much more important, unilateralism gave the new movement its sharp cutting edge.

The new policy statement was very much tougher. Here it is:

> The purpose of the Campaign is to press for a British initiative to reduce the nuclear peril and to stop the armaments race. We shall seek to persuade the British people that Britain must:
>
> a. Renounce unconditionally the use or production of nuclear weapons and refuse to allow their use by others in her defence;
>
> b. Use her utmost endeavour to bring about negotiations at all levels for agreement to end the armaments race and to lead to a general disarmament convention;
>
> c. Invite the cooperation of other nations, particularly non-nuclear powers, in her renunciation of nuclear weapons.

This was followed by the short-term ban on tests, missile bases, overflights, and provision of nuclear weapons to other countries. It was also written in rather better English.

This was not the only reaction from the Central Hall meeting. Some of the audience, stirred by the excitement, demanded that they should all set off for Downing Street, conveniently nearby. The canon, who had not yet acquired his instinctive reaction to calls for direct action, told the audience that if they wanted to go there, they should. Quite a number did. Among those who turned up there were Mervyn Jones, Doris Lessing, and some students. The police, taken on the hop, reacted hastily. A few turned up, accompanied by dogs. Among those arrested were Mervyn and a Labour Party Member, David Owen Evans, who was later fined ten shillings. He rang up Canon Collins and said that since he had told him to go there, and had not come himself, the least he could do was to pay the fine. The Executive Committee, rapidly acquiring a tactful response, agreed to pay any fines which could not be met by the sinners.

The press, however, remained calm. Practically no newspaper even reported the meeting. *The Times* said not a word, though it subsequently included the meeting in its 'Events of the Year'. This, again, was a reflection of what was to follow.

The Campaigners

What were they like, these campaigners who from that day on flooded into CND? Who were they? Where did they come from? Frank Parkin, in his book *Middle-Class Radicalism* (1968), reduced them to a sociological analysis. He found that they were mainly from the more creative and socially orientated professions and that they were more interested in the humanities than in commerce – surprise! surprise! They came from a very wide spectrum of politics and non-politics, yet for many years CND held them together. Freda Ehlers, a Bristol campaigner, told an early CND conference all about the CND umbrella long before it became an issue in the campaign. 'In CND', she said, 'I have to mix with so many odd people that the sooner we ban the bomb the better.'

There were, of course, the pacifists and among them a great many Quakers. They helped to set up the local and regional committees, like Damaris Parker Rhodes in East Anglia, Kenneth Lee in Kent, Alec Horsley in Yorkshire, Francis Jude and Maeve Wilkins who ran Christian CND, like Norman Frith who chief marshalled the Aldermaston marches with magnificent tolerance in the later years when they were really difficult. We must have used in those years nearly every Friends Meeting House in the country for our meetings and for housing marchers overnight. I remember the Friends Meeting House at Hammersmith where we took the press one year, when they were looking for 'Sex on the March', to find a group of Quakers there singing hymns by the fire. I remember the Friends Meeting House at Scarborough out of which we got thrown by the (non-Quaker) caretaker because David Boulton was smoking in the library. I remember the Meeting House at Jordans where the litter team used to stay after we abandoned Aldermaston and marched from High Wycombe. I remember, too, Bob Wickenden, who year after year organized the collection of litter on the marches, and often the Elsans as well. Lovely people; we could not have survived without them.

But at first we did not have all the pacifists with us. Some, like Stuart Morris of the PPU, rejected our 'partial' campaign and saw it as a threat rather than a step towards peace. I remember one Fellowship of Reconciliation branch in Halifax who wrote and telephoned persistently because they would not agree to work with Edward Thompson, then living in Halifax, because he had once been a communist. Yet gradually, as the years passed, most of them worked and walked with us.

Then there was the Labour Left. Dejected and disrupted by the débâcle at the 1957 Scarborough Conference, they moved into the campaign with alacrity and agreed with very little persuasion to close down their Anti-H Bomb Campaign. Labour Party members and Labour Party banners were out in force in the early years. Nearly every party in the country in 1958, 1959, and 1960 was passing or supporting unilateralist resolutions. They, too, saw victory coming easily through the Labour Party. Yet, oddly enough, the Executive Committee in those early days refused to have MPs on it. Michael Foot was not an MP then. They took the view that their job was to influence Parliament and thought they could do this better without MPs. This did not last long. But after 1964, when Labour won power, many of the rank and file wanted to reject them, as the Executive Committee had in its earliest days.

Communists were also there, but in the early days only as individuals. From 1957 to 1960, the Communist Party supported the Bevan line on nuclear weapons. Nevertheless, from 1958 on, a great many individuals in the party supported the campaign, took part in its marches and were quite unable to reject its militancy. Hundreds of Young Communists worked in the Youth Campaign and many of them were certainly as loyal to CND as to the Party, if not more so. Then in 1960, the Party, and the British Peace Committee, changed its line, though for many years it went on holding its annual conference at Easter so that the high-ups always turned up late. This produced problems because the press was always too ready to label us as 'communist' even when they weren't there. After 1960 the TV cameras would always find the CP banners on the marches.

In fact, the communists inside CND always played a centre, steadying role. They never attempted, or at least never succeeded in, dominating the campaign, its national or regional committees. They remained loyal long after many Labour Party people had left. They were usually not very radical. I remember one who proposed, for instance, that we ought never to march to or from or by any controversial place!

The Direct Action people were important, more important, because they brought to the campaign a commitment to and an understanding of non-violent techniques which was supremely important at that time and which set a tone and produced a quality for demonstrations which lasted for many years. The dominant people were Hugh Brock, then editor of *Peace News*, April Carter, Pat Arrowsmith, still demonstrating around and about, and Michael Randle. They brought to the Direct Action Committee, to the Committee of 100, and to the campaign as a whole, a quality which was both non-violent and radical. It was they who initiated and ran, with an *ad hoc* committee, the first, 1958 march from London to Aldermaston.

Then there was the New Left, nowadays known as the 'old new left'. They were important in the campaign because they brought politics to it, independent of the Labour Party, together with an understanding of the urgency of this new movement. It was they who were largely responsible, in 1960 and 1961, for extending the aims of the campaign to withdrawal from NATO and to positive neutralism. It was Stuart Hall, Peter Worsley, Edward Thompson, and young New Left people from the universities, like Alan Shuttleworth and John Slater, John Gittings and Richard Gott, who provided a political leadership and a hard background of political analysis to what was basically a moral crusade, especially after many of the Labour Party people moved out. In the early years they organized, from that well known New Left address, 7 Carlisle Street, the distribution of millions of leaflets before each Easter march. Yet, in one way, CND did them no good. It swallowed them up as a political force in Britain.

Finally, there were a lot of people who could not be classified. They belonged to no political party. Many of them belonged to no church. They had no politics. Their interest in banning the bomb was mainly ethical: they thought it was wrong. Most of them were young. Years later, when sociologists moved in on the campaign, they discovered that the great majority of them were absolutist (Lancaster Peace Research Unit and Claus Iverson and Anders Boserup of Copenhagen) and that they were more interested in working for a more just and humane society than in finding themselves a good job (Frank Parkin, *Middle-Class Radicalism*, 1968). They believed that the bomb immediately threatened the future of civilization, that it had to be banned very quickly or armageddon would come first. My daughter-in-law, who was one of them in those early years, told me later that she really believed then that a nuclear war could start any moment, would start if nothing was done. To put this into sociological terms, the movement, most of it, was absolutist and compulsive. It wanted to get rid of nuclear weapons, all of them. It wanted to do it very quickly.

This explains the way it behaved. It was in a tremendous hurry. From the Central Hall meetings on, there was a sense of urgency, a feeling of emergency, almost a fanaticism which made life very uncomfortable for the Executive Committee, and the office, as well as the Government and opposition.

All those clamorous campaigners and committees moved rapidly from the Central Hall meetings into the first march to Aldermaston and into a hurly burly of setting up groups, arranging public meetings and every sort of local activity. But they also wanted constant national activity. So, as soon as the march was over, there was Jean Jenkins, then wife of Clive Jenkins, setting out to organize a Mass Lobby on 23 April. The Executive Committee, unused to such haste and ebullience, was lukewarm and refused to give money but had no hope at all of stopping it. The project won immediate support from campaigners and hundreds of committees. The lobby duly took place and thousands of people queued outside the House of Commons to see their MPs. It seemed useful then and probably was. Some years later, not many in CND could be bothered with queuing to see MPs.

Immediately after that, we were off on another march. This time it was a four-pronged march in central London. Since the campaign was full of ardent, amateur organizers and the office was certainly over-busy, this was organized by an *ad hoc* committeee working from Pioneer House in Gray's Inn Road. In theory, the National Office remained in charge of finance, policy and press. It was not until Easter 1959, when the campaign itself organized the second Aldermaston March, that the campaign really took over its own demonstrations.

From the early days there were a number of local committees, regional committees and individuals who saw the Executive Committee as a conspiracy to keep the campaign down. Some London groups, especially Hampstead and Sevenoaks CND, regularly circularized all London groups, and sometimes all groups in the country, urging pressure on the Executive Committee for this or that. A spate of rude letters would flow into the office and to the poor Executive Committee.

Such campaigns were frequent, but when it came to the point, when groups from all over the country sent their delegates up to London for a CND Conference, the Executive Committee, and later the National Council, rarely failed to hold them. There were occasional successes, like the addition to CND policy of withdrawal from NATO and support for positive neutralism, but there was very little real opposition to that. The rebels were mainly concerned with activities. For years any suggestion that the annual march from Aldermaston be abandoned was heavily defeated. On matters of strategy the Executive Committee usually had its own way. There were two reasons for this. First, the campaign had so many divergent groups and all of them acted to a certain extent as pressure groups for their own point of view. They rarely combined widely enough to carry the day. The second reason was that while most of them were certainly absolutist and compulsive, they were basically very British, conservative and rather naive. They thought banning the bomb was a fairly simple matter and they never recognized the revolution in British politics that it required. They wanted to get rid of the bomb, leave NATO and abandon the American alliance without upsetting the pattern of life in Sutton, Totnes, or Greenwich, SE3. So while the leadership was constantly under fire for its slowness and hesitancies mainly on tactics, in terms of radical politics it was often to the left of the movement.

They hoped that at some stage, sooner rather than later, so many marchers (or sitters) would gather in Whitehall that the Government would fall, and Lord Russell or Canon Collins, or both, would ride into the Kingdom on a white horse. What they would do then they rarely thought about. Occasional conferences on the positive aims of the campaign were very wishy washy.

Also, most of them, though they often seemed hypercritical, wanted those big names on the Executive Committee and Council and after they got democracy continued to elect them year after year, even if they rarely attended. In spite of that, in the meantime, most of them saw as one of their main functions a constant battle to goad, prick into action, whip and scourge those lackadaisical people who met from time to time at 2 Amen Court or worked feverishly in slum offices in Fleet Street, Carthusian Street (known as Confusion Street), and, latterly, in 14 Gray's Inn Road.

I suppose that a movement which was so anti-establishment was bound to be against its own establishment. I got a lot of practice in writing the 'soft answer that turneth away wrath ...' but it rarely did. Times of crisis, as when Russell resigned, were sheer hell. But somehow we survived them, and when the campaign started to write polite letters I began to fear that we had passed the peak.

The Aldermaston Marchers

They were always anonymous. Though they carried their banners – 'Twickenham CND', 'Harrow Society of Friends', 'Gorbals Young Socialists' or 'North London AEU' – they had no names. There were many to recognize as they passed by on the road, but they did not require names. They were just the sort of people who marched, most of them young, wearing anoraks and sandals, a few with bare feet, a few with funny hats, and, with them, mothers and fathers and prams and babies and toddlers and all the rest of the marchers, clergymen, scientists, trade unionists, Members of Parliament, professors and students, teachers and schoolchildren, librarians and nurses, actors and printers, entomologists and engineers, philosophers and plumbers, doctors and draughtsmen, firemen and farmers, every possible profession and trade.

When they joined the march, they were lost in it. They became homeless and faceless. We never could find the 'big names' for whom the press was looking. Like everyone else they had merged into something which was simply 'the march'.

It was a community. 'Those not marching', said the *Observer* one year, 'seemed the outsiders'. But it was a community for which no vows were required. All you had to do to belong was to step off the pavement and join it. While the bomb was its main occasion and theme, it was much more than that. It was a mass protest against the sort of society which had created the bomb, which permitted it to exist, which threatened to use it. This is why so many of them were young – still free enough to reject it.

The march spread around the world. First, they came to join it: French and Germans and Italians and Scandinavians and all sorts of Africans and Asians and Japanese and Iraqis, Icelanders, Irish, Cypriots, Greeks, Americans, Australians, New Zealanders, Canadians and South Africans. We must have covered most of the United Nations, but we were united.

Then the march spread to other countries, to Denmark, to Sweden, to Germany, to Athens, to Washington, to Selma. By 1963 sixty other countries had marched in its wake – not always with the same theme, but in the same spirit, with the same mass refusal to conform, the same mass determination to change the world. That was what was so compelling about it. It really seemed for a time that the sort of people who marched and the sort of world they wanted might become a reality. 'The Aldermaston marchers,' said René Cutforth in a BBC programme, 'are the only people in Britain left alive.'

They existed for a time, shared a rich experience, contributed to something which seemed then more worth while than anything they had done before or might do afterwards. They created, briefly, a new sort of politics. I wonder where they are now?

From the Falcon Field ...
It always began, of course, in the Falcon Field at Aldermaston, except in 1958 when it ended there. Opposite were the gates of the AWRE, the Atomic Weapons Research Establishment, looking, as Mervyn Jones once said, like a cross between a comprehensive school and an oil well.

Early on Good Friday morning there would be just the field, damp and almost empty. A few small tents of early comers, a few early marchers. The catering team boiling up water for teas. The Elsan team putting up their small tents on the edge of the field and on the triangle of grass opposite the Falcon Inn. Then the police would gather outside the field. Then the pantechnicons for the baggage, seven tonners each – six, eight, ten, twelve – more of them each year as the march grew. Sometimes even now I pass in London one of those enormous vans with that odd name 'GRIFF FENDER' printed on the side. It takes me straight back to the car park outside the Falcon Inn, to the car park by Peg's Cafe where they used to park on Good Friday and, all around them, piled high, mountains of baggage, rucksacks, duffle bags, cases, sacks, sleeping bags, bundles of blankets, each with its own coloured label to match the colour hung on the van – so that the baggage went off with the van to the right school in the next stopping place, and when you got to your school, wet and exhausted, there was your baggage, waiting for you. At least, usually it was. There were occasional slip ups!

Then the Co-op van would arrive with Bob Tapson. 'The real leader of the March,' said the *Guardian*, one year, 'is the Co-op van.' Someone else said that if you drove it across London soon after Easter by the time you got to the other side you would find a march behind you.

Bob Tapson who drove it was wonderful. Patiently, day after day, he would answer questions from marchers, make tea for us, and drive, slowly and carefully, at the head of the march. One year we left a bottle of whisky half full in the van on Easter Monday. Next year, on Good Friday, he turned up with the bottle still there and the whisky too, untouched, ready for action.

By that time there would be all the rest of our transport – child care and medical, litter vans and vans for the bands, catering vans and marshals' vans, and the banner wagon.

One year we borrowed an elderly BOAC coach for the banner wagon. Late on Maundy Thursday evening it set off for the Harrow Road where the Architects' Group had been making banners in a basement for weeks. On its way, in the middle of the Easter traffic jams, it broke down on a main crossing. Infuriated policemen commanded it to move on. 'If I could,' laconically replied the driver, 'I would, but I can't.' Garages were closing for Easter. Mechanics had all gone home. Eventually, very late, it was mended, reached the Harrow Road, and was loaded up. It even arrived safely and on time the next morning at the Falcon Field. But there, directed by a not very efficient policeman, it drove into the ditch right across the only exit and entrance to the field. Luckily, no mechanic was needed that time. Hundreds of marchers heaved it out of the way.

It was this coach which was nicknamed 'the brothel', because apart from the architects busily mending banners, it was usually full of all the lovely young girls from St Pancras Youth CND – most of them, probably, virtuous.

Then the coaches would start to arrive from all over Britain; first

▲ 5a   People rushing to see the Ruth Ellis execution notice outside Holloway Jail on 13 July 1955.

▼ 5b   Peggy Duff at Aldermaston, 1961.

▲ 6a   The CND symbol on the poster for the 1962 Aldermaston March.

▼ 6b   Ken Garland's tall banners lining the street outside Windsor Castle, 1963.

of all one or two, then more and more, queuing outside the Falcon Inn to drop their passengers and then away up the road to the A4. Hundreds then thousands of people milled around the baggage wagons, in the road, and into the field. Meanwhile, the marshals were putting up their markers for the different contingents and all around the field banners were being assembled and raised. In the middle of the field, there would be a small crowd around the Good Friday service.

Then, out with the catering vans and all the other transport that had to get away before the march. Up to the gate with the Co-op van. Raise the head banner with its bunch of daffodils. Call up the head party and off we went. In front the TV cars with their cameras precariously perched on top. Next to them the Alberts, complete with trombone and whippet. Then the head banner, and behind it, mile after mile, the Aldermaston March.

On the road to Burghfield and beyond ...
It wasn't really very difficult to take five, ten, or fifteen thousand marchers along country lanes and the A4, or even fifty thousand or more through the streets of London. They knew where they were going, and they had to cooperate with each other to get there at all, so they did. Yet the march had a will of its own. If you left it too long at a stopping place it would get up and go off on its own. There was always a trail of marchers, in front and behind.

I remember one year at the Seven Stars at Knowl Hill, where we stopped for lunch, the marshals decided to have a meeting. They got together in a corner and the chief marshal was addressing them through a loudhailer, from the top of his car. But meanwhile the march had got bored and wanted to be off. Someone put up the head banner. The canon stood in front of it. Someone else said: 'Off we go.' And off they went.

When we went and told the marshals they were furious. They sent a car down the road after the march with a loudspeaker which said: 'Stop! Stop! You cannot go without the marshals.' But they could and did. They did not like being shouted at through loudspeakers and loud hailers and it was a wise chief marshal, Andrew Murray, some years later, who realized this and threw his away. But they liked to know the essential information – which way? How far? What time? Which school?

They didn't like being diverted and they felt very strongly that the march had a right to go through the centre of towns, right down the main streets, especially when they were busy. The police did not like this but they learned to live with it. I remember one year the police suggested that in order to miss the centre of Reading, packed with people and cars early on Saturday morning, we should leave by a short cut round the back, passing, as the chief marshal Michael Howard said, derisively, 'the town gaol and the biscuit factory'. That simply wasn't on.

When they were wet and tired, they didn't understand what you said to them. You had to point them towards their school or to the room they were to sleep in, and gently push them towards it. All they needed was a road to march along, food to eat, a floor to sleep on, and a banner to carry.

It was always good to arrive at a lunch or tea site twenty minutes or so before the march was due to arrive. It would be crowded and busy with those who served the march, fed it, made its tea, put up its Elsans, collected its litter and bandaged its blisters. The grass would be dotted with tables loaded with food, with bins for litter, and people selling pamphlets to make more litter. The pubs and lavatories were gloriously empty. Then down the road it would come, the big black and white banner swaying at the head, with all the banners behind and all the people.

The names of those sites will always be familiar: Burghfield where the green was always too small; King's Meadows by the river at Reading; the Seven Stars at Knowl Hill; the Wheatsheaf at Littlewick Green; Kidwell's Park at Maidenhead; the lay-by at the Procea factory near London Airport and the pub opposite where Michael Craft put up a picket line because the food was so dear; Uxbridge Common where it was so hot one year that the catering team sold water for a penny a cup, when soft drinks ran out; the park in Hounslow where the mayor, in 1959, insisted on making a speech though it was pouring with rain; Turnham Green where one year the canon and I actually managed, non-violently, to take the Trotskyist banner off the head of the march; Acton Green where we moved when Turnham Green was too small; and, of course, all those different bits of Hyde Park that we used from year to year.

We had to cope not only with the march, but with the police. Gradually they began to learn that the marchers would do what we asked but not usually what they demanded. They also learned, for instance, that if you turn a march right, it cuts across traffic, but not if you turn it left.

That was the mistake the superintendent made in Slough in 1959. He drove out towards Reading in the afternoon to take a look at the march, disbelieving our reports that it was several thousands strong and expecting to find only a few hundreds. He was appalled by what he saw and panicked. He insisted on diverting a very tired, cross march, which had come some nineteen miles, right across the main road, down a long, bleak, back road into the town. There was chaos for cars and anger from the marchers. The next morning, just to show him, we took the march back and out through the High Street.

The following year they knew better. They even fixed us up with schools all to the *left* of the road. So right down the High Street came the march, and half way down the marshals made a mistake and directed the band, the head banner and the front party left into a side street. The police sergeant marching with the head of the march was terrified. He turned to Clive Jenkins and said: 'Please, sir, bear witness. It wasn't my fault.' So the rest of the march continued on down the High Street, led by a banner which said: 'Slough welcomes the marchers.'

The oddest incident with the police took place at Slough in 1963. Fearful of trouble in the West End on Easter Monday, the Metropolitan Police sent down one of their top coppers, called, I think, Burgess, with beautifully curling moustaches, to issue all the organizers and marshals with a copy of a Public Order Act notice they had issued covering the route of the march on Easter Monday afternoon. Swiftly, the rumour spread. The marshals and organizers had been 'sworn in' as special constables. I often wonder what Burgess would have said if he had known what they thought he was doing.

The Metropolitan Police were professionals. They knew how to get a march through, how to turn it ... but they also knew how to cut it, to slow it, when they wanted to. They sometimes made mistakes ... like trying to box the anarchist group in near Parliament Square in 1963 – a stupid manoeuvre which deserved to fail.

But we also learned a few lessons. We learned that on Easter Monday, when we had fifty thousand or more marchers behind us, it was difficult for them to say no. That was how in 1962, after the first trouble at the end of the march (when some of the marchers spread across the road in Victoria Street and marched round and round from Whitehall into Horse Guards Avenue, along the Embankment and back again up Whitehall) we took five thousand and more of them silently into Grosvenor Square and stood them all round the north, east and south sides of the square, packed tight on the pavements, and held them there, in silence, for two minutes. That was one of the most impressive things we ever did. But it seemed a very long two minutes, and the police nearly spoilt it all by bringing up squads of coppers just as they started to leave. (There were, of course, no Maoists there then.)

In the schools and the tents ...
In 1959, in Reading, we had only one school for two thousand marchers to sleep in. Luckily, just in time, we found the Deputy Education Officer in the Butcher's Arms in Hosier Street, where we had an office. He gave us another school and they all slept under cover.

But at Slough the next night, we had no schools at all and only a few halls. Desperately I negotiated with councillors and committees all day as the march moved steadily nearer, but in vain. When the marchers arrived, weary and furious about the diversion, there was incredible chaos at the loading bays of the local Co-op where that year they had to collect their baggage. The march was so late that it was dark and nobody could see whose baggage was whose. Michael Howard solved that problem by lining them up in a queue and bringing in cars to light the bays with their headlights. But there was still nowhere to sleep for many of them. They sat patiently waiting on the pavements. At that time I supposed that they believed that God or CND would provide. Someone who sat there told me recently that he was just too tired to care.

Then TV and radio took a hand. 'Thousands of marchers,' they announced, 'are sitting on the pavements in Slough with nowhere to sleep.' It must have been Nigel Calder, who was always our press officer in those years, who laid that on and saved the situation. Gradually, out of their vicarages and rectories and manses came the clergymen. A hall for one hundred here ... off they went; a hall for two hundred families here ... off they went; 150 women only, here ... not so easy that one ... but off they went too. And then, at last, triumph – a councillor risked his local reputation and his honour and let us have the Town Hall. We put all the rest of them there. They slept in the Council Chamber. They slept in the corridors. They slept in the Rating Office, in the Health Office, in the Parks Office, in every office they could find. They slept on the stairs. Slough took weeks to recover from the shock and one Tory woman councillor probably never did. She turned up to inspect and found men, women and children, all sleeping together (how terrible) and worse still, the Queen's portrait with her face turned to the wall ... 'What else could I do?' asked the guilty man, 'I couldn't take my trousers off with her looking!'

That was how they always slept – not in Council Chambers – but all mixed up, men, women and children together. They marched side by side all day. They slept side by side all night. It was usually crowded. It was always uncomfortable. It was often noisy. But it was part of the march. Then when councils changed hands, as they did in Reading, schools became more difficult to get and finally in desperation we had to use tents. I never ride in to Reading on a train passing King's Meadows by the station without remembering the finest head of canvas ever raised in Europe in which the marchers slept in 1962 and 1963. In 1963 there was an enormous marquee which housed at least two thousand. By then we were sleeping around fifteen thousand each night.

The first year of the tents it was bitterly cold, frost on the grass and icy mist over the river – not only ice, either, there were fascists too, throwing fireworks and ready to slash guy ropes. All night we patrolled around the tents where inside all those thousands of people were trying to sleep, in spite of the noise, in spite of the cold. The next morning they stood patiently waiting to wash at the few stand pipes and in long queues for the few lavatories. (The Elsans went lost that night.) I don't think I shall ever meet people again who were so unreasonably patient as the marchers so often were.

The next year we had to use tents in Slough as well. This time the fascists struck earlier. During the week before Easter (it took a whole week to erect the tents) they slashed a number of the big marquees. High winds added to the damage. This was one of the occasions on which the police really helped. In spite of the difficulties with the local education committee, late in the day as the march began to come in, they got us a school. 'The Education Committee,' said the superintendent, 'insists that there must be an official in charge. We are trying to find a caretaker, but have failed so far. If we can't find one, will your marchers accept a policeman?'

The marchers were too tired to care and the North West Region marchers who slept in the school were far too reasonable to object, but in any case they found a caretaker, so the problem did not arise. The marchers in the school were far luckier than those in the tents. The tents were all lit by one solitary line from a lamppost. It failed, and for more than an hour there were no lights at all in any of the tents. We found one elderly woman crying in the middle of an enormous marquee, lost in the darkness, without her baggage. So we got someone to drive her up to the medical centre where they bedded her down for the night. We arranged to send others back to Leighton Park School in Reading for the night in the North West Region's coaches ... and then we lost the coaches, or rather the drivers, which came to the same thing. Somehow we got them to Reading and then, the next morning, forgot to collect them. Somehow they caught up with the march. Next morning, heads and banners high, they all marched through Eton and up through the main street of Windsor, lined with the beautiful, tall, black and white banners which Ken Garland designed. They were wonderful people.

Into London ...
The final day was always different. It began to change on Sunday afternoon as the march came near to London. More and more people came out to meet it, to join it. By 1961 it was so large that even though there were two marches, one from Wethersfield to the east of London, and one from Aldermaston to the west, the school playground at Spring Grove in Hounslow, where the western march stopped for tea, was too small for it. So Andrew Murray took the front half of the march, which had rested and eaten, out of one exit, while the back of the march was still corning in through another gate. We left the police miles behind that day ... not that that mattered. He did it again the following day at Kensington Gardens, but then he took the front half, which had rested for an hour, out of one side of the gates while the back half was still arriving through the other side.

We also found that even a march as large as that was much more flexible, less unwieldy than it seemed. In the later years when there was a sort of guerrilla war with the anarchists we found we could divert the march at a moment's notice, that we could leave to the last moment the decision on which gate you would use to leave Hyde Park, that if there was trouble at one point, you could take the march down a side street and round, back on the route. But this was only possible because the great majority were our people and trusted us. Mind you, neither the police nor the anarchists like that sort of tactic very much. The police liked things cut and dried and the anarchists preferred to put rings round you.

As the march came up on Easter Monday through Hammersmith Broadway and Kensington, the pavements were thronged with people waiting to join it and to see it pass. As it became bigger and bigger, reluctant authorities put up notices saying 'AVOID TRAFALGAR SQUARE' but they never said why. And as the march came up Whitehall, in those early years, the crowds parted to let it through into the square, like the Red Sea before Moses.

We never could decide what to do about Whitehall. The end of the march up that great wide street with the square at the end of it was the climax of it all. There was always a feeling that we ought to take it all over, spread right across it. For many years some groups did, at least for a time. The trouble was, as we found in 1964, the year of the one day two-pronged march from Kennington Park and Hyde Park, that it wasn't as easy as it looked. Even when you had two columns, one from the east and one from the west, Whitehall was so wide compared with Victoria Street that in order to fill it you had to keep halting the marchers at the foot of Whitehall, then wait till you had enough people to send them up right across the road in a significant mass. It wasn't until 1968, when the 27 October Vietnam march came the other way, and came as one march, no splits, no cuts in it, that Whitehall was really taken over at last.

We never found a really effective end to the marches. (Neither did they, in 1968.) Perhaps this was mainly because what mattered was the march and all those thousands of people coming up Whitehall into the square. After that, what was said was not so important. The end was bound to be an anticlimax. Perhaps it just wasn't possible to put into words what the march was about, what it meant, what it wanted. So we had speakers, nearly always too many and nearly always too longwinded. Members of Parliament and all sorts of politicians and orators would stand there, begging to speak, with their mouths watering at the sight of that enormous crowd. There was always much more enthusiasm to speak than to listen. We had poets, always too few, bands and singers, always popular, speakers from abroad ranging from Russian archbishops to American pacifists like Bayard Rustin and Staughton Lynd. Finally, in 1966, we had the puppet show written by Adrian Mitchell and Mike Kustow and those twenty-foot high puppets on the North Terrace with the bitter faces drawn by Gerald Scarfe. That, at last, was right, for the march was bitter by then.

Maybe the annual disappointment in the square was just a reflection of things to come. Yearly we learned at the end of the march that anticlimax must follow, the banners be furled, the marchers depart. Yearly we read the press with impotent fury. Yearly we saw at the end of the march the image of failure to come: the failure of CND to create something stronger, more enduring and victorious; the failure of the Labour Party to make room for it; the failure of politics in Britain to change.

Seeking a Revolution ...
For it wasn't then a nice, cosy, minority movement. It wasn't a collection of well-meaning people seeking limited reforms like capital punishment abolition or abortion reform. It was much more than the stage army of the good grown rather larger than usual. It wanted a revolution – and there were times when it marched up Whitehall and when, as on 17 September, it sat in Trafalgar Square, when the smell of revolution was in the air, insistent, compulsive and heady, like Paris in May 1968.

But it frightened its own leadership, scared the politicians stiff, and ranged against itself all the careful, unimaginative, conservative forces of all the establishments, including its own. They fought it, and fought it, and fought it again, and beat it.

It didn't last. How could it? It came up against all the hard inanities and harsh realities of politics. It had no programme, no ideology, no plans for alternative policies, let alone alternative governments. 'What splendid people they are,' said the press. 'What a pity that what they want is so unrealistic.'

So the march changed. It failed to get what it wanted either through marching, through the Labour Party, through civil disobedience, through Voters' Veto, through independent candidates, through any of the strategies marchers advocated. Frustration turned it in on itself. It ran furiously across roads, shouted at itself, barred its own passage, trumpeted at MPs who tried to speak, and yet persisted long after many of the early marchers and most of the big names had stopped turning up. Some lost heart. Some learned to live with the bomb. Many stayed at home when a Labour Government came to power. Some carried the black and cherry banners of the anarchists. Some went on trying.

For it was OK to have a rather colourful carnival gathering of sincere but misguided moralists – but when great trade unions fell under its spell, when it started to win votes at Labour Party

Conferences, when it really became a threat to the powers-that-be, enough was enough.

So they fought it and beat it. Not only the Tories, but the 'Socialists'; the Gaitskells, the Wilsons, the Healeys, the Stewarts, the democratic socialists, the bright young technocrats seeking power, accepting megaton and megadeath, the monstrous doctrine of nuclear-power politics. They fought it and won.

Then, year after year, they congratulated themselves that it was dead, that unilateralist resolutions had vanished from conference agendas, that Labour Party and trade union banners had disappeared from the march. They didn't notice that when it died something died, too, in the Labour Party. 'Mr Gaitskell,' said Christopher Driver in his book *The Disarmers* (1964), 'virtually completed a process which had already taken almost fifty years: he turned a party of protest into a party of power.' He also made it almost indistinguishable from the Conservative Party and created the same political dilemma, the same unspeakable lack of choice, as in the United States. If CND declined, at least protest has survived and is putting forward new roots and invading new constituencies – which is more than can be said for social democracy. 'The man recovered of the bite, the dog it was that died.'

The Other Marches

The Aldermaston Marches were not the only marches. Campaigners were always marching, and still are. During my nine years in CND there can be few towns in Britain to, by or from which I have not marched, no bases I have not protested outside.

There were occasions when I wondered whether there might not be better things to do. I remember one year remonstrating with the West Midlands Regional Council of CND because once again it was planning its annual march around the outer circle of Birmingham. 'Why not do something different?' I asked. 'You don't understand,' they replied. 'We have people here who can march, who like marching and can't do anything else. They're too shy to canvass. They can't speak at meetings. They don't know how to run bazaars. But they love marching. So, once a year, we run a march for them.'

We did, of course, do lots of other things. We organized hundreds – indeed, over nine years, thousands of public meetings. We distributed millions of leaflets. We sold hundreds of thousands of pamphlets. We must have sold millions of copies of our monthly newspaper, *Sanity*. We raised a lot of money, but never enough. Especially we wrote letters to local newspapers – and, unlike the national press, they published them. But in between all this, we marched ... and since marching around a base is as good a method as any of drawing attention to it, we must have done a lot of good with all that marching.

East Anglia was the luckiest region. It had more nuclear bases, of one sort and another, than all the rest of the regions put together. Essex, and Suffolk, and Norfolk, and Cambridge were pitted and dotted with Thor bases (those antediluvian, solid fuel, nuclear missiles which were rushed into Britain after the Sputnik went up in October 1957, to meet a nonexistent missile gap), with British V Bomber bases, with American Strategic Air Command and

NATO bases. Unfortunately, most of them were very remote, but the East Anglian campaign was undaunted. They ran innumerable demonstrations of all sorts and sizes.

One of the early ones was to a Thor base at Mepal, near Cambridge, which was run by Cambridge and Cambridgeshire Labour Party with the support of CND. Then we organized a series of meetings, pickets and marches around all the bases. I remember one in particular which started with a picket at a Thor base at Feltwell and finished with a march from Feltwell to the enormous American base at Lakenheath. I remember it for three reasons. First, it was bitterly cold and the RAF police brought in to man the gates at Feltwell shared their tea with the kids picketing outside. Second, the march passed through some of the loveliest country in England – why do they always choose the best of Britain for their worst excesses? Third, the last part of the march, to Lakenheath, was led by the wife of the vicar of Lakenheath who had become infuriated by a day and night influx of US bombers from France narrowly missing their church tower. (It must have been one of those times when de Gaulle was being difficult.) So she turned out on the march, on a pony, immaculate in riding kit, not a hair out of place ... and behind her round the endless verge of the Lakenheath base the usual mixture of hairy, bearded and beardless, rag, tag and bobtail, plus the mothers and fathers and grandfathers of a CND march. Then, of course, there was Fylingdales, where they built the Ballistic Missiles Early Warning System – again choosing one of the loveliest stretches of moor in Yorkshire. We ran a long march off the moors, down into Scarborough to finish with an open air meeting under the Castle.

Then there were the towns which housed Labour Party Conferences and TUCs – usually Blackpool, Scarborough and Brighton. Blackpool was marvellous for marching, because you actually marched on the front and, because of the illuminations, there were thousands of people about to see you pass by, to move out of the way as you came. But for everything else it was lousy – the food, the lights, the traffic. There's only one worse city in the world, said James Cameron once, and that's Mukden in

Manchuria. Scarborough too was good for marching, but there were never so many people about. Brighton, in spite of being so close to London, was never so good. If it was wet and windy the front was a wide open space, miles long and deserted.

There was the Scottish Aldermaston in June 1962. I missed it because I was in Ghana for the Accra Assembly. It started at a NATO store near Loch Lomond and finished in Glasgow.

It was in many ways a great success, but there was one snag, long remembered in CND. Either they over-estimated the number of marchers, or their eating capacity. When it was all over there were hundreds of fruit pies left uneaten.

Janey Buchan, wife of Norman Buchan, MP, took them back to her flat in Glasgow and stored them in her spare bedroom. She sold or gave them away as fast as she could to any social occasion that offered itself. But still there were hundreds left.

Then Ewan McColl, the folk singer, arrived in Glasgow and asked for a bed for the night. When he came down in the morning Taney said to him: 'I bet that's the first time you have shared a room with five hundred tarts.' He was not amused.

Then there were the long marches. In 1960 we marched all the way from Edinburgh to London. It was George Clark's idea, but he went sick and left it to us. We found ourselves with a four hundred mile long march and practically nothing arranged for it.

We started off from Edinburgh, swinging down Carlton Hill with a pipe and drum band at the head and out through Edinburgh to Dalkeith where we stayed the night. This was another occasion on which we slept in the Town Hall, but not so happily as at Slough. The local burghers insisted on segregation of sexes and some university marchers went home in disgust. Typical, puritan, spoilsport Scots!

We set off the next day into the lowlands. Though arrangements had been made for overnight stops, nothing had been done about lunch or tea. We had to buy food as we went on most days and find some convenient place to stop. On the second day, as it neared lunchtime, it started to rain. Not a house or a barn or anything with cover in sight. Only a railway station. So we went there. The stationmaster, porter and general factotum, was delighted to see us. He gave us the freedom of his station. He unlocked the waiting rooms and opened up the lavatories. We set up our boilers on his platforms. It must have been a pretty lonely life on that very remote station at which trains rarely stopped. We made his day.

That same afternoon we discovered the joys of Scottish licensing laws. Pubs with seven-day licences stay open all Sunday to serve bona fide travellers, which we certainly were. We spent a very comfortable tea break in a seven-day licensed pub.

Day after day we made our way slowly down through the lovely Scottish country, crossing the Ettrick and the Tweed and many other beautifully clean and clear streams. Mostly city dwellers, the marchers had never seen rivers like that before. Every evening and sometimes at midday we would march, singing loudly, into a small lowland town, Hawick, Selkirk, Galashiels, and many more, and hold open-air meetings in the town and lots of little meetings in the pubs and coffee bars.

Then we moved through Carlisle and over Sea Fell down into industrial Lancashire. By then the march had built up a tight, hard, community spirit. When local marchers came out to meet them, when speakers came up from London, they would eye them with the deepest suspicion. They were outsiders, not the hard core of the march. They even gathered up marchers off the road as they passed. There was one called Brighton Jo, a boy in his teens, living rough. They took him along, washed him, cut his hair, cleaned up his clothes, and made him a 'member of the march'.

The big cities were different with thousands of people to greet them and march with them. But there was trouble in Macclesfield. There we had the Friends Meeting House for the marchers to sleep in, but it had been let to a local religious sect. The place was just a hall with a table and chairs. The marchers went out and bought fish and chips, coke and beer, came back and sat around the table to eat. Then the minister arrived and was furious. They were desecrating his altar – how were they to know? Canon Stanley Evans, who had marched all the way from Edinburgh, tried to reason with him and gave up. What made matters rather worse was that two university students, a boy and a girl, turned up at the minister's home where accommodation for two had been offered. His wife looked at them with surprise and said: 'I am sorry. I have only one double bed.' 'Never mind!' they cheerfully replied. 'We always sleep together.' So Alec Leaver, then Assistant General Secretary of CND, and Sam Collins from Manchester, had to load most of the marchers into all the transport we had and take them back to Manchester. When they got back the next morning, tired out and unwashed, there was the mayor to see them off.

But there was worse trouble in Wolverhampton. Two of the marchers were arrested, leaving a local cafe carrying under their coats bowls of sugar. They were charged with stealing the bowls and the sugar!

At that stage CND had a reputation whiter than white. To have two marchers appearing in court was almost as unthinkable as nuclear war. The local police, surprisingly, accepted this. There was absolutely no mention in court of the campaign nor of the march. I turned up just in time to pay their fines. Needless to say, the press got hold of the story and played it big.

But that night, mystified by this curious incident of stealing sugar bowls, Alec Leaver went through everyone's baggage. He discovered that all down the march, every night, they had been pinching things, as mementoes of the march. He confiscated and hid the lot just as the police, who had got the same idea, arrived to search. They found nothing. The next night, on the outskirts of some dreary Midland town, we chucked over the walls of a big house a curious collection of souvenirs ranging from a plaque of the arms of Preston to telephone books, beer mugs, ashtrays – the flotsam and jetsam of the Edinburgh to London march.

On and on it went until it neared London stopping at Watford and Willesden on its way to Trafalgar Square. There was one interesting incident between Watford and Willesden. It had been agreed from the beginning that no party banners would be allowed until the last day of the march. But the London Communist Party organizer turned up at Watford with their banner and put it up in the march. I took it down. He put it up again. As the march was early we stopped for a break at a large pub at opening time. There we had a meeting of marchers in the public bar. By a large majority, including many young communists who had marched all the way and the Glasgow *Daily Worker* correspondent who had also joined at the beginning, they voted the banner out, until the next day.

The following day, with thousands of people with us and led by the same drum and pipe band which had headed the march out of Edinburgh, we marched into Trafalgar Square to be greeted by Lord Russell, CND's president. A week and a half later the Labour Party had passed its unilateralist resolution at Scarborough and Lord Russell had resigned. That was his last appearance as our president. We never had another.

The other long march, from London to Holy Loch where the United States had a Polaris base, set off from the 1961 Easter March. It was the last operation of the Direct Action Committee. I saw little of it until it reached Glasgow and set off on the last leg of the march to Holy Loch. It marched out through Partick around 3 p.m. on a Saturday afternoon. Just as the Edinburgh to London marchers had never seen streams so pure and clean, so the London to Holy Loch marchers had never seen Partick on a Saturday afternoon when the pubs shut. The streets were packed with drunken Scots and Irish. One especially drunken Irishman was absolutely infuriated by the sight of the march. He ran along beside it, screaming with rage. Then, because he was too drunk to keep up with it, he boarded a tram going the same way and stood on the platform, hanging on to the rail and screaming foul epithets at the marchers as the tram passed by. There were also at the head of that march, I remember, two brawny boilermakers with their banner. '10,000 Boilermakers against the Bomb,' they shouted as they marched. 'Where are the other 9,998?' asked the marchers.

In Dunoon and all along the shores of Holy Loch the sun blazed down. Londoners who had never seen the Clyde before certainly got an over-glamorous view of Clyde weather which is usually wet and misty. Pat Arrowsmith's little ships buzzed and floated around the Polaris supply ship, the *Proteus*. One at least got near enough

▲ 7   On the plinth of Trafalgar Square in the summer of 1959.
Bertrand Russell, Lady Russell, Victor Gollancz, Jacquetta Hawkes, Peggy Duff,
Ernie Roberts of the A.E.U. and Michael Craft.

▲ 8a   The Direct Action Committee pickets the Court House at Swaffham after their first
action at the Thor rocket base nearby.

▼ 8b   Head of the March, 1962, with John Collins, Ritchie Calder, Jacquetta Hawkes,
Anthony Greenwood, James Cameron, John Horner, Frank Allaun, Michael Foot,
Arthur Goss and Sydney Silverman.

to be hosed. Meanwhile, others sat at the entrance to the pier. *Proteus* must be still there, and nearby at Faslane is Britain's own nuclear 'deterrent', her four Polaris submarines, which both the TUC and the Labour Party Conference rejected in 1961.

Not all demonstrations were marches. We ran one campaign in East Anglia for which we printed thousands of small, bright yellow, diamond-shaped posters. 'FIFTEEN MINUTES TO ANNIHILATION', they said. That was the space of time then provided by the Early Warning System to get Britain's bombers off and away before we or they were wiped out by incoming missiles. The little posters were used most effectively in that very horsy town, Newmarket. One morning some local supporters got up early and pasted one of them on every lamp-post in the town, just high enough to be out of reach. They were lovely lamp-posts, slim and steel and painted a deep brick red. I drove into the town about 10 a.m. and the effect was fantastic. Even the horses must have noticed them. The powers-that-be in Newmarket were convinced that hordes of foreigners from Cambridge and London had invaded the town to desecrate it. They sent us a bill for a few pounds for taking them down. We were happy to pay. It was worth it.

Then there were the placards. London Region CND invented them. They were made of hardboard, two feet high by four feet long, and they were made in series for a series of linked slogans. They were intended for carrying on marches. We found a better use for them. We took them out to the NATO base at Wethersfield in Essex on their Open Day. The road leading to the base had a broad grass verge on both sides. In the morning we set up the placards in the grass on the left-hand side of the road. Then we sat by them in the sun all morning as thousands of cars queued and drove slowly past them into the base. When they were all in, we took up the placards, crossed the road and set them up again, facing the other way. Then we sat again enjoying the sun all afternoon as the cars left. They certainly got the message. It was a beautifully lazy way of campaigning.

Then we developed these placards for another purpose. We would decide to 'bomb' a town, that is, to drop a nuclear weapon on it. Leaflets were produced with accurate information about the effects of a nuclear bomb on the Town Hall, or the Palace Pier, or the Aquarium, and the placards would then be erected on the various perimeters, fire zone, complete destruction, moderate damage, and so on, on every road into the town, up to several miles outside it. This was a good sort of demonstration for a seaside town on bank holiday. One year, in Scarborough, during the Labour Party Conference, we dropped a one megaton bomb there, bang on the Spa, a near miss for Fylingdales.

Fallex '63 in the autumn of 1963 was a development of this sort of activity but this involved not just one bomb on one town, but a medium attack on Britain. It was based on a NATO exercise, Fallex '62.

A group of scientists were brought together, mainly physicists and experts in the effects of fire and fire storms. Together they worked out the effects of about fifty fairly small nuclear weapons, either 1 or $1/_2$ megaton missiles, on the most obvious targets in Britain: US, NATO and British bases. In addition, it was presumed that the major conurbations would be hit by rather larger bombs or missiles. The results in terms of damage, fire, death, injured, and radiated were put into a pamphlet, *Civil Defence and Nuclear War*. We spent a lot of time and trouble locating the bases, though a great deal of this was simple – we had been demonstrating outside them for many years. Enormous maps showing the path of radiation, the destruction and the fire areas, the bases attached, were produced.

The pamphlet, the maps and the lists of bases were the tools for this operation. In addition we produced thousands of posters and hundreds of thousands of leaflets to be distributed around the country by local CND groups. The idea was that every city, town and village should be clearly informed about what would happen to them if there was even a fairly small nuclear attack on Britain.

At the end of Fallex '63 there can be few who did not know the facts. Some years later Peter Watkins finished the job for us with his film *The War Game*.

On the whole, however, the campaign preferred traditional types of demonstration: traditional marches, traditional sitdowns, pickets, vigils, motorcades. But campaigners were always delighted when the movement hit the headlines with anything unusual. They loved any highly imaginative, highly expensive project like sending the Everyman to Leningrad or marching from San Francisco to Moscow. When a group of campaigners went over one Easter to join the West German marches and were refused entry at Dusseldorf, the campaign was jubilant when they sat on the floor in the plane and refused to move. Since a plane cannot take off unless everyone is strapped to a seat, they anchored the plane there on the airfield.

They were not so keen, however, to be unorthodox in their own home town where they battled away against prejudice and apathy, year after year. It was easier to feel militant on an Aldermaston March with fifty thousand others; not so easy in a suburb of Birmingham, in Cheltenham or little Wootton on the Wold.

Yet it was there, in those early years, that the message got through. These people who marched, and planned the marches, who booked the halls for the meetings, flyposted the posters, gave out the leaflets, sold the pamphlets, wrote letters to the local press and every year organized the contingent to the Aldermaston Marches – these were the people who created a fever of opinion which for a time the orthodox political leaders could not stay. They were the ban-the-bombers – and one of the reasons why they confounded the pundits was that a great many people, some openly, some tacitly, learned to respect them, the logic and the ethics of their gospel, and the sincerity and urgency which drove them on.

The Committees

Like most organizations in a so-called free society, CND spawned an incredible number of committees, groups, regional councils, specialist sections, *ad hoc* committees, planning groups. The number was not always directly related to its vitality. They tended to increase as its impact lessened. During those seven years from 1958 to 1965 I must have sat through thousands of such meetings, long into the night.

The first and foremost was the self-appointed Executive Committee of 1958 with all its big names. During those early years they stumped the country, travelling from hall to hall, preaching the message, putting the case against the bomb. The climax of this sort of operation was the Nuclear Disarmament Week of 1959 when no less than forty top speakers appeared on our platforms in hundreds of towns and cities. There is no doubt that their attacks on the bomb to large audiences, reported at length in local newspapers, made a major contribution to the swing of opinion between 1958 and 1960. Yet there was always this curious dichotomy, that the campaign both loved and hated them. They wanted them as speakers. They wanted them on the marches. Also, because a movement so anti-establishment had to fight its own, they belaboured them without mercy for their sins of omission and commission.

Since the Executive Committee was so clearly unrepresentative, some form of contact with other organizations supporting the campaign, and with CND Groups and Regional Councils as they were set up, had to be provided. The Coordinating Committee, which met on the day following the Central Hall meetings for the first time, was intended to meet this need. It inevitably became a two way channel for the virulent criticism which was always around, and for proposals for actions.

Oddly enough, in 1959, just before the first conference when the

Executive Committee was enlarged by a delegate from each Regional Council, Lord Russell informed the Executive Committee that he thought it ought to resign to allow elections to take place, and also that the campaign ought to have membership. Canon Collins was asked to convey to the president the view of the Executive that they had been appointed by the sponsors (which was a slight exaggeration), could not be changed without consultation with them (which was not exactly true, there had been cooptions without any consultation), that they were not in favour of resigning, and did not favour membership.

In demanding elections, of course, Lord Russell was lining up with the militants, but not in demanding membership, which the campaign continued to reject, quite rightly in my view, for many years. It accepted membership only in 1966, reluctantly, when some sort of stabilization was essential if it was to survive.

The new 1959 Executive Committee with its regional delegates was a large and rather unwieldy body. Mostly, its policy and approach were very similar to that of the first committee, but it was less disciplined, less friendly. Meetings lasted longer. This was probably due to the fact that the new members came up to town for the day and had time to spare. The older, original members were all very busy people. Nevertheless, there were no major changes under the new regime. This was one of the troubles with CND. It frequently democratized its institutions, but they remained basically the same.

In 1960, with some reluctance, Conference voted down proposals for a fully democratic constitution. The Executive Committee, in spite of its self-perpetuating conservatism, saw the writing on the wall, and itself prepared and tabled proposals for a fully democratic constitution for the 1961 Conference. It was largely my brainchild and has survived with one or two minor alterations to this day.

The new constitution provided for a chairman, a vice-chairman (later three of them), a treasurer, and ten individuals nominated by CND groups and elected at Annual Conference. In addition, each Regional Council and each specialist section (Christians, Labour

CND, Students, YCND, Scientists, etc.) were represented on the council which met about four times a year. The council elected an Executive Committee which had to include four representatives of the regions and, later, one from YCND. The first elections were carried out by a postal ballot and the result was not very different. Those who had believed that once democracy was won, the ordinary campaigner would take over and these old fuddy duddies would disappear, were bitterly disappointed. The ordinary campaigner showed a normal and understandable desire to elect big names to its council and continued to do so, even when it was clear that the names in question would rarely attend its meetings. There was at least one big name who disappeared – A. J. P. Taylor. He quit. He didn't approve of democracy for CND.

With the victory of democracy, the Coordinating Committee died, but many other committees, groups, and ad hoc committees took its place. One of the problems of movements ideologically opposed to bureaucracy is that they tend to establish multitudinous bureaucracies in order to avoid it. I remember one occasion when George Clark proposed that we ought to have a liaison committee to liaise between all the committees and the Executive and Council and then, presumably, you have to have a committee to liaise with the Liaison Committee – it's an anti-anti-missile type of escalation.

However, the specialist sections were a really profitable development. They represented sectional interests in the campaign and, since they had a clearly defined function, they made a great contribution. I do not intend to write a detailed history of their operations, only to define the area in which they operated, the sort of flavour they had.

Christian CND was not established for some time after the campaign was founded. In May 1959 Christian Action and the Friends Peace Committee organized a big meeting at the Royal Albert Hall: Modern War: a Challenge to Christians. The main speakers were the Bishop of Southwark, the Dean of Berlin, Victor Gollancz, Trevor Huddleston, Kathleen Lonsdale and Harold Roberts. Richard Acland, Jill Balcon, Pamela Frankau, Christopher Hollis and John Neville also took part and Canon

Collins took the chair. Until then, Christian Action had largely covered the campaign in the churches, but it was always a little frightened of the CND and, so far as I know, never unilateralist. Shortly after, Christian CND was set up by a Quaker, Francis Jude, then Field Secretary of the Friends Peace Committee.

It was never a mass organization. It produced excellent literature which was very widely used by CND groups and by sympathizers in the churches. Later, when Maeve Wilkins, another Quaker, became secretary it organized a number of pilgrimages and significant, small, thoughtful demonstrations, marches to Canterbury, to Winchester, to Parton.

Women: this was a small, national group which came together from time to time to organize special projects. It also produced some very good pamphlets, like *Tomorrow's Children* by Antoinette Pirie. Their first activity was a meeting on 27 June 1958 at Church House at which only women spoke and only women were admitted, except for the press. Like the first Central Hall meetings it was beautifully planned and timed but it was also in some ways more effective because it had a quietness and a conviction which remains with me even now, thirteen years later. The speakers were Jill Balcon, Peggy Ashcroft, Margaret Lane, Iris Murdoch, Jacquetta Hawkes, Annabel Williams-Ellis and Diana Collins, but mostly they read: letters from a Hiroshima widow, a poem by Jacquetta, a series of statements by politicians and the press.

Over the years that followed they came together from time to time to organize a meeting or demonstration. In between, the group rested on its laurels and never met unless there was a reason – commendable restraint.

Right at the beginning there was a small Press and Publicity Group, led by J. B. Priestley and Gerald Barry. It aimed to break through the press barrier – not a very easy task. Probably its major success was a television play, written by J. B. Priestley, called *Doomsday for Dyson*, which was shown by Granada Television and gave the new campaign a great lift. Marghanita Laski's play which was both shown on television and published as a book, *The Offshore Island* (1969), was equally useful but appeared some time after the Press and Publicity Group had disappeared.

The Scientists' Group was an obvious. Since nuclear weapons had been invented by scientists, they had a clear obligation to CND and many of them recognized it. Because the issue of the tests was important, it is not surprising that many of those who established and ran the Scientists' Group were biologists and bio-chemists, like Dr John Humphreys and Antoinette Pirie. They produced for a time a very professional CND Scientists' Bulletin, probably too academic for most campaigners. But they also provided a series of leaflets and pamphlets on radiation and fall-out. This was important, for it became one issue on which we won a victory. The attempt by governments to play down the dangers of tests and of fall-out failed because the truth, particularly the uncertainties, was widely distributed by movements like CND and SANE in the US, in leaflets, in pamphlets, in the press, and from public platforms. Nobody now pretends that fall-out isn't dangerous.

There were also physicists, Professor Nick Kemmer, Felix Pirani, Gerald Elliott and many others. They gave us reliable information on the effects of nuclear weapons, in terms of damage, fire, etcetera, and they were always accurate. They helped us to destroy the viability of civil defence.

This was immensely important for CND, for gradually over the years the public came to accept the facts as we put them and governments were forced to abandon the half truths and half lies they had been handing out for public consumption. We never produced, nationally, a leaflet, a pamphlet or a demonstration on the bombs or on tests which was challenged. Without their help and the aid of many other scientists in the States and in Europe, I doubt if the Test Ban Treaty would ever have been achieved. They also helped us to create in Britain and throughout the world an awareness that nuclear war meant annihilation.

Quite early in the campaign, on 22 September 1958, we laid on a meeting at the Central Hall, Westminster. The title of the meeting was Scientists on Trial. The scientists were Professor Marcus Oliphant from Australia, Dr Linus Pauling from the States, Professor C. H. Waddington from Edinburgh, and the late Professor C. F. Powell from Bristol. They answered questions and comments from Margaret Lane, Ludovic Kennedy and Keith Kyle.

This meeting got far more publicity than most. Some 159 weeks before the meeting, Dr Pauling visited Britain on his way to a Pugwash meeting in Austria. As he left, he was informed that he would not be re-admitted for the Central Hall meeting. A very considerable row broke out and the Home Office had to retract. In the meantime some scientists were so angry that they agreed to speak, though earlier they had refused. The meeting needed little advertising.

The Architects' Group was quite different. It was ebullient and extrovert. It was established very early in 1958 and a great many of its members worked for the London County Council. They made and designed hundreds of banners and operated a repairing unit on the marches. They made exhibitions, one of which, the Hampstead Exhibition *No Place to Hide*, travelled all around Britain, and then with John Brunner around the continent.

They were great people. Jim Bath used to turn up on marches wearing a fur bonnet and once got mistaken for an expected Icelandic visitor. Gordon Redfern, big, burly, and bearded, was incurably enthusiastic. One year he insisted on booking a few places for posters on the back of buses. We could only afford a few and he disregarded criticism that so few would be lost. For days he searched London for a bus with his poster on it. Then at last he saw one driving down Kensington High Street. Desperately he ran after it, but didn't catch it. He never saw another.

The designers were never a group, though we did, at one time, have a team which farmed out the work between them. In the early days our posters, leaflets and pamphlets were fairly undistinguished. Only the black and white made an effective impact. But gradually we recruited top designers. CND and Committee of 100 posters, especially the Easter posters, created a style, still in the black and white, which was distinctive and immediately recognizable. Ian McLaren's NATO poster won a prize in the annual competition of the Council of Industrial Design. Ken Garland, who designed the tall, slim, black and white banners produced for the 1963 march, headed the team. Many others helped with banner, poster, leaflet and pamphlet designs – Ray Carpenter, Ivor Kamlish and, of course, Robin Fior.

The doctors, of course, operated as a team only on the marches. David Pitt was the first medical officer of the march and in the early days we usually had a team of two dozen or so, together with nurses and chiropodists, who worked in shifts a twenty-four hour day. Their main concern was blisters, and yearly we purchased yards and yards of adhesive tape and hundreds of sheets of plastic foam. I remember going into a chemist's shop in Maidenhead one Easter Saturday afternoon to buy fifty sheets of plastic foam, a hundred packets of toilet paper and twenty tins of Elsanol. The shop attendant seemed a little surprised.

Later we had doctors who would like to have had a field hospital and demanded plasma and all sorts of other refinements. They must have been disappointed that we never actually had a birth on the march. One year we had a case of German measles and, as it was the year of the smallpox scare in Wales, it caused quite unfounded rumours.

I have left to the last the two largest and most dominant sections, the university campaign (CUCND, the Colleges and Universities CND) and the Youth Campaign (YCND).

From the very beginning there was widespread support among university students and university CND groups rapidly sprouted in every university. In many, they were soon the biggest political societies. They were largely autonomous, though they used our literature and came to us for speakers. They ran their own projects, like the Oxford marches to and from the US airbase at Brize Norton. They came out in thousands on the Aldermaston Marches. The university contingent was always one of the largest on the march.

CUCND represented them on various committees and coordinated their activities as best it could, lacking paid staff and always short of funds. It ran a yearly conference and usually produced a freshers' leaflet for each new university year. It organized an International Students' Conference. Needless to say, they were well to the left of the movement. Michael Craft, who chaired it for many years, was one of the most virulent critics of the CND powers-that-were, both as chairman of CUCND and later as chairman of London Region CND.

The one I remember best was the Campaign in Oxford University for Nuclear Disarmament. This was not only because under cover of some *ad hoc* group they ran the very successful Brize Norton marches. Many of its leaders and officers became well known names in CND after they left the University. Alan Shuttleworth and John Slater both worked for CND as research officers. Nigel Young was regional organizer of London Region CND and later of the West Midlands CND. John Gittings and Richard Gott came onto CND Council, wrote many of our pamphlets and played a big role in CND activity against the war in Vietnam, until they both left Britain for Chile in 1966. Mike Kustow, who organized theatre-in-the-round in the schools for the 1960 Aldermaston March, putting on three of David Campton's plays, later wrote and produced, with Adrian Mitchell, the Giant Puppet Show which ended the Aldermaston March in 1966.

There were occasions when university CNDs clashed with town CNDs. This happened in Oxford when the students painted CND symbols on the ancient walls of Magdalen. Olive Gibbs, local councillor, later to be chairman of CND, went down with pails and scrubbing brushes and cleaned off the offending symbols. But on the whole relationships were good and they often cooperated. I cannot remember any of the more active students in CND who later moved into conventional, professional politics. John Slater told me recently that he knew of only one from Oxford, who succeeded Frank Cousins as MP for Nuneaton. He also told me that he had never met one who had changed his political views or his opposition to the bomb since those days in the late fifties and early sixties when CND was the biggest political stimulus in the universities.

The Youth Campaign was very different. It was much younger. While officially the age limits were from twelve to twenty-five, most of the young campaigners were under twenty and many of them still at school. YCND was started early in the campaign by A. J. P. Taylor's son, Giles, and my own son, Euan. After that it operated for a number of years under the leadership of Elizabeth (known as Lou) and Daniel Elwyn Jones, Mischa Goldman, who was chairman, John Hoyland, who edited its excellent newspaper,

Youth against the Bomb, Jo Taylor, who came down from Edinburgh to be organizer and who later married Lou. Pete Latarche later took over from Mischa as chairman. Bob Gregory was also organizer for a time and now works with Ken Coates in Nottingham. Their politics were mixed. Some were communists, some were Labour. Many had no party allegiances. Most of their time they gave to YCND.

CND was always sensible about the youth movement. They recognized that the thousands of young people who worked in YCND and marched annually from Aldermaston were an asset no other political movement possessed. So we provided office space and paid for their organizer but also gave them complete autonomy to run their own affairs. They organized their own demonstrations, including two coast to coast marches across the north of England, one from east to west, one from west to east, produced their own literature, published their own newspaper, and ran their own conferences. While there were one or two occasions when council members talked of 'mothering' them, they never really got a chance. YCND shared our offices with very few ructions and the constant stream of young people in and out of Carthusian Street helped to give the campaign office a permanent Aldermaston March image. But there were occasional explosions. Jimpy Mendham, who for many years did all the essential jobs around the office from packing to driving, from duplicating to the post, from stores to catering, from mending pipes to making banners, one cold day in winter smelt smoke. He ran upstairs and discovered that the Youth Campaigners on the top floor had put a lot of copies of Sanity into a dustbin and set them alight, in order to warm their office, since the electric fire was broken.

It was nearly always as crazy as that ... but it was also amazingly sensible and the political content was often very high, as high and higher than that of many adult CND groups. Also, while many of them sat with the Committee of 100 or worked for independent candidates, the Youth Campaign as a whole didn't get involved in the lobbies and in-fighting within the campaign. They were far too interested in banning the bomb to get diverted. They concentrated on young people, recruited them, activated them, convinced them.

That was their job – and they did it very well. One of the reasons why they did it so well was that they were slightly crazy, but not so crazy as the world they were trying to change.

Later, after 1963, when victory through the Labour Party, victory through civil disobedience, and victory through independent candidates, had all failed to break through; when the Test Ban Treaty and the Cuba Crisis had begun to blunt the campaign; some people in CND decided that the failure to make progress was due not to any of this, but to a failure to organize the campaign in a way which effectively involved the grass-roots campaigner. Planning groups were to be the remedy. No more stuffy committees. No more directives from on high. Just ordinary campaigners setting about the task of banning the bomb.

They may have been partly right. Maybe what went wrong was a failure to bridge the gap between the canon and the Executive Committee sitting in Amen Court and all these young and middle-aged and older people frantic to get on with the job. Maybe we failed to find a method of working suited to this extraordinary body of people. The orthodox were probably too intolerant of the unorthodox, and vice versa. But by 1963 it was too late. So the new planning groups, the new attempt to get all the wings of the campaign working in harmony together, didn't really work. Too many of the planning groups were just like the old ad hoc committees and while in some places and on some issues we got a temporary revival by elevating the importance of the individual campaigner, it did not last because inevitably the campaign was beginning to lose its momentum.

One of the problems was the leadership. Canon Collins really wanted a movement like Christian Action, Save Europe Now and the Campaign for the Abolition of Capital Punishment. He wanted a Victor Gollancz type of set-up where the chairman called the Executive Committee together to get their approval. This is what he tried to make of CND, and it isn't surprising that he had so much trouble because it wasn't that sort of a movement.

In the early days I had little to do with policy decisions. I rarely spoke at Executive Committee meetings. I loyally defended, at considerable risk, the Executive Committee from attacks and explained to CND groups and to campaigners the reasons for their decisions. It was not until the sixties that I won the right to put my own point of view, but even then I recognized that to get my way I had to convince people. John Collins always wanted to bring the tablets down from on high. The difference between our approaches is clearly revealed by him in his book *Faith under Fire* (1966):

> There were times when she infuriated me; for example, there were occasions when, as chairman, I was trying to steer through a committee some awkward or controversial point or some carefully worked-out compromise, and she, with her forthright bluntness, would upset the applecart; and whereas it was my desire to get committee meetings over as quickly as possible, she seemed to enjoy them and would never seem to mind how long they dragged on – perhaps this was only an unusual outlet for self-denial. I suspect she hoped for someone more easy-going as chairman and was disappointed to find instead one who liked to get his own way, even sometimes, I fear, to the extent of obstinacy; and there were, I know, occasions in committee when I rather brusquely used to bark her into silence.

Canon Collins was immensely devoted and committed to CND, as he saw it, as he wanted it to be. He expected me to be loyal to him, to his conception of the campaign, and because I wasn't that sort of person there was bound to be trouble. My loyalties were to the movement. Yet though he often offended campaigners' sensibilities and so often infuriated the militants, it would be quite wrong to believe that many of them wanted to be rid of him. They did not always like what he said to the press or on television, but they admired his commitment. They wanted him there at the head of the march ... but they wanted Russell too. This leads to the story of the Committee of 100 and the part that it played in the Ban the Bomb Movement.

The Direct Action Committee and the Committee of 100

There was trouble over direct action almost as soon as the campaign was set up, and long before the Committee of 100 was even an idea in the mind of Ralph Schoenman.

The first Aldermaston March was, of course, run by the Direct Action Committee enlarged into an *ad hoc* March Committee. But there was little difficulty about that. Direct action in terms of marching was hardly civil disobedience, and the campaign supported the march, announced it at the Central Hall meetings, and gave it some money. The march was tremendously successful and gave the movement a great lift. At the meeting of the Executive Committee on 14 April 1958, however, the question of the Direct Action Committee and other *ad hoc* committees was considered and the proposals agreed show some signs of that anxiety about rival organizations which later became almost an obsession with some of the leaders of CND. The minutes reported a decision to appoint an advisory group on direct action and stipulated that:

> Any organization or activities outside the scope of the Advisory Group, such as the Nuclear Disarmament Mass Lobby Committee, must be asked to make it clear that they were independent of the Campaign. Pat Arrowsmith, Organizing Secretary of the Aldermaston March Committee, should be invited to be Assistant Secretary of the Campaign.

If this proposal had been accepted by Pat Arrowsmith and the Direct Action Committee, superficially a lot of problems would have been solved, but a tussle between the canon and Pat Arrowsmith would have been inevitable. So perhaps not too much was lost when she and the committee rejected the proposal, seeing it clearly as a take-over bid. The only real solution, then and later, was parallel organizations working for the same ends, by different methods, mostly with the same troops, maintaining friendly relations. Unfortunately, that did not happen until very late in the campaign.

Trouble followed very quickly. The London University Students' Committee, with a general election expected shortly, put forward a proposal for a Voters' Veto campaign in places where no candidate supported unilateral nuclear disarmament. The proposal was quickly taken up by the Direct Action Committee. This was directly in conflict with the Executive Committee's aim of changing the policy of the Labour Party, and then putting it into power, for a Voters' Veto campaign would obviously alienate Labour Party members. Throughout the summer and autumn, therefore, the proposal was rejected again and again by the Executive Committee. But in spite of a visit from the chairman, the London University Students' Committee, together with the Direct Action Committee, proceeded with its plans first for a veto campaign during a by-election in South-West Norfolk, and, later, during the general election. The argument went on for months but at least by January 1959 some recognition was given to its existence. The CND *Bulletin* carried two articles. One, by Michael Foot, was entitled 'A Policy for Hermits'. The other, by Michael Craft, was called 'Everything in our Power'. Here are some extracts:

... Only through the election of a Labour Government and the political pressure which we may exert afterwards can we succeed. A renewed mandate for a Tory Government, which has shown itself adamantly opposed to any concession in the direction of nuclear disarmament, would be a serious, and possibly fatal, set-back to our campaign. To refuse to take any of these factors into account in deciding how to vote would in my view be an act of complete irresponsibility. [Michael Foot]

... the greatest tragedy for the Campaign would be the return of a Labour Government with its policy unchanged. It is pious to hope that we could change their policy in office and disillusion would spread in the Campaign. The great merit of 'Voters' Veto' is to force the Labour Party to think again before it is too late. [Michael Craft]

By that time there was more trouble. From its foundation, CND had proposed that 'Britain must not proceed with the agreement for the establishment of missile bases on her territory.' This was a reference to Thor missile bases, fifteen of which were built in Britain, five in East Anglia, five in the Midlands, and five in Yorkshire. The Thor missiles were slow and cumbrous affairs and the bases were established in a feverish attempt to close a mythical 'missile gap' following the launching of the first Russian sputnik in 1957. The missile bases were grand targets for demonstration, especially because it was very unlikely that any of the missiles could be launched in time, in the event of a hostile nuclear attack. CND ran many demonstrations around them, especially in East Anglia. The Direct Action Committee, however, went ahead towards the end of 1958 on a direct action project at the Thor missile base at North Pickenham, near Thetford in Norfolk.

Mervyn Jones, who went to this demonstration, told me that this was one of the most effective he ever saw them undertake. The missile bases looked very sinister. In each, there were three long black sheds in which the three missiles were housed, surrounded by a galaxy of gantries and miles of barbed wire. They were usually situated on a high, bare plateau.

It was dusk when the Direct Action group reached the missile base at North Pickenham and as they attempted to enter it the sun was setting, red and fiery, behind the base. The operation was non-violent only on one side. Irish labourers constructing the site threw Pat and some others into their cement-mixers. Of course, the affair got an enormous press and the *Manchester Guardian*, as mimsy-mamsy as usual, promptly accused CND of undertaking sabotage. This was one of the first occasions when the press showed itself quite incapable of distinguishing between the various wings of the movement. I don't know who was most annoyed – the Direct Action Committee which lost the credit for the operation, or the campaign whose leaders didn't want it. Canon Collins on this occasion immediately issued a statement:

> Supporters of nuclear disarmament have been widely criticized in the press for abandoning the methods of persuasion and undertaking civil disobedience at the weekend demonstration at North Pickenham. I would, therefore, like to make the position of the Campaign clear. We aim to change public opinion and the policies of the political parties through the usual democratic channels. We work in friendly cooperation with a number of other organizations, including the Direct Action Committee against Nuclear War which was responsible for the demonstration at North Pickenham. It is an entirely independent organization with which we have cooperated on many projects, including the Aldermaston March and Vigil. The National Campaign for Nuclear Disarmament is not in favour of civil disobedience or sabotage so long as reasonable opportunities continue to exist for bringing democratic pressure on Parliament. It recognizes that those taking part in the North Pickenham project did so in full knowledge of the risk involved of violence or legal action. We also realize that many who support our aims have been encouraged to take part in such activities through the failure of a great part of the national press to report either fairly or adequately our legitimate activities.

There were three difficulties about this statement. First, it implied that sabotage had been intended. Second, it also implied that the action had provoked violence or was responsible for violence occurring. Third, it was unquestionably a dissociation and as such infuriated both the Direct Action Committee and thousands of campaigners who were delighted with the project and the publicity it got.

The campaign exploded in wrath and the next meeting of the Executive Committee was forced to issue a statement that, in future, it should not, as far as possible, publicly repudiate nor formally associate itself with actions involving civil disobedience. This, with a long explanation, was published in the bulletin. But it did not really help for the fact is that if you fail to associate yourself with an activity, you inevitably repudiate it. CND ran into this trouble throughout its existence, even as late as 1968 when it refused to join in officially on the 27 October demonstration on Vietnam and yet insisted that it was not 'dissociating'.

That was not the end of the DAC/CND confrontation by any means. At its first annual conference in March 1959 the Executive Committee found itself faced with a resolution moved by Pat Arrowsmith that CND itself should undertake civil disobedience. It seemed very likely that it would be accepted by a considerable majority. The Executive Committee, in a panic, made it clear that if this happened they would resign in a body. The motion was then defeated, but narrowly enough for the protagonists of civil disobedience to be able to claim that, but for the action of the Executive Committee, CND would have been committed, from that time on, to civil disobedience.

Trouble continued between the two organizations. The Direct Action Committee organized a vigil at Aldermaston on the night of a CND Central Hall meeting. That didn't help. The Committee continued to campaign for Voters' Veto with very little support, and to plan direct action projects, with a great deal of support. It was only when they announced a sit-down at the Thor base at Harrington, near Rothwell in Northamptonshire, that there was a brief pause in the hostilities and a truce seemed at last possible.

The DAC had planned a march from Rothwell to the base, to be followed by a sit-down. I suggested to John Collins that CND should organize a supporting march from Rothwell, past the base to a small village about two miles further on. It would be clear that CND was not involved in the civil disobedience, but it would also be clear whose side we were on; that we, too, opposed the base. So, on a bleak wintry day, the two columns set off from Rothwell. First, the Direct Action group together with its supporters, then the CND march led by the canon. It was agreed that there should be no sit-down until the CND march had passed by.

So in the dusk we came up a short hill to the gates of the base, surrounded by those waiting to sit, by the press and rubberneckers from near-by towns, and, behind the hastily erected wire, by a cordon of Home Office police in curious black short capes, looking like rather sinister blackbirds or crows. We passed by in silence, and when we had gone the Direct Action group sat down. In the confusion, for there were still hundreds in front of the entrance to the base, the police behaved in a way which astonishes Europeans, used to different police methods. Anxious to arrest only those who had come there for that purpose, they walked around asking people if they wanted to be arrested. If the answer was 'no', they passed on. If the answer was 'yes', they obliged.

Harrington seemed a model for a future, happier relationship. It had avoided repudiation. It had registered support without involvement in civil disobedience. The campaign liked it and at the 1960 annual conference they passed a composite resolution which opened the way to coexistence along those lines.

It seemed then that all our troubles might be over ... but we reckoned without Ralph Schoenman.

I first heard of Ralph during the summer of 1960. I went, rather late, to the annual conference of YCND. Mischa Goldman, the chairman, told me that someone from Hampstead YCND (Ralph Schoenman) had moved a resolution in favour of mass civil disobedience which had been narrowly defeated. Throughout that summer rumours abounded but there was nothing hard about them. A man from Special Branch, Scotland Yard, came in to see me and told me he understood that mass civil disobedience was planned. I told him I knew nothing about it. This happened to be true, but even if I had known, I would not have said so. Not a word of presidential support for such a project or of any new movement leaked out until after I had gone north for the Edinburgh to London March.

On 3 September, the day on which the march left Edinburgh, Lord Russell wrote to John Collins to tell him that when he spoke on 24 September in Trafalgar Square, at the end of the march, 'I plan to say something in a respect for those who practise direct action.'

Naturally, the canon was alarmed. He tried to dissuade Lord

Russell in a letter and saw him about the matter on 16 September. Lord Russell then agreed that Frank Cousins should be consulted. If he thought that such a statement might prejudice the crucial decision expected at the Labour Party Conference in early October he would postpone, but not abandon, his action. Frank Cousins did not think such a statement would be helpful and Lord Russell obligingly postponed his statement. What is odd about this incident is that Russell said nothing to Canon Collins throughout about any plans to set up a new movement for mass civil disobedience.

About a week after his meeting with Canon Collins, rumours started to circulate again. One or two people received letters from Lord Russell and the Rev. Michael Scott inviting them to join a new Committee of One Hundred people to organize mass civil disobedience, and reported this to Canon Collins. He became more and more alarmed. Mass civil disobedience was bad enough but a new movement was even worse.

Then, of course, the whole story came out because one of the letters was sent by mistake to the wrong John Connell and the man who received it was a journalist who immediately gave the whole story to the *Evening Standard*, which published it on 28 September, only a few days before the opening of the Labour Party Conference.

Panic spread like wildfire, fanned by the press. Statements and counter-statements were issued and published, many of them inaccurate. A brief and very badly attended meeting of the Executive Committee issued a statement emphasizing that neither the Executive Committee nor the campaign had been informed of Lord Russell's plans, which was true. One newspaper, however, reported inaccurately that this meeting had called for Lord Russell's resignation. Lord Russell riposted with a further statement which made the headlines on 1 October when delegates to the Labour Party Conference were assembling in Scarborough to composite several hundred resolutions on nuclear disarmament. John Collins was in Newcastle where he had been speaking and drove south to Scarborough with Alec Horsley and his family in a considerable state of perturbation.

That was a chaotic weekend. There was a very large CND demonstration in Scarborough and the town rapidly filled up with campaigners from all over Britain, easy to identify by the little black and white symbol pennant flags mounted on long poles that they carried. On the Saturday night, some people plastered the town with anti-H Bomb posters. The police were convinced that I was responsible and questioned the hall porter at my hotel as to whether I had spent Saturday night in bed! I was the North St Pancras Labour Party delegate and I had to attend a meeting on the Saturday morning which we had arranged for delegates whose parties had tabled unilateralist resolutions, the usual Saturday afternoon meeting for compositing and, in addition, I had been mandated to raise in the Conference the question of John Lawrence's expulsion. Add to that this bigger than ever row between the president and chairman of CND.

We persuaded John Collins to telephone Lord Russell to ask for a meeting. After a lot of telephoning it was agreed that they should meet at Lord Russell's Chelsea flat on the following Monday evening. But Lord Russell insisted on 'seconds' or 'witnesses' and John Collins insisted that I come back to London to accompany him.

So, after one of our most successful marches, I waved goodbye to the marchers setting off home in their coaches, slept briefly, and went off early the next morning to London, hoping to get back in time for the Defence Debate on the Wednesday.

I was lucky. I was black-balled by Lord Russell – an honour I shared with Kingsley Martin. So I took the next train back to Scarborough. In my absence, the chairman and president met four times that week, with Arthur Goss and Michael Mitchel Howard for company, and with a tape-recorder to register every word. Again and again statements were agreed and then rejected as Lord Russell changed his mind. At last, on the Friday evening, they produced a brief 'Statement of Amity', which expressed the intention of both parties to the dispute to work together for nuclear disarmament and the hope that a joint statement might emerge later when the CND Executive Committee met on 5 November. That was quite a way off, for Canon Collins was going abroad on holiday. It was also agreed that no further action would be taken and no further word said, until then.

I must say that in retrospect, even more than at the time, the whole business seems to me extraordinarily childish. Luckily, the tape was never widely heard. It rests now with the Russell Archives at McMaster University, Ontario.

For a week or two there was peace. The brief statement was given to the press and sent out to CND groups, all in a state of high excitement. Meanwhile, we got on with the job and concentrated on ways and means to exploit and perpetuate the Scarborough victory.

But there was more trouble to come, even before Canon Collins returned and the Executive Committee met. Michael Scott prepared and sent out to all CND groups a seven-page statement supporting Russell, ignoring the Statement of Amity, and Canon Collins returned home rather earlier than expected, because the weather was bad, to find on his desk a letter from Lord Russell resigning as president. The Statement of Amity agreed on 7 October was forgotten or brushed aside – 'I cannot countenance the chairman of an organization of which I am president permitting the policy of that organization to be misstated in public statements which are said to have come from him and have not been publicly repudiated by him.' The letter was dated 21 October. Chaos was come again.

Chaos remained with us for a long time. Campaign groups and campaigners joined in the battle, on both sides, and letters of abuse flooded into the office and into 2 Amen Court. And when, at last, the Executive Committee met on 5 November, it was faced with a new problem. Lord Russell had arranged for a statement by him to be published in the *Observer* and Canon Collins was invited to reply. The statement was certainly contentious, possibly libellous. Canon Collins refused to comply, but there seemed little chance of dissuading the *Observer* from publication as David Astor had agreed with Lord Russell to publish it and had then gone off to Switzerland.

The Executive Committee was in a quandary. Lord Russell had certainly behaved in some ways outrageously but the public row was doing the movement a great deal of harm and most campaigners were warmly behind the new movement, even if they did not want CND to get involved in it. The Committee agreed that John Dennithorne, who was secretary of the Welsh Council of CND of which Russell remained the president, should telephone him in Wales and try to persuade him to withdraw the article, informing him that the Committee had passed a resolution 'confirming CND policy on civil disobedience, expressing its unreserved confidence in the chairman, accepting the resignation of the president, and recording their great appreciation of his past services' – *nem con*, but with three abstentions.

I think Lord Russell was probably surprised. He may have been misled by the width and warmth of the response from the movement to the Committee of 100 as such. He probably expected and hoped that the Executive would repudiate the chairman and beg the president to come back. They did not do this, partly because Lord Russell's tactics had been unwise, had laid him open to charges of bad faith, and had enormously helped the canon; partly because the great majority of campaigners were quite unreasonable. They did not want to choose between the president and the chairman. They wanted them both.

So after long telephone calls, Lord Russell agreed to withdraw the article and the Executive Committee agreed to moderate their statement to:

> The Executive Committee regrets that false statements, purporting to come from the chairman, about CND policy and concerning the president's actions, have been made to the press.
>
> It expressed its unreserved confidence in the chairman, Canon L. John Collins.

The next tight corner for CND was the annual conference which took place on 4 and 5 March at Hackney Town Hall. While the non-involvement of CND in civil disobedience was re-affirmed, Conference accepted that the methods of the CND, the DAC and of the Committee of 100 must be regarded as 'three techniques in a united attack on preparations for nuclear war', congratulated the Committee on the timeliness of its first demonstration (it had coincided with the arrival of the *Proteus*, the US mother ship for polaris submarines to be based in Holy Loch), and urged full cooperation between the Committee and the Scottish Campaign on anti-polaris actions. Also a liaison committee was to be set up between CND, the DAC and the Committee. This was not too bad for those who were trying desperately to keep CND legal. The principle survived, though only just. The real trouble arose over a resolution from Sydenham CND proposing that Lord Russell be invited to resume the presidency. There was little doubt that this resolution would be carried by a large majority. The danger lay in the debate, in which it was possible, indeed likely, that the whole sorry story of the row between the chairman and president might come out into the open. It was a dilemma that somehow had to be solved. It was difficult to solve it because there were people on both sides who wanted to speak out. It was Alasdair Macintyre who found the way out.

After the resolution had been moved with commendable restraint by Sydenham CND, Alasdair rose to his feet and moved that the vote be taken. The canon, who was not very familiar with Citrine rules, asked me what he should do and I told him he must there and then, without any further discussion, take a vote on whether or not the vote on the resolution should be taken. He did. It was carried by a large majority. The canon again asked me what he should do. I told him: 'The mover of the resolution may speak. After that you must take the vote on the resolution, without any further debate.' It took a bit of time to convince him, but in the end, the mover having declined, he took the vote. It was passed by a large majority.

Those who stood for conciliation rather than confrontation heaved a sigh of relief.

More than a month later, Canon Collins wrote to Lord Russell to report on the decision, asking him to resume the presidency. There was some little difficulty because the new constitution did not provide for a president and J. B. Priestley had resigned as vice-president mainly because the post became redundant when the president had gone. But the Sydenham resolution could not be ignored. Certainly the new council could not ignore it. Since the chairman was not to be elected until the meeting of the new council in May, he asked Lord Russell if he would be willing to serve as president 'regardless of whosoever they may elect to the other offices'.

Lord Russell took a month to reply. But in the meantime he agreed to speak at the final rally of the Easter March which, in 1961, was a dual affair from Aldermaston and from the NATO base at Wethersfield, in Essex. It was the wettest Easter we ever had and the platform party was not exactly a happy one, in spite of the size of the march which was bigger than ever. Lord Russell refused to shake Canon Collins's hand or to share his umbrella – but the marchers were happy, in spite of the rain, to see them both there.

Lord Russell replied to the invitation on 15 May and apologized for the delay, due to his illness. Here is most of what he said:

> In regard to the query that you put to me, the answer to which you would like to tell the newly elected Council at their meeting at the end of May, as to whether or not I should be willing to reassume the office of President of the CND:
>
> 1. Largely from your public pronouncements and those of various members of the Executive-during-the-past-year of the CND, I have gathered that a great number of the supporters of the CND do not believe in methods of nonviolent civil disobedience to achieve their ends and that many of them, in spite of the policy outlined by the Annual Conference, do not even tolerate their use by others. Since I am President of the Committee of 100, it seems to me that the CND would lose the support of those who feel in this way if I were again to become the President of the CND. I myself believe that there is room for and, indeed, need for various methods – legitimate and of civil disobedience – if the movement for disarmament is to succeed. I think that the CND has done excellent work by pursuing legitimate means and that it would be a great pity if such work were discouraged or brought to an end. None the less, I believe that

methods of non-violent civil disobedience are also necessary both in order to break down the barrier of silence or misrepresentation in organs of public information and to show the breadth and gravity of the movement – both of which are methods of persuasion, not force, equally with the legitimate methods of the CND. For the sake of the CND as well as the whole movement towards disarmament, therefore, it seems to me that it would be a mistake for me to become its President. It may be, however, that I have misunderstood the general situation and that the number of members of the CND who disapprove of non-violent civil disobedience and object to it on moral grounds is small and of less importance than I have been given to understand and that the loss of their support would not injure the Campaign.

2. Further, it seems to me that I should be in an untenable position personally were I to become President of the CND, many members of which – even members of the present Executive and possibly of the future Executive – disapprove of what I am doing as President of the Committee of 100.

3. As to your final query concerning my willingness to serve as President regardless of who the new Council may elect to the other offices of the CND: as you know, in the hope of making evident the unity of aim of the Committee of 100 and the CND, I agreed to speak in Trafalgar Square at the end of the last Aldermaston March, and did so speak. But the occasion made it clear to me that I must hold to the reasons of my resignation of 21 October from the Presidency of the CND. As you no doubt remember, we wasted more time and energy than we can well afford in mutual misunderstandings during the days before the Trafalgar Square meeting. I think, therefore, that I must hold by what I said in my resignation of 21 October.

He was, of course, begging the question. He knew very well that few campaigners disapproved of non-violent civil disobedience, that most of them accepted that there was room and a need for varying methods. It is significant that in his final sentence he stood by the letter of 21 October in which he said that 'he found it impossible to work with the present National Chairman of the Campaign'.

The letter, of course, went to the newly elected Council, where it was accepted and where Canon Collins was elected as chairman. Had it gone to Conference, there is every likelihood that the campaign would have insisted that there was no reason why the president of the committee should not also be president of the campaign. By the next time that Conference met, the committee was past its peak, Ralph Schoenman had been permitted to remain in Britain only if he ceased to organize demonstrations, and Russell's interests were moving to other fields. His abrupt departure from the committee was probably as much resented as his departure from CND was regretted.

The failure to hold both Collins and Russell in the campaign seemed to me, and to a great many others, very sad. Maybe he was wise to stay out, maybe the council was wise in accepting his decision. After all that had passed it would have been very difficult to have started again.

Meanwhile, the struggle at the top went on and on, while the campaign around the country and in the National Office continued to get on with the job of recruiting more and more support, demonstrating more and more widely. The Berlin crisis loomed up and testing was resumed by the Russians on 31 August, and by the Americans on 6 September. CND laid on an almost instantaneous March of Shame to the Russian Embassy, which numbered several thousands and gained it some respect from the rightest of the right-wing press. It was living up to its professed non-alignment. But while the size of its demonstrations steadily climbed higher and higher, support in the Labour Movement declined and it soon became clear that unilateralism in the Labour Party was doomed.

It is not my intention to write here a history of the Committee of 100 – I would not presume. In any case, I know very little of what went on inside it, though the *Manchester Guardian* regularly carried reports of its secret and private meetings. All I want to do here is to retail its activities in relation to the movement as a whole, and to outline the impact of its major demonstrations on CND.

Certainly, throughout 1961 the escalation of the nuclear threat, combined with the de-escalation of support in the Labour Party, gave the Committee great impetus and brought them mass support.

The first demonstration on 18 February brought out thousands. They sat by the Ministry of Defence, then on the corner of Parliament Square. Nobody was arrested.

In their second demonstration, planned for 29 April, the Committee aimed to take over Parliament Square. They marched down Whitehall and this time the police were not so amenable as they had been on 18 February. They marched into a pocket of police in Whitehall where they sat. 826 were arrested. Most of them were fined £1. *In toto*, quite a lot of money.

The biggest of all their demonstrations and the peak of the Committee's activities was on 17 September 1961. There was a parallel demonstration the same day at Holy Loch. The Government made a tremendous contribution to its success. In the first week of September they arrested thirty-six of the better known members of the Committee, including both Lord and Lady Russell. They appeared at Bow Street and, under an Act of 1361, were asked to bind themselves over to keep the peace. Thirty-two out of the thirty-six refused. The other four had commitments they could not break. Most of them were sentenced to two months in prison, including Lord Russell. It was an enormous piece of stupidity on the part of the Government. Russell's sentence was later reduced to one week, but a week was bad enough. The sight of the old philosopher being driven away in a black maria stirred not only the campaign but the whole of Britain.

Then the police, or rather the Home Office, put a Public Order Act on a large area around Trafalgar Square, stretching as far east as Temple Bar at the junction of the Strand and Fleet Street.

The CND Executive Committee met at 2.30 p.m. on the day of the demonstration. It considered the situation in relation to the arrest and imprisonment of members of the Committee and the imposition of the Public Order Act. It was agreed, as I had planned, that 'the Executive Committee would proceed as a body to the periphery of the area covered by the order, and should then seek, as private citizens, and with no intention of causing a breach of the peace, to make their way to the square to do what they could', as they rather pompously recorded, 'to prevent the outbreak of any violence and to protect the right of individuals to ...' etc.

This was one occasion on which there was excellent liaison between the CND Office and London Region CND. Just as this proposal was agreed, there was a knock on the side door of 2 Amen Court. There was Ted Hilley, chairman of London Region CND. 'Peggy,' he said, 'if the Executive Committee is thinking of walking down to the square, there are one or two people out here in Ludgate Hill who would like to go with them.' So out we went into Ludgate Hill and there, thanks to a last-minute circular and a lot of phone calls, were several hundred campaigners from the London Region.

We marched together down Ludgate Hill and up Fleet Street to Temple Bar where we met a cordon of police. 'Can we go on as individuals?' we asked. They agreed. So we broke up into groups, jumped onto buses, and all of us somehow got to the Square.

It was an extraordinary sight. In the square itself there were many thousands. It was impossible to tell how many. And all around it there was a thick queue of people perambulating round, because the police would not permit anyone to stop. So round and round we went, and as we went we kept meeting people we knew or recognized – Elwyn jones, later Attorney General, Marghanita Laski, Fenner Brockway, many MPs, a great many campaigners.

Round and round we went, and always there was this almost irresistible impulse to join the others in the square itself, always this uncomfortable, unhappy feeling of being shut out. Canon Collins, of course, as soon as he appeared, was nobbled by TV. I thought he made a great mistake that day of all days. Committed as he was to the need to keep CND legal, he concentrated on telling Britain over the air that this was not a CND demonstration, that CND did not involve itself in civil disobedience. While there in the square itself were thousands of people who had marched with him from Aldermaston, worked on the local committees, helped to make CND what it had become, sitting to defy the Government.

There was a feeling about the square that day which I found later in Paris during May and June 1968 – a feeling of revolution, of real challenge. You felt it sometimes at the end of Aldermaston marches as all those thousands of people marched up Whitehall, but it was never as clear and evocative as on that day. Gradually, it began to get dark.

Gradually, people walking around the square started to go home. Only the thousand or so in the inner square stayed and sat undeterred. Then as dusk came down, and as the police realized that they might well stay there all night and into the next day, they began to lose patience. It was then that they arrested Fenner Brockway and Canon Collins, the only two then left in the square who might successfully have testified against them. After that, they got rough with the people in the square, threw Adam Roberts into the fountain, and arrested 1,314. At Holy Loch a further 351 were also arrested.

That, for me, was the peak of the Committee. Nothing they did after that was on a par with that day and night. The next demonstration, the next big sit-down confrontation, was planned at Wethersfield, the base in Essex from which the 1961 Easter March had started. That was a colossal mistake. For the confrontation both of the Committee and of the campaign in that year was with the Government, with the Labour Party, with power; and power was in London, not at a remote Essex base. This was why, quite rightly, CND turned the 1959 march round, started it at Aldermaston and ended it in Trafalgar Square.

The Government made the same mistakes as before, raiding and searching the Committee offices and the homes of five of the leading organizers Ian Dixon, Terry Chandler, Trevor Hatton, Michael Randle and Pat Pottle; but they left Lord Russell alone. On the day preceding the demonstration, the five of them, together with Helen Allegranza, were arrested and charged with conspiracy under the Official Secrets Act, and were remanded on bail. Enormous precautions were taken at Wethersfield. They built a twelve-foot high wire fence around the base. A Braintree School was requisitioned as a Court House. All police leave was stopped and three thousand civil and military police mobilized.

In spite of the fact that very few pledges had been received, several thousands turned up at Wethersfield. But the base was too remote. The weather was lousy – wet and misty. The feeling of challenge, of confrontation, that had been so strong in the square in September, was missing in the wilds of Essex in December.

It was never the same again. In January, when the trials of the six were due, Pat Arrowsmith proposed a return to Wethersfield, as an act of defiance. She was defeated by 31 votes to 12. Quite rightly, I think. It is never wise to repeat a disaster.

CND mustered a massive march in Blackpool for the Labour Party Conference, but it failed to save the unilateralist resolutions. Something more like a demonstration than a meeting filled the Albert Hall and an overflow in November, and showed that the campaign still had more young people, more vitality, more force than any other movement in Britain. But the heyday was over – both for CND and for the committee.

I still wonder, I can't help wondering, whether it would have made any difference if, on 17 September 1961, or even earlier, the whole of CND had swung behind the committee.

Part of me says No, because in some ways the confrontation was a phony one. Most of the people who sat, paid their fines and went home again. They never filled the gaols, as Thoreau advocated. Only a gallant few went to prison, some of them again and again. Yet, I suppose, in very conservative Britain, it is still amazing that people like that actually came up to London and sat in the middle of Whitehall! Unfortunately, there were too many in CND who believed its purity must be defended; there were too few in the Committee prepared to go to prison; and both sides were intolerably self-righteous and holier-than-thou. Fusion or fission simply wasn't on.

Yet I still wonder what might have happened if on 17 September

Canon Collins had led CND down into the centre of the square and had sat with them there with the Committee. Not a major revolution certainly. Not even a change of government. Possibly the salvation of unilateralism within the Labour Party. The extra pressure on Macmillan and the Government might have forced through some unilateral gesture. Even if it had been only a British independent move to ban testing, it would have had two important results. The channel between public opinion and the policies of the Government would have been held open – instead it was closed (except from the right where opinion on racialism, for instance, operates freely). It would have given the movement the lift, the impetus it needed to maintain and consolidate a new sort of counter-politics. Instead, with both roads, progress through the Labour Party and through civil disobedience closed, CND and the Committee gradually sank into a morass of frustration.

The Labour Party

Certainly most of those who established the campaign in 1958 aimed to achieve nuclear disarmament through the Labour Party. The October 1957 decision of the Labour Conference was seen as an unfortunate error, which could be quickly reversed. Then all that would be necessary would be to get Labour elected, and we were home and dry. A short, brisk campaign, said the canon.

Many of those who came out on the early marches, set up the local groups, served on regional committees and involved themselves in CND in many different ways, were the traditional old Labour Left. These were the people who had supported Nye and the Bevanites in the early fifties, who had stormed down Whitehall on the Suez demonstration of 1956. They were left-wing MPs, left members of local Labour Parties, trade union branches, left-wing cooperators.

But from the beginning there were a great many also, especially among the rank and file and the young, who were not in the Labour Party, whose position varied from uninterest to outright hostility. For many, CND became the only politics they knew and even though most of them accepted for a time the strategy of victory through the Labour Party, their first allegiance was to CND. The pro-Labour brigade was much more strongly represented in the Executive Committee than among the rank and file.

On the eve of the Labour Party Conference of 1958 the Executive Committee meeting on 25 September discussed a proposal from Ted Bedford, Secretary of the Political Committee of the London Cooperative Society, who had become treasurer of CND, that the H-Bomb Campaign Committee, a Labour group, should be asked to close and merge itself into a Labour Advisory Committee of the campaign. It was felt that this merger would strengthen the 'victory through the Labour Party' wing of the campaign and provide an answer to wild suggestions like Voters'

Veto. A meeting of Labour Party campaigners was called during the Conference and the committee was established shortly afterwards. Its first chairman was Frank Beswick, a Labour MP (now Lord Beswick) who was also chairman of the LCS Political Committee. Other members included John Horner, then General Secretary of the Fire Brigades Union, Harry Knight, secretary of ASSET, the late Stephen Swingler, MP, and an Oxford City Councillor, Olive Gibbs, who later became chairman of CND. Fearn Jenkins of Mass Lobby fame was its secretary. The meeting at Scarborough was notable for me because it was my first encounter with Olive Gibbs and the beginning of a long friendship partly sustained by a common commitment to nuclear disarmament and partly by the fact that I never succeeded in beating her at shove ha'penny.

The campaign laid on public meetings both at the TUC in Bournemouth (the speakers were J. B. Priestley, A. J. P. Taylor and Kingsley Martin) and at the Labour Party Conference (speakers were J.B.P., A.J.P.T. and Benn Levy). The results in comparison with later years were modest. A resolution opposing missile bases in Britain gained only a million votes.

However, there was very little trouble with the anti-Labour people in 1959 and 1960. This was partly because the Voters' Veto campaign won very little support from campaigners. It was too negative and seemed anti-democratic. But mostly it was because the campaign was being fantastically successful in the Labour movement. In 1958 our gains had been comparatively small. The *Daily Herald*, on 23 February, suddenly came out for unilateral nuclear disarmament by Britain and against missile bases, a fact that considerably annoyed Morgan Phillips and Transport House who regarded the paper as theirs. Later, in April the Labour Party acknowledged the existence of CND by attempting to answer its arguments in a pamphlet by John Strachey, *Stop all the H-Bombs*, to which Hugh Gaitskell wrote a foreword. This was a sort of official, non-official document.

But 1959 was very different. On 4 June I was telephoned by Dick Clements, the editor of *Tribune*. 'Are you feeling strong?' he asked. 'I have some extraordinary news. Sit down while I tell you .... The Municipal and General Workers' Union has passed a unilateral resolution!'

The news was breath-taking. The M&GWU was probably the most reactionary union in Britain. It had never done anything revolutionary. Yet by 150 to 126 votes, and with 75 abstaining, they had come out against the British independent nuclear 'deterrent'. It was, I once told an American pacifist friend, like the Daughters of the Revolution tearing up their draft cards. It was a major victory and, though it was reversed a month or so later by a recall conference, it changed the whole climate of the battle to win the Labour Party. It began to look possible.

Alarm began to spread at Transport House, especially when the Transport and General Workers' Union passed a similar vote and made no attempt to reverse it. Forced into counter measures, the NEC sent the TUC a proposal for a Non-Nuclear Club, a new version of dis-engagement. Nobody was actually against this, but it made no impact as an alternative to the much more radical demands of the campaign. The vote at the TUC improved considerably. Although the T&GWU motion was defeated by 5,133,000 to 2,795,000, a further resolution opposing missile bases in Britain was carried by a small majority. There was no Labour Party Conference that year. Gaitskell was saved by a General Election, which he lost. CND played only a small role in this. Foreign and defence policy hardly got a mention. The Executive Committee issued a questionnaire to candidates and lists of MPs supporting unilateralism to local CND groups. There were a few difficulties about this list, because some candidates who considered themselves unilateralist, at least at election time, didn't get on to it, and others who did were not recognized as such by the local CND group. CND also, very carefully, advised groups to 'support any candidates considered to be genuine supporters of CND, but to pay due respect to, and recognize the existence of, the party allegiances of individual members'.

It was after the election, during 1960, that the tide flowed strongly with CND. In a statement issued after the October 1960 Conference of the Labour Party had accepted unilateralism, we said:

> The vote at Scarborough was the outcome of a massive shift of opinion within the Labour Party and the trade unions. Those who complain of a block vote wielded by a few leaders who allegedly misrepresent their members are very wide of the mark. Every one of the big unions which voted unilateralist had taken its stand by majority vote after full debate at its own conference; and in all of them except the Transport and General Workers' the leaders had bowed reluctantly to a rank-and-file decision. Those unions which have no internal democracy and have never debated the issue all voted for Mr Gaitskell's policy.
>
> This swing of opinion, however, was not achieved by lobbying and infiltration but by a public campaign which affected trade unionists along with the rest of the population. It was at Aldermaston that the victory of Scarborough was won.

This was certainly so. Yet we were also very greatly helped by events, especially the Blue Streak disaster. In April the Government announced the cancellation of the Blue Streak project. The Blue Streak was to be a British manufactured missile to carry Britain's own nuclear warheads from the mid-sixties on. £87 million had been wasted on it. Later the *Daily Mail* (6 August) revealed that £312,700,000 had been wasted on Government defence projects, including the Swift Fighter, the Victor II Bomber, the Avro 730 Bomber, the Blue Streak missile, five known missile types and thirteen known aircraft projects.

The Government tried to patch up its nuclear policy with talk of purchasing the Skybolt Missile from the United States (another non-runner), but the effect of the cancellation was even more devastating for the opposition. Gaitskell was abroad, and when the debate on Blue Streak took place on 27 April there was an abrupt change in the Labour Party line. Speaking for the opposition, George Brown came out against any further attempts by Britain to manufacture her own independent nuclear 'deterrent'. By the time Gaitskell reached London it was too late.

This was a sort of half-triumph for CND but the decision stemmed far more from impracticability than from a political or ethical decision. When the Labour Party's new Defence Policy Statement was issued later that year, CND lambasted it in its little bulletin, under a headline 'Old Lamps for Old':

> ... The statement proclaims conversion to the view that 'a country of our size' should no longer seek to be an 'independent nuclear power', but it omits to define this phrase. Does it mean that we should refuse not only to make nuclear weapons but also to wield them? If Skybolt, say, materialized and was offered to us, would the Labour Party decline it? The statement is ominously silent. We can only presume that, if it meant that Britain should henceforth have nothing to do with nuclear warfare, the statement would scarcely have failed to say so ...

Before the Blue Streak disaster, the debate and the change in Labour policy, there had been three signs of the way the wind was blowing. During April, the Co-operative Party, USDAW and the AEU had all passed unilateralist resolutions. By late June they had been joined by the Miners, the National Union of Railwaymen and the T&GWU. It was not really surprising that opposition within CND to the strategy of winning through the Labour Party declined steadily throughout that year.

The TUC, meeting in Douglas, Isle of Man, met the difficult situation, with the aid of the AEU, by voting both ways. It accepted the Labour Party Statement of Policy. It also accepted both the AEU and the T&GWU resolutions, and the last got the biggest majority.

The Labour Party Conference in Scarborough in October 1960 was one of the highlights of the campaign. The fact that it was all mixed up with the row between Collins and Russell hardly seemed to matter. It was as if we had started to move a great boulder down a mountain-side. It seemed that nothing could stop it. There was a small meeting of delegates concerned with unilateral resolutions, before the compositing took place. There was very little choice. It was obviously essential to ensure that both the T&GWU and the AEU resolutions were tabled in order to secure the backing of the big unions, especially the AEU which had voted both ways at

Douglas. In any case, Frank Cousins always refused to composite, and who would argue with a million votes! All the rest of them, all those constituency parties and smaller unions who had painfully worked out carefully worded resolutions, had to be persuaded to withdraw. When we met on the Saturday afternoon, in that school behind the station at Scarborough, it wasn't difficult. There was little scope for argument. It was agreed that Frank Cousins should move the T&GWU Motion with John Horner as seconder and that the AEU should move their own, with Ian Mikardo as seconder – an unusual combination.

On the Sunday, coach after coach drove into the town with loads of CND marchers. Usually during a Labour Party Conference in places like Scarborough or Blackpool, or Margate, it is easy to see that the Labour Movement is in town. All those rather solid, square men, some in cloth caps, parading along the front. But in Scarborough in 1960 it wasn't so easy, for all around them and in between them and in the pubs and the cafes, and at the usual Sunday morning meetings, were all those campaigners carrying their black and white pennant flags. We took over the town that day and in the afternoon we marched solid and miles long through the town, down along the front and then up past the hotel where the NEC was meeting, singing lustily 'Ban the Bomb for Evermore'. And that year, the march was full of Labour Party and TU banners.

Then the marchers departed, Canon Collins went back to London to tussle with Russell and the conference began. It was the AEU vote which was crucial, for at Douglas they had voted both ways. Here it was essential that they should vote for their own resolution and for Frank's, but not for the NEC's statement. The AEU delegation included that year Stan Orme and Norman Atkinson, both ex-members of the Bevanite Second XI and, of course, many other left-wingers like Norman Dinning and Jock Stallard. At that time the delegation still had the right to decide how the AEU voted, how it applied conference policy to the resolutions to be voted on. later Sir William Carron claimed this right for himself and kept the voting cards firmly in his pocket – but not that year. The left-wingers sorted out the floating voters among the delegation and followed them around. Whenever one of them went out for a cup of tea or a glass of beer, he would be accompanied by a campaigner, and always the conversation swung to the Bomb. They did a magnificent 'Parkinson' job.

The delegation met on the Tuesday night when the main conference party – the Civic Reception – was held. We hung around the halls and watched the doors, waiting for news. We were in the bar, I remember, when Stan Orme and Norman Atkinson turned up to tell us: they had decided to vote for the AEU and the T&GWU resolutions, and to vote against the Executive's statement. We were home and dry. Joyously, we sang 'Ban the Bomb for Evermore'. It was a great occasion. Never before had there been a victory like that. In the Bevanite days we had won seats on the Executive, but never a major resolution.

The next day the temperature was lower. Maybe it was because there is something artificial about a debate the result of which has been predetermined. Maybe it was the shadow of trouble to come. Frank Cousins moved the T&GWU resolution and, so it seemed to me, wasted a lot of time on irrelevancies. John Horner was magnificent. The high-ups of the AEU declined the honour of moving their resolution and left it to the Left, to Len Missindine from South London. Ian Mikardo followed him. There was little outstanding about the debate until Gaitskell rose to reply.

In his book, *Middle-Class Radicalism* (1968), Frank Parkin tried to justify a theory that for the left the issue of the bomb was only a means to change the leadership. I don't agree with him. It is true that they fought the leadership on the Bomb, on Clause Four, but a direct fight for the leadership was remote, because there was now no clear alternative. Harold Wilson, who was nominated that autumn, opposed Gaitskell on the issue of acceptance of conference decisions. He was never anything like a unilateralist.

I think it was Gaitskell who made the issue one of leadership. He had an alternative. He could have accepted the decision. He refused to do this and even, later, to accept any compromises put forward. He had a very clear idea of the sort of party, of the sort of Government, he wanted to lead. So, just as in the early 1950s, he fought. In that over-heated, over-tense hall he fought for his leadership, for his position in the party, for the sort of Government he wanted to lead, but never did.

He was extraordinarily effective, though he made the same mistake as in 1952, when he labelled his opponents as 'pacifists, neutralists and communists'. But still as he spoke you could feel the Constituency Party votes falling like heavy rain around you. Only the fact that the unions stood firm saved the day. But it was a hollow victory.

The AEU resolution was passed by 407,000, the T&GWU by 43,000 and the Executive Statement was defeated by 297,000. But the Labour Party promptly invoked a constitutional rule that changes of policy required a two-thirds majority and a resolution moved by John Stonehouse attempting to reaffirm the sovereignty of conference was so hemmed about with amendments that it was worthless.

Why did we fail to hold it? After all, the world situation in 1961 was, if anything, worse than in 1960. There was the Berlin crisis and the resumption of testing. The 1961 marches from Aldermaston and Wethersfield were larger than ever. CND continued to extend its support. By marching against tests to both the American and to the Russian embassies, it earned itself the reluctant approval of the Beaverbrook Press. The committee's sit-downs brought out more and more, culminating in the Trafalgar Square confrontation on 17 September 1961. Those who, like Canon Collins, believe that civil disobedience harmed the campaign, would probably contend that this was partly responsible. I think they would be wrong. Most Labour Party people respected those who were prepared to go to prison for their beliefs. In 1961 Polaris, which was the main committee target, was still voted down by the TUC and Labour Party Conference. I think there were three reasons why we failed to hold what we had gained.

First, the left in the Labour Party was unused to winning and neither the left nor CND really knew what to do about their victory. One or two went around squaring their shoulders, saying: 'We are the masters now', which sounded fine but was obviously untrue. There was no lack of orthodox campaigning. Some excellent pamphlets and leaflets were published. Speakers continued to stump the country. But because the swing of opinion in the movement had been partly irrational, a reaction to the attraction of a militant movement unlike anything the Labour Party had seen for many years, the people in the Party did not know what to do to hold it.

Second, in many constituency parties and trade union branches the majorities for unilateral nuclear disarmament had been small. The victory and, in particular, Gaitskell's reaction to it brought out from the backwoods many right-wingers who were normally rarely seen at party meetings. The backwoodsmen swung the balance.

Third, because Gaitskell made it an issue of his leadership, many people in the Labour Party came to see the Bomb as a threat to the unity of the party, and to its electoral ambitions. It had been out of power for ten years and, when it came to the point, for many in the Labour Party loyalty to the party came before loyalty to CND. Yet in spite of this, the reversal in 1961 resulted more from confusions and uncertainties than to any major, clear change of position within the Labour Movement.

Shortly after the Scarborough Conference, the left in the House of Commons sharpened its challenge by nominating Anthony Greenwood for the leadership. He subsequently withdrew in favour of Harold Wilson who was willing to stand on the issue of conference sovereignty, but not on the Bomb. He had, of course, a much better chance of winning, though he failed. Five MPs who voted in the Defence Debate in accordance with the Conference decision, promptly had the whip withdrawn (Michael Foot, Sydney Silverman, Emrys Hughes, Will Baxter and S. O. Davies). They stayed out for quite a long time. They were not, however, expelled from the party. If that drastic step had been taken there might well have been a revolt in Ebbw Vale!

The confusion began when Dick Crossman and Walter Padley, the general secretary of USDAW, started to try and find a middle way, a compromise. The document they produced was not very different from the Policy of Peace produced by the Labour Party.

Both argued for staying in NATO, both opposed a first strike by H Bombs, both supported a non-nuclear club and disengagement in Europe. The Crossman-Padley document, however, opposed a first strike by strategic weapons and in this respect was slightly better than Policy for Peace. A third document was produced by Frank Cousins which added to the confusion for it argued for staying in NATO and reforming it from within, but it was firm on rejecting American nuclear bases in Britain and insisted that NATO strategy be based on conventional rather than nuclear weapons.

The campaign remained absolutist and rejected all of these compromises, though some within the campaign, like Michael Foot and *Tribune*, were attracted by them. This did not make them popular in CND but they were forced back in line by Gaitskell who, like CND, rejected them all. But although they got nowhere, these compromise proposals created sufficient confusion to undermine the situation in the Labour Movement, especially in the trade unions.

By the late summer, we knew that we could not win. The one resolution we got through at the TUC and later at the Party Conference was for opposition to Polaris bases. Yet, in spite of that vote, Polaris remains all that is left of the British independent nuclear 'deterrent'.

The defeat was a major catastrophe for the leaders of CND. Victory through the Labour Party had been their one, basic, strategy. What could they do now?

They decided to go on doing the same thing. Many of them, and especially the leadership, still felt that a Labour Government would be more friendly to nuclear disarmament than the Tories, and more open to pressure. Donald Soper, writing in *Sanity*, CND's newspaper, in November 1961, put this point of view. 'It is a myth,' he said, 'that the Labour Party is a great monolithic bloc within which it is no longer possible for the nuclear disarmers to find any room for effective action.'

In 1961, as defeat at Blackpool became more and more evident, it seemed to me at that stage that much tougher action must come from CND, after the reversal. I felt that something had to be done, if CND was to survive, to sharpen the challenge both inside and outside the Labour Party, and that this might be done if CND occasionally put up a candidate at a by-election. I was never in favour of fighting general elections, when people choose a government, rather than an MP.

The movement was still growing. If we were lucky and a vacancy appeared at the right time (during an international crisis – and there were many of these), at the right place (where CND was strong on the ground and there was a right-wing Labour candidate), CND could successfully put teeth into its campaign by such a direct challenge.

I talked to a number of people. Stuart Hall and the New Left were keen. So was the treasurer, Laurie Kershaw, and, of course, Michael Craft and others who had been pressing for this for a long time. The canon was non-committal. We even approached James Cameron with the suggestion that he should be our first candidate. He was willing, but only if we would guarantee that he wouldn't get in ... he totally refused to be an MP.

I produced a document, outlining the proposal and the logic behind it. We recognized, of course, that such action would be very embarrassing for Labour Party members but it seemed possible for them to continue to operate within the party, while CND operated outside – particularly as there seemed no alternative except to go on as we had in the past, which seemed a dead end.

We invited John Horner up for a meal, and tried it out on him. He did not like it at all. Then, unlike most pressure groups in the campaign which would have started at the grass roots, we took the bull by the horns and arranged to discuss the proposal at a meeting of CND supporters in the Labour Party during the Blackpool Conference of 1961.

In spite of our expected defeat in the Defence and Foreign Policy debate, thousands of campaigners turned up to march along Blackpool front on the Sunday before the conference opened. The New Left was producing a daily hand-out for delegates, a project that CND later took over. The New Left, however, on an operation of this sort invariably stayed up all night. The consequence was that when Stuart Hall and I set off for the confrontation with

Labour CNDers, he had not slept for several nights and was in a state of dormouse-like torpor.

Not that it made much difference. The meeting, to a man, was wholly opposed to the proposal. Michael Foot said it was 'poison'. All the old arguments about progress through the Labour Party and only through the Labour Party were trotted out. It was rather like going to a meeting of catholic fathers and putting forward a proposal for free and unlimited abortion. We really got thrashed. Olive Gibbs was there with her husband and drove me home to my hotel, in tears. 'I don't agree with you at all,' she said, 'but I don't like to see you get such a bashing.'

Conference duly disposed of unilateralism and accepted the bomb, though not Polaris. We returned to London. It soon became clear that there was no prospect of persuading the EC and Council to agree to so revolutionary a proposal. Yet the movement was still growing, not only in numbers but in style, as the Albert Hall meeting showed in November. But I had to recognize that I could not continue with my private campaign for candidates and remain the general secretary. It seemed more important to stay, so I did.

Others were not so tied as I was. The New Left and various other groups and individuals held a series of meetings, some of which I attended. They set up a new organization, INDEC, the Independent Nuclear Disarmament Election Committee. It concerned itself not only with by-elections, but also with general elections which I thought a blind alley.

The 1962 Conference of CND took place in June. INDEC and the question of candidates was the prime issue of the weekend. Michael Foot himself moved a resolution from the Labour Advisory Committee: 'In order to retain the character of a pressure group influencing all political parties, the campaign shall not support any one candidate.'

This was, of course, a major change of line. Previously campaigners had been urged to support unilateralist candidates and asked to seek out the nearest unilateralist within their own party. Under the threat of independent ND candidates, the Labour Advisory Committee was putting them all out of bounds.

Twickenham CND, where Michael Craft stood in the 1964 General Election, moved that CND 'give earnest consideration to sponsoring their own candidate where no other unilateralist is standing'. Michael Foot's resolution was carried by a large majority and Twickenham's was similarly defeated. But Conference carried a further resolution which put INDEC on the same footing as the Committee of 100, and putting up candidates on the same level as civil disobedience. CND did not do it, but campaigners were free to do as they please and could, as individuals, support any candidate. This was a realistic approach as campaigners did what they liked anyway. But on this occasion there was no attempt, and no move, to keep the dissidents off the council and executive. Laurie Kershaw continued as treasurer. Unlike Russell, he didn't resign. Michael Craft remained chairman of London Region and a member of the council.

INDEC was not very successful, partly because it mainly fought general elections and never found a really suitable by-election to fight. That did not happen until early 1966 when Richard Gott fought Hull on the issue of the war in Vietnam, and even then it approximated to a general election situation because Labour's majority was so small that the loss of Hull could have unseated the Government. In spite of that Richard's campaign was enormously exciting, but also because of that, his vote was deplorably low. I missed the election because I was in Canada. I read the result in an early edition of a newspaper at 2 a.m. in a Chinese restaurant in Toronto. It was a depressing moment, but not unexpected.

Meanwhile CND proceeded on its way still aiming to win over the Labour Party, the trade unions, the public at large, and attended by growing frustrations within its ranks. In 1963 it moved into a period of intensive study of its own navel. It was generally accepted that it was getting nowhere very fast. (Though, indeed, even in the early triumphant days, campaigners went around asking why it had failed.)

What actually happened, so far as the Labour Party was concerned, was that gradually support within the Labour movement drained away. As the 1964 General Election approached, leading party members like Anthony Greenwood and

Judith Hart, who had come on to the council only a year earlier in response to the threat of CND candidates, withdrew, and Michael Foot went with them. Many remained faithful both inside and outside the House of Commons, but unilateralist resolutions disappeared from TUC and Labour Party Conference agendas. In August 1963 *Tribune* dropped its front-page banner claiming that it led the campaign against H Bombs (always resented by the anti-Labourites in CND). and neither the TUC nor the Labour Party discussed defence that year.

Campaigners were faced with a painful choice in the 1964 General Election. Stuart Hall, speaking at a rather dreary pre-election CND meeting at St Pancras Town Hall, described it as a choice between black and dark grey. It was in that spirit that many campaigners voted for Labour in 1964. By 1966 the situation was much clearer but for every campaigner who abstained, there were half a dozen others who couldn't care less about the bomb, voting for Wilson. By 1970 there seemed no point in it.

Naturally CND became more independent of the Labour Party. The Labour people in CND became just one of a number of groups within it. Desperately we tried to create an independent image at elections, both by and general. Committees were set up and sat interminably. Special issues of *Sanity* were produced. Elaborate brochures were sent out to groups. *Sanity* featured a wide range of candidates from Labour to INDEC. But the independent presence inevitably lacked body and sinews because it had no electoral presence. It was just one of the many pressure groups, trying to pressurize candidates. It had no real impact on the electors, little to attract them. In any case, its interests were too narrow, too much concerned with one issue only for it to be able to build itself an independent political position outside the party systems.

Frustration grew. CND was no longer in a position to move the Labour Party (this became dearer after the 1964 election and clearer still after 1966). It continued to march at Labour Party Conferences in spite of the lack of resolutions to press. But year after year it produced at Labour Party conferences and TUCs its daily *Focus*, a regular, duplicated, six- to eight-paged document, distributed early in the morning to delegates as they went into the hall.

We produced our first *Focus* at Scarborough in 1962. We collected together quite a formidable team: there was Stuart Hall, Alan Shuttleworth, Bob Rowthorne, Douglas Gill, David Boulton, editor of *Sanity*, Peter Worsley, Alec Leaver, Assistant General Secretary of CND, and myself. Others came up and helped for a day or two during the week.

We started our operations in the Friends Meeting House in the centre of the town. There we set up our typewriters, our two electric duplicators, our large stacks of paper, the staplers and all the other paraphernalia needed for producing a *Focus*. But we ran into trouble on the first night. The caretaker, who wasn't a Quaker and was very aggressive, late that night found David Boulton typing in the library and *smoking*! He promptly chucked us out. Hurriedly we loaded one of the duplicators, one of the typewriters, some stencils and bundles of paper into our dormobile. There we held a council of war. There was only one hope – that the hotel at which we had booked two rooms (one for me and one for the member of the team writing 'What the Papers Say', which had to be done very early in the morning) would let us finish the job there. We drove up the hill and sent Alec Leaver in to negotiate, because he was the cleanest, the tidiest and the most courteous, while we sat outside eating a couple of chickens Stuart had bought. After a time Alec returned and told us it seemed to be OK.

So we unloaded everything into the bar. Unfortunately there were two visitors at the hotel who insisted on going on drinking. Eventually, when they were too happy to object, we started work again and hour after hour ran our copies off through the night. We had assured the hotel manager that it wasn't noisy and would not disturb his guests but Stuart, who actually went to bed when there was nothing more for him to do, said he could hear the old duplicator clearly going thud, thud, thud, through the small hours of the morning.

So the first issue was out to time and the following day we managed to get an old school, scheduled for demolition. It was large, it had electric points, it was unheated, and bitterly cold, but it sufficed.

We kept on producing *Focus*, year after year, at Blackpool, at Scarborough, at Brighton. We produced it in the Labour Party rooms at Blackpool and slept on the floors beside the duplicators. We produced in luxury in a shop in Brighton. We produced it once in a top back bedroom in a Blackpool boarding house. Beggars couldn't be choosers and we were always hard up.

Each year, as the situation in the Labour movement worsened, *Focus* got tougher and tougher. It upset Labour campaigners and often we got complaints from the next Council meeting or Executive Committee. The first time this happened was at a TUC at Brighton when *Focus* actually criticized Frank Cousins! Not everyone understood that it had to be bright, sharp, impertinent and virulent. This is why delegates liked it and queued in the morning to get their copies. But those who objected could do little about it because they never stayed up late enough, or got up early enough, to be able to censor it. There were times when even I had to censor it, as in Blackpool in 1965 when we had John Gittings, Richard Gott, Terence Heelas and Tony McCarthy, then Research Officer of CND, on the team. Richard wanted to slip in the words 'Judas Iscariot' in a sentence referring to a member of the Old Left. There was also a very irreverent attempt to introduce into a rhyming ABC an abbreviation of Gunter rhymed with a once unmentionable four-letter word.

Focus was certainly the best method we found, after the days of the big resolutions, of putting the CND case at Conference. Even the right read it avidly. First thing in the morning, the hall would look like a sea of the colour we had used for that day's issue, for we changed the colour of the paper daily. Yet I sometimes think now that the reason why so many delegates liked it so much was because they lacked the ability, the know-how to get their own way, to rape the platform; they found in *Focus* a sort of masturbation for their frustrations. It certainly provided us with considerable relief for our own bitterness. But when all had been written, stencilled and given out, the policy of the Labour Party remained unchanged. We were still exactly where we were in October 1961.

It was, nevertheless, probably the best we could do in the circumstances. Any really independent presence required a much more radical analysis of politics and a very considerable broadening out of the concerns of the movement. Issue-orientated campaigns carry within them the seeds of their own extinction, unless they can be rapidly attained. And our particular issue could not be quickly achieved through the Labour Party because it required a major revolution in foreign and defence policy. The Labour Party was not that revolutionary. To have maintained its momentum, the campaign would have had to extend itself at least to the whole field of foreign politics. This it steadily refused to do.

The Policy

After early 1958 when unilateralism was written large into CND policy, there was really only one major change. In the first two years, unilateralism was seen to involve British renunciation of testing, manufacture and stockpiling of nuclear weapons. The halting of overflights of nuclear bombers, the rejection or withdrawal of nuclear missile bases, and a refusal to sell nuclear arms to any other country were a part of this.

The major change occurred at CND's conference in early 1960, and was amplified a year later. In 1960 Croydon CND, of which Walter Wolfgang was a leading member (he was then a parliamentary candidate in the borough), tabled a long and rather verbose policy statement which contained one new proposal – a rejection of nuclear alliances.

From the ethical point of view, this was a simple extension of the campaign's aims. If British nuclear arms were wrong, obviously alliances relying on nuclear weapons must also be wrong. Certainly not all campaigners realized the political implications of the step they had taken. It would have been possible for Britain to have rejected an independent nuclear deterrent (and the Labour Party at one time did) while remaining in NATO and other alliances, and without any major change in her foreign policy. Such a limited step might have had some influence in stopping the spread of nuclear weapons. Certainly Robert McNamara, American Defence Secretary, who opposed small independent 'deterrents', would have supported this. He would have liked to restrict the 'nukes' to the two hegemonies. But such a limited step was unacceptable to CND, both to its political people and to its pacifists. The inclusion of withdrawal from NATO meant that CND was now asking for a revolution in the foreign and defence policy of Britain as it had been under Ernest Bevin and every Foreign Secretary since then, both Labour and

Tory. It called for a rejection of the American alliance. By 1961, CND had recognized the political logic of its early decision and added to its aims, as an alternative to the American alliance, a policy for Britain of positive neutralism, of non-alignment. Gaitskell was quick enough to recognize the implications of the change and he spelled them out clearly in his Scarborough speech in 1960.

Positive neutralism, or non-alignment, was much in the air in those days, since the emergence of the group of non-aligned nations, including Yugoslavia, India, Egypt and Ghana, anxious to free themselves from the domination of the Great Powers and to act as a restraining influence, especially on nuclear policies. In 1961 CND published a pamphlet, one of its best, *Freed from Fear* by Mervyn Jones. This spelt out the consequences of a withdrawal from the alliances and the possibilities for a non-aligned Britain. It was the best and most detailed analysis published by CND in those early years.

This pamphlet was an answer to those who complained that CND was purely negative. It put forward a wide range of positive acts that would transform Britain's position in the world. The fact that non-alignment has declined rapidly over the past seven years (though now reviving) does not undermine the argument, for the situation in the Far East, in Europe, in the Middle East, steadily worsened as non-aligned influence declined.

During the years that followed there were no further major changes in policy. Rejection of biological and chemical weapons was merely a logical extension of opposition to weapons of mass destruction. Yet there were a number of major battles on policy which arose mainly from the wide diversity of approach of campaigners, from differences of view between various wings of the campaign, between the political people, the pacifists, the absolutists.

The first of these came to be known as the Crewe Resolution. At the 1961 conference, bemused and confused by the running battles on civil disobedience and the presidency, the Executive Committee allowed a resolution from Crewe CND to pass unchallenged. It called on all nuclear powers to renounce nuclear weapons, *unilaterally*.

When the new council, elected under the new constitution, met in May 1961, they were horrified by what had been done. It seemed to them utterly unrealistic to call on the United States and the Soviet Union, *unilaterally*, to renounce nuclear weapons. They felt that to include this in their new policy statement would lay them open to accusations of political naivety. So they went ahead and produced a policy statement which included the new policy of positive neutrality, and omitted the unfortunate Crewe resolution.

Naturally Crewe, and Malcolm Pittock who had moved the resolution, were furious. A long battle followed between the Executive, council and Crewe CND. The council excused itself by pointing out that a policy statement had been agreed at Conference, with one amendment only, the addition of positive neutrality, which was true; that in a brief statement it was difficult, if not impossible, to include the Crewe resolution with the explanations required, which was partly true. Crewe was not satisfied and drew unfortunate comparisons between CND and the Labour Party.

It was only in 1964 that a compromise was reached. Conference then rejected by a narrow margin a call to the US and the USSR to take unilateral initiatives, but it agreed a resolution calling on all nations unilaterally to renounce the use, manufacture, and possession of nuclear weapons, and for unilateral action 'in any country'. That was the end of a battle, in which I personally veered from one side to the other, sympathizing with both.

The rest of the arguments were on much the same lines. Unilateralism became a sort of religion, almost an ideology. No multilateral actions by Government could be acceptable. Only unilateral moves could be trusted – which was highly illogical both because governments can as easily repudiate unilateral actions as multilateral, and because not all unilateral steps are commendable (as in Rhodesia). The Test Ban Treaty was, after all, a multilateral agreement (some of our pacifists rejected it for that reason). George Clark produced one of the finest examples of this reasoning when he insisted that unilateralism was 'a way of life' ... a statement which drove Professor John Rex out of CND.

There is no doubt at all that the demand for unilateral action by Britain gave the CND movement a sharp cutting edge. This was partly because attempts in the late forties and in the fifties to reach multilateral agreements on disarmament were so insincere, so bogged down, that they deflated the peace movements. Jacquetta Hawkes's definition that unilateralists were multilateralists who meant it seemed to me much nearer the point. For me, it was always a strategy, a way to open up the road ahead, to prime the process of disarmament.

But the absolutists set themselves up as a sort of witch-hunting court in the campaign, seeking to destroy anyone or any group attempting, in their view, to water down the pure milk of CND doctrine.

The first row of this sort arose out of a short-term programme which was the brainchild of Stuart Hall. Shortly after the Cuba crisis, travelling from Hull to London by train, it occurred to him that, in the aftermath of the crisis, Governments might be sufficiently shaken to consider at least some steps towards a reduction of tension, to a lessening of the nuclear danger. He came to see me and suggested that CND should launch an interim programme for a few initial steps along these lines. It seemed eminently reasonable to me.

We sold the idea to the canon. Then we took it to the Executive Committee and Council. It was there that the mistake was made. They insisted on enlarging the initial steps from our original three which comprised withdrawal of nuclear weapons from all territories outside the USA and USSR, a test ban treaty and priority for the UN, to almost all the policy of CND with only one exception, withdrawal from NATO. It was this that did the damage, for *Steps Towards Peace* came to be seen in the campaign as a deep-laid plot to drop the issue of NATO.

While the leaflet putting forward these demands made it perfectly clear that there were not the full CND aims, it was, of course, distorted by the press. The *Daily Herald* reported a 'significant shift of policy'. The *Observer*, in spite of an article in its own columns from Anthony Greenwood which stated that there was no question of going back on the campaign's long-term aims of withdrawal from NATO and acceptance of positive neutralism, yet announced that CND 'no longer demands that Britain should leave NATO, provided that NATO itself is denuclearized'.

The reaction within CND was immediate and catastrophic. The absolutists swept into the attack. They saw the *Steps* as treason, in spite of the fact that Stuart Hall, always a popular militant, was concerned in them. They howled down any suggestion that the campaign's aims could be called 'long-term'. Withdrawal from NATO had to be immediate, if possible by next Monday.

The battle went on until the next Annual Conference, where we won. While Conference criticized the manner in which the statement had been issued, immediately after the Cuba crisis, they passed a resolution endorsing the right of the Executive Committee to issue statements providing a set of interim objectives, while reaffirming CND's fundamental opposition to nuclear weapons everywhere, by an overwhelming majority. We were home, though not exactly dry.

The next trouble of the same sort arose over the publication of a CND discussion pamphlet by John Gittings and Richard Gott, called *NATO's Final Decade*. A leak appeared in the *Guardian* before it was published. It reported, quite erroneously, that the pamphlet suggested the point at which CND might begin to accept the idea of NATO and that it supported another interim objective – Professor Blackett's scheme for a 'minimum deterrent', the scaling down by the Great Powers of their nuclear stockpiles, as a step towards nuclear disarmament. Again, the absolutists, led by George Clark, swept into attack. The contention in the pamphlet that the crisis in NATO, the 'death throes of the alliance' could lead to its abandonment in 1969 when it came up for review, was regarded as treason by those who held that we should aim to be out within a week.

While CND was a fairly libertarian organization, *NATO's Final Decade* nearly got censored out of existence and it looked likely at one time that everything we published would be subjected to minute scrutiny by both Executive and Council – horrible thought. But we survived, with a lot of patient help from Professor Wedderburn at council meetings. It was finally accepted that only the annual policy statement should be vetted by the council and we were left free to publish discussion pamphlets which were the responsibility of the authors, and which carried at least a brief statement of CND's full policy.

The third row was closely connected with the others. During 1963 and 1964, when the Labour Party people were gradually moving out of active participation in the running of the campaign, we began to feel the need for a more detailed political and strategic background to campaigning. It was for this purpose that the Disarmament and Strategy Group, known as the Dis and Strat, was set up. It was not a policy-forming group. It provided advice for the campaign's Executive and Council, and for literature to be published. It worked very closely with CND's research officers, Alan Shuttleworth, John Slater, and Tony McCarthy. Its members included John Gittings and Richard Gott, Terence Heelas, then a vice-chairman of CND, Professor Wedderburn, John Westergaard, Sheila Oakes, Douglas Gill, David Boulton and I, and some others. For a time it was regarded with the deepest suspicion by the absolutists. When George Clark resigned from the council in May 1964, shortly after the canon left, he issued a statement containing an attack on the group:

> Attempts are being made, more particularly by the Disarmament and Strategy Group (Terence Heelas, Sheila Oakes, etc.) to change the principled stand that the campaign has been taking against all nuclear policies during these past six years. This group has the sympathy of the Executive, the General Secretary, and the Editor of *Sanity*.

In spite of these attacks, the group survived.

The only other argument, which was very different, was about widening the aims of the campaign. It was twofold. There were those who would have liked to extend the range to cover the whole field of foreign and defence policy. There were also those, especially the activists of INDEC, and in the Committee of 100, who wanted a much broader dissenting programme, including other social ills, such as housing and race, which could be linked, but only just, to the campaign's original concerns, financially, because the money spent on arms could be used for housing, and racialism in some countries could lead to war. But neither the one nor the other succeeded in carrying the campaign or winning at Conference. Most of the local groups wanted to campaign on the Bomb and only on the Bomb. Too many of them did not want to get involved in 'politics'. So they insisted on relating everything they did to the Bomb. After 1965, they inevitably got involved in the protests on the war in Vietnam, but they related this by stressing the danger of a nuclear war in Indo-China, which in my view was pretty remote. Long afterwards, in 1968, I went to a Council or Executive meeting and found them trying to justify a statement on Biafra through the danger of nuclear war in Africa, which was even sillier, for both the great nuclear powers were backing Nigeria.

This is the main reason why I left CND in early 1967. I found the continuing determination of most of the campaign to stick to the issue of nuclear arms and only nuclear arms entirely illogical. For me, the war in Vietnam seemed a more immediate and urgent concern and American intervention there and elsewhere more threatening to the future peace of the world, in 1967, than the possibility of a nuclear war. This was probably partly because of my growing associations with the American peace movements. Many there had come to see that the Bomb was a symptom and not a cause and that the real threat to peace lay in the hegemonies of the super-powers, and especially of the United States. It was this which had fed the arms race, which had obstructed national independence in Vietnam and elsewhere. Many dreadful, non-nuclear arms were being used daily in Vietnam. It seemed to me ridiculous to have to justify one's concern about this by 'creating' the possibility of nuclear war there.

This is why I went to the International Confederation for Disarmament and Peace. It had a wider, more global outlook and, there, peace in Vietnam was accepted as the priority.

The CND Style: the Umbrella

There were a great many issues on which Canon John Collins and I were agreed. We had two big disagreements. One was the umbrella.

CND achieved its amazing successes during its early years because it united under its flag a very wide spectrum of people and organizations with widely differing approaches in terms of politics, morals, religion and methods of working. So odd a collection could only work together effectively so long as CND was accepted by them as an effective means to protest and a road to achieving changes they all wanted. But if so disparate a company was to be able to operate at all, even to march down a road together, a great deal of tolerance was required both between the different groups in the rank and file, and between them and the leadership.

In the early days the mass quality of the movement bred the tolerance that was needed, which is not to ignore that there was widespread dissension even at that stage. But, at that time, the sheer fact that there were so many people who could and did work together was more important than the differences between them. This overcame the difficulty that, ideologically, there was really very little unity.

It was its indiscipline which was so attractive, particularly for the young. They came into the campaign precisely because it was not authoritarian, or never succeeded in becoming so. The variety and the diversity of the marches, the multiplicity of banners, the enormous range of political and apolitical opinion, this was the most distinctive thing about it. It was very uncharacteristic of British society. So peculiar and crazy a collection of people had never before in Britain managed to set up so large a fraternity, mainly a self-governing community, for in many ways the Executive Committees and Councils ran after it rather than led it.

It wasn't possible or even advisable to turn them into well-regimented, disciplined, membership types of organization. You had to take from each of them, and from each group, what they had to give and persuade the rest that it was acceptable. And precisely because it was grand that there were so many who actually shared the same aim, at least on the Bomb, they learned to respect and even to like each other and to live with all those idiosyncrasies, for a time. There were, of course, occasions when people carrying red flags competed with people carrying gold crosses, as in Maidenhead one year. There were always authoritarians who wanted to censor the banners on the march. They would have liked to standardize them. But always, year after year, they came up against the technical difficulty that when you have a march of five thousand, let alone fifty thousand, it is simply not logistically possible, at least in Britain, to make them carry only the banners you like. And that was just as well, for all those different banners reflected the march and the movement as it was, and not as some of its leaders would like it to be.

There were always some who wanted to march in silence. There were always a lot who wanted to shout. That was a problem to which we never found a solution, though we tried to encourage them to sing and the style of the movement was also linked to the songs it sang as it marched along the roads, all over Britain.

We learned to accept the contribution that people had to make. Designers who made us our posters were given a free hand, although there were always some on a committee who wanted to alter them, who disliked the designs. We even managed to avoid, to a large extent, allowing committees or councils to scrutinize or bowdlerize pamphlets and leaflets, and we accepted with gratitude the songs and the singers – from Joan Baez to Meg the busker – the actors and writers, the poets and playwrights who made the movement what it was. So when a group got together to write a puppet show for the Easter Rally I gave them a free hand, even though there was bound to be trouble afterwards about some of their four-letter words. They were the people who made the movement what it was. If we had tried to make them conform, it would have been a different sort of a movement.

The meeting in the Albert Hall in November 1961 was an excellent example. We decided to hold a meeting there, at that time, just to show the Labour Party that even if it had rejected us, we were still much more alive and kicking than it was. So we aimed not just to fill the Albert Hall, an achievement on its own, not just to fill an overflow, which we did, but to show the sort of a movement CND was, the sort of people we had, the style of CND.

We persuaded Joan Littlewood and Sean Kenny to help. We told them that we wanted to run something more than a meeting, to hold a mirror up to the movement, to show its variety, its confidence, its ebullience, its political content, its diversity. They got the idea. We went down to the Albert Hall, and they looked at it, and shuddered, but didn't give up. The result was that we had many of the big names – J. B. Priestley, A. J. P. Taylor, Michael Foot, Anthony Greenwood, Stuart Hall, and Canon Collins – in the chair (though there wasn't a chair) but also we had moving coloured lights on a great white backcloth, and Humphrey Lyttelton (who really understood what we were trying to do) and his band, and George Melly, the Polaris Singers from Glasgow, and, real old Aldermaston March stuff – the Alberts who had always led the early marches with whippet and trumpet. It was a crazy mix up of jazz and folk and farce, and colour, and speeches about the Bomb – hard and soft politics, but which was the hard and which the soft I am still not sure. Some of the speakers thought it was horrible but the audience loved it and even the *Guardian* was rather impressed. The manager of the Albert Hall was very, very hostile, I have never dared to go back there since that night. But it wasn't juvenile either. I still meet people, adult and sophisticated, who tell me it was one of the greatest evenings of their lives. That was the style of the umbrella.

CND offices had the same sort of style. We started in two rooms on a second floor in Fleet Street and then humped everything down two floors and up four floors in a house two doors down the street. There, for about a month, we had hell, for the offices had been used only as an accommodation address and when we moved in with duplicators and electric fires we overloaded the electricity supply and about once a day all the fuses blew.

A year later we moved to Carthusian Street. There we had three floors in a slummy old house on the borders of the City and Finsbury. Later, at the height of the campaign when we had as many as twenty on the staff, we took over also the basement and ground floor. It was known in the movement as 'Confusion Street', and it certainly was. We were there for about four and a half years. Millions of sheets of paper must have shot through our duplicators. Thousands of parcels of leaflets and pamphlets and posters came in and went out again. The walls were covered with multitudinous posters of movements and campaigns all over the world and with all the graffiti of campaigners. It was always full of people ranging from ten and a half to seventy. It was certainly international and poli-political. At one time, we had two Kenyans and a Sikh running the accounts office, under the watchful eye of Jessie Goodchild who looked after our money. When the Kenyans wanted to confuse customers and annoy the Sikh, Gurmukh Singh, they talked to each other in Swahili.

Regularly people tried to break in, and sometimes succeeded. We put Banham locks on the doors, and Banham grilles on the windows, even in the lavatories, but still they tried. We never really knew whether it was fascists, MI5, or just local toughs. Then when they couldn't get in they painted foul epithets on the doors and windows. Every time I came in in the morning and found Jimpy, our man around the office, outside with paint and a brush, I knew they'd been at it again.

But we had our moments. We discovered, for instance, that taxi-driver trainees, because Carthusian Street was small and not on the map, had CND office on the list of places they had to know, and one day as we walked along the street to the filthy old pub a few doors up we saw a continental coach full of continental visitors and heard the guide saying over the loudspeaker: 'On your left you will see the offices of the Campaign for Nuclear Disarmament, the Ban the Bomb people.' Fame at last!

Down in the basement we stored piles and piles of banners and Aldermaston lost property. This was sheer hell. There were always hundreds of rucksacks and bags, and blanket rolls, and books, and sponge bags, and towels, and food which went bad. But it was never the stuff that people wrote in to claim. One year, when the Peace Boat, the *Everyman*, was down in the river, all ready to sail for Leningrad, they asked if we could let them have some blankets. That was wonderful. We collected together all the lilos, the bed rolls, the sweaters and sleeping bags and took them down to the boat. Later, on its way back, it sank in a Norwegian port, so, thank goodness, we never saw them again.

Then there was the rock. One year YCND ran a summer project, On the Beach. They ordered a lot of seaside rock, with the symbol, rather distorted, in the middle. But they overestimated their selling techniques. Hundreds of tins of rock were left and stacked down in our basement. Gradually, year by year, it was sold or eaten. Luckily, rock doesn't go off.

The vehicles were in the same style. There was the *Feather Bedder*, a London Region ex-army or ex-farm truck. It always broke down and never reached its destinations. There was the Campaign Caravan coach. It was never the same after a cow jumped over a hedge right in front of it somewhere in deepest Dorset. But the cow suffered more than the coach. It eventually gave up the ghost somewhere in Yugoslavia and was never seen again. There was the Youth Campaign coach which was parked on a temporary car park on the Barbican site not far from the office. Then they closed the site because building was about to begin. But the coach wouldn't budge. Eventually, I believe, someone towed it out, but I am not sure that they didn't build the Barbican on top of it.

Nowadays I work in beautiful, clean, centrally heated offices. It's lovely to sit there in the sun in the summer, or in the warmth in the winter. But often still I remember the squalor and hustle and bustle of Carthusian Street and wish I was back there again. It was fantastically exhausting. It was tremendously invigorating. I wouldn't have missed it for worlds.

Sanity, CND's monthly newspaper, was in the same style. CND did not have its own newspaper until fairly late. Up to October 1961 there was only a very small bulletin, edited at different times by Mervyn Jones, Wayland Young and Nigel Calder. Then, in the autumn of 1961, David Boulton who was working for *Tribune* became the editor of a four-paged CND newspaper, *Sanity*, which merged with a news sheet published by North West CND. The paper was much brighter than the old bulletin. It had a lot more space. After a year, David left *Tribune* and came to work for us full time and *Sanity* was enlarged to eight pages and sometimes twelve. From 1961 on, it became an important and integral part of campaigning and its circulation at one time reached forty-five thousand.

It was an umbrella paper. It reported and reflected the movement. Everything that was done, no matter who did it, whatever group was involved, was covered in Sanity. It always had and still has the dilemma that it has to be both a house journal and a propaganda sheet. This was a seemingly insoluble problem, but David solved it by making sure that it was always bright, controversial and challenging. Philip Bolsover who took over when David left carried on the same tradition.

David had problems, of course. There were some who thought the paper should be the mouthpiece of the Executive Committee and Council, and that it ought to confine itself to CND affairs, ignoring the heretical wings. There were others who thought it too controversial and wild. There were always complaints from Birmingham. One month, David had a picture of a gentlemen's lavatory in Fleet Street on the front page (it happened to be listed as an air-raid shelter!) Birmingham sent a severe letter. Another month it had a picture of a mother feeding a baby. Birmingham sent that issue back. Then, another month, there was a review by Bruce Page of *Fanny Hill*. I re-read that recently and wondered whether the *Sunday Times*, for which Bruce now works, would print it. *Sanity* did.

But *Sanity* had one enormous advantage which silenced its few critics. It sold like hot cakes. Most campaign groups sold it regularly at weekends in shopping centres and markets. When the campaign started to decline, many CND groups which had actually closed down still went on selling *Sanity*. So while it was often a bone of contention, it survived and flourished and helped to hold the campaign together. And anyone, or any group, who did something, here or there, about the Bomb, was sure to get a mention.

David Boulton worked for CND for one year part-time and then for two and a half years full-time. He left in March 1965 to work for Granada Television. I hope they enjoy him as much as we did. He was always invigorating and often infuriating. Once a month there was a meeting of the editorial board. There he told us what he intended to do. He then went away and did it regardless. Luckily, we usually agreed with him. I soon found out that it required a major operation to persuade him to change his mind. But he really did understand the campaign and the paper reflected his understanding.

He was lovely when he was angry. He seemed, somehow, to levitate himself off the floor. I remember one furious row he had with George Clark on the first floor of Carthusian Street when I thought he would, literally, hit the ceiling. He seemed to bounce, higher and higher, off the floor.

Then there was his lunch with Colonel Sammy Lohan of the Defence Ministry, now writing on food for the *Evening Standard*. He wanted to persuade David to accept D notices. D notices are Government handouts asking you not to print. David was much too wise to fall for that one, but he went out to lunch with him at the Savoy, wearing a beautiful Ministry of Defence tie which the colonel brought along because the Savoy refuses to accept the tieless. David returned from the lunch, still refusing to accept D notices, but gorgeously tight.

That was all part of the umbrella and the trouble was that those who would have preferred a nice disciplined movement never had a chance. It wasn't only that the black and white symbol was used by everybody and gradually became not only the symbol for banning the bomb, but a general symbol of protest, of challenge. The initials, CND, also became for many people, and especially for the press, the movement rather than just the Campaign. So if thousands of marchers swept into the square on Easter Monday, it was CND. And if thousands sat here or there, it was CND. And if people came out with banners, booing the Queen of Greece, that was CND. It must have been infuriating for both Canon Collins and for Lord Russell.

After we had failed to win the Labour Party and after civil disobedience had failed to change the government, because there were still thousands and thousands of people, but no way through, frustration built up, particularly but not only among the young. We started having trouble on the Easter March, first in 1962, when some of the marshals tried out an idea they had that if only they could get enough people into Whitehall at the same time, some miracle would happen. There wasn't any miracle, of course, but a lot of people marched gaily round from Whitehall into Horse Guards Avenue, onto the Embankment, back to Parliament Square and round and round again. Canon Collins who was standing in Horse Guards Avenue on the steps of the Co-op van, saying, 'Well done' to the marchers as they came through, turned to me and said, as the banner of Gorbals Young Socialists passed by, 'I'm sure I saw that one before.' He was dead right. It was their third time round. But that was a fairly minor riot and as the press had all gone off to get their copy in in time, nobody really noticed it.

After that there was trouble every year with groups labelled as 'the anarchists' though certainly not all of them were. But many of them carried the black and cherry banners of the Anarchist Federations (contradiction in terms, anyway) and this is what they were called whatever group or mini-group they came from. It wasn't really surprising that a lot of the young people who had come into politics through CND, finding no way through, should turn to anarchism, rejecting the system that thwarted them. It wasn't surprising either that they picked on CND establishment as one of the targets for their wrath.

So one year we had the scaffold pole held across Hyde Park Corner, barring the road of the march. Another year we had them down in the square, below the North Terrace, frantically blowing on trumpets, trying to drown the voice of the one MP who was speaking that year, Stan Orme, because for them he represented everything they were against. Year after year their banners waved above the march, rushing here and there and trying to get to the front, yelling 'Stuff Duff' at the top of their voices.

One year, I got involved in a long march against atomic weapons around Paris. It finished outside a *Mairie* in a Paris suburb. As we stood on the steps, waiting until the march was in, there I saw in the crowd the black and cherry banners of the English anarchists (the flags of the French anarchists are black). 'Stuff Duff,' they yelled at me. It made me feel at home.

Of course, they were very unpopular with other marchers, more disciplined, more long suffering, less frustrated and older. Year after year we had trouble with people and groups who wanted to get tough with them, to get them out of the way and out of the march. Basically, Canon Collins disliked the 'umbrella' because he did not want the Committee of 100 or the anarchists under it with him. There were some who agreed with him and the number grew each year, as the dissidents became more obstreperous. But there were others, especially those who had to marshal and organize the march, who recognized that a march has no boundaries, no electronic fences to keep people out, that the anarchists and those who marched and ran with them were a part of it just as much as the well-behaved. So there were times when for a brief period we let them march at the head of the march, when the orthodox were furious. And there were times when we diverted the march to avoid them, when the anarchists were furious. But in spite of it all, a sort of respect built up, at least between some of them and some of us, based on our understanding of what it was that made them so angry not only with the Government and MPs, but with CND too, which had failed to get them where they wanted to go. And while some complained that they battened on the march, using it for their own purposes, this was just as true of the hundreds of salesmen who followed it along its way, selling their multifarious wares – *Tribune, Peace News, Solidarity, Socialist Leader, The Week,* all the cacophony of the left, parking their cars and vans all over our lunch and tea sites, rarely, if ever, marching. At least the anarchists marched.

The worst year we ever had on the march was 1963. That was

the year of the *Spies for Peace* and the *March Must Decide* campaign. The latter was not very difficult. It was just Peter Cadogan and one or two others trying to decide, unilaterally, how the march would end. Eventually, rather too late, the march decided it did not much care for Peter's proposals, but by then we had made so many mistakes over the *Spies for Peace* that trouble at the end was inevitable.

The *Spies for Peace* issued very shortly before the march, and throughout it, a duplicated report about the results of a NATO exercise called Fallex '62, which was based on a Russian attack on Europe including a limited nuclear attack on Britain. Very little was known about this for the press had been frightened off with D notices. A lot of the information in their report related to a Regional Seat of Government, at Warren Row, about a mile off the Saturday route of the Aldermaston March, north of Knowl Hill, between Reading and Maidenhead.

The existence of RSGs was not widely known though some of them, including the one at Warren Row, had existed during the Second World War. They were underground, heavily reinforced centres for an alternative government covering a region, which would take over after a nuclear attack. The report revealed the existence of these Regional Seats, and also, in some detail, the results of Fallex '62. Naturally, the marchers were enchanted. The press were also interested, for no newspaper or journalist enjoys being censored and they like to see someone who defies a government on this sort of issue. It also provoked widespread responses all over the country. Hundreds of CND groups went out looking for their RSGs. A great many people, hearing of the RSG at Warren Row, promptly sat down and wrote a letter to their MP, asking what arrangements had been made for them, in the event of a nuclear war. It was a good question because no effective arrangements had been made. Indeed, even the police at Slough complained to me rather tetchily that they knew nothing about Warren Row RSG and had no places there, so far as they knew.

By the evening of Good Friday, it was clear to Norman Frith, chief marshal of the march that year, and to me that on the following day a lot of marchers would respond to the suggestion publicized on the march that they should go off from Knowl Hill to visit this interesting RSG at Warren Row.

On Good Friday evening, after we had, somehow or other, fitted our thousands of marchers into their tents in King's Meadows, we went off to a meeting with the chairman, Canon Collins, the vice-chairman, Ritchie Calder, and some other members of the Executive Committee and Council. Norman had already talked with Philip Seed, a Quaker, who was either working with the *Spies* or closely in touch with them. After a lot of argy-bargy we persuaded our people that it would be better to accept the fact that a lot of marchers would want to go to Warren Row and to make provision for it. It was agreed that those wishing to go should march in the third contingent (we usually divided the march into groups of about a thousand with a gap between them to allow traffic to pass and to prevent concertinaing). But because there had been earlier occasions when marchers had complained that we had not told them what was happening (for instance, on Ralph Schoenman's first diversion to Grosvenor Square in 1961), we also agreed that loudspeakers should tell marchers at Knowl Hill where the march would divide, and what was going on.

It would certainly have been better if we had agreed to take the whole of the march down to Warren Row. This would have united it and while there would have been difficulties in taking so many people down a narrow lane and back again, it would have been better than dividing them as we did. Nevertheless, it seemed a fairly reasonable arrangement.

We got very little credit, then or later, for the agreement. Also, the competing loudspeakers at Knowl Hill merely inflamed the situation and since the anarchists are very serious people, one or two of my irreverent remarks over the Co-op Van speaker further infuriated them. Several thousands went off to Warren Row and joined the march again later. What really surprised me at the time and later was that so many actually stayed with the march. I suspect that a lot of them had no idea about what was going on. Tired and footsore, they merely followed the marcher in front.

But two further developments added fuel to the flames. That

year we published two issues of *Sanity* for the march, one for sale on Good Friday and Saturday, one printed on Saturday for sale on Easter Sunday and Monday. David Boulton and Stuart Hall went off to the printer all Saturday to put the second issue to bed.

They turned up fairly late in Slough with the copies all ready for sale. There on the back page were all the details from the *Spies for Peace* report. This was a bombshell for us, for it was one thing to produce an anonymous, unsigned, duplicated report and something quite different to produce it in a newspaper, with an editorial board, an address and a number of known people who could be held responsible. Would the police confiscate it? Some copies of the *Spies'* report had already been taken. Would the editorial board, most of whom knew nothing about it, be liable for prosecution under the Official Secrets Act? We had no idea. If we went ahead and ran into trouble, would the Executive and Council back us up? The answer was, for a lot of them, definitely no. So, in the end, having consulted Ritchie Calder (John Collins had gone back to London) we reluctantly decided to tear the back page off. Naturally, this further infuriated the *Spies for Peace*. Later, but too late, in the next issue, David reprinted the lot.

If it happened again I believe that, older and wiser, I would fight for taking the whole of the march down to Warren Row, that I would leave *Sanity* as it was, whatever the consequences. But things don't happen twice and all one can do is to recognize the mistakes one makes.

We reached Hyde Park on Easter Monday, still arguing with Peter Cadogan about who should decide. By then, it was too late and it certainly wasn't Peter who was deciding. The head of the march set off happily to march through Victoria Street, up Whitehall and on through the West End back to Hyde Park where the rally was held that year. The first two sections reached the park in good order. The third section, including the anarchists, the *Spies*, the solidarity mob, battled their way slowly through Grosvenor Place, Victoria Street and Whitehall to the park. At one time we diverted part of the rest of the march through the Embankment, up Northumberland Avenue, back on the route. I remember standing on the island in the middle of the north end of Whitehall and seeing them come out of Northumberland Avenue, solid and singing, led by Yorkshire Region CND. They were lovely to see. Later the march started again up Whitehall and there was the International Section, under the care of Dan Elwyn Jones. He came over to me on the island and said: 'Peggy, I have a group of Spanish anarchists here and they say if you would like them to *do* the English anarchists, they are ready and willing.'

When everyone, somehow or other, got to Hyde Park, we had an enormous rally. After it John Collins told me he was to go on the Panorama programme that night. I told him then that most of the marchers were enchanted with the *Spies for Peace*, with the revelations, that they had shaken the Government and raised the morale of the campaign. I said he ought to say so on television, that it would be disastrous to attack them.

He didn't take my advice. Always loyal to CND as he saw it, he was quite unable to see this as a part of the movement, as a contribution to the campaign. He didn't see it as a lift for morale when such a lift was urgently needed. He was blind to its originality, its ingenuity, its value in the fight against nuclear weapons. So he attacked it. What a row there was about that!

The leadership, the centre, found itself more virulently criticized than ever before, although the next issue of *Sanity* printed everything, and although the next Executive Committee, after some pressure, welcomed the revelations. What had gone wrong? Why was it possible for the leadership to be so stupid? Why, with all these hundreds of thousands of people, were we no nearer success than in 1958? Why wasn't it possible for CND to bind and blend and absorb all these different initiatives? It was this which started off an immense argument about the umbrella.

It wasn't an argument about policy. It was a conflict about the way you did things, about the way you campaigned. Five years later, Staughton Lynd, writing in the American *Guardian*, outlined briefly what it was all about, in a country and at a time when the issues had become much dearer. He wrote about two styles of politics: 'political paternalism as against political self-reliance, plebiscitary democracy in contrast to participatory democracy, vicarious politics opposed to political direct action'. This was the problem in CND, a problem that was never solved, because too many of the leadership, too large a part of the centre, was paternalist, plebiscitary and vicarious, and basically lacked the imagination or the courage to accept and lead the movement as it was.

The argument about the umbrella was waged on the one hand by those who wanted open doors, participatory self-reliance, and those who preferred a smaller, disciplined movement, working along orthodox lines. In June 1963, at the height of the controversy, CND held a discussion conference, which was an attempt to bring the argument out in the open, to find a new, freer approach which might liberate the movement and recapture its momentum. Here is a brief extract from my own contribution to that conference:

> Dissociation has never worked. Partly because the press has ensured, however the centre has tried to protect its own image, that the public image reflects not only the activities but all the heresies as well, and most of all the heresies. Some of us have realized over the past five years that maybe the press is right. The Campaign for Nuclear Disarmament is not only the Executive and Council, Regions and Groups, but the Committee of 100, the Direct Action Committee, all the *ad hoc* committees, the anarchists, the beardies and weirdies and the Solidarity Mob. However hard we try to pretend we are all different, our common aim binds us together. What each one of us does affects the operations of the other. The successes and failures are shared ...

It was for this conference that Nigel Young attempted to define the 'style' of CND:

> We have failed in five years to spell out unilateralism; we have failed in education and organization and central leadership; we have failed to experiment; and we have failed to show political courage. What we have succeeded in doing is in creating a 'style' – a new kind of politics in which policy is not of paramount importance. But even

this style regularly wilts, and is in as much danger as the organization itself .... With respect, this style has nothing to do with Canon Collins's pipe or Peggy Duff's red coat; it is the way the movement does things – the symbols and the pennants, the songs, the typography and lay-out of its posters and literature, the atmosphere of the marches and sit-downs, the attitude to direct action and to individual participation. Moreover, it is the way in which the bomb is related to other issues, local and international. It is an ambience which is contagious; it has spread to North America, to Scandinavia and the rest of Europe, it is still spreading; a new sort of politics.

The conference argued frenziedly through the weekend. There are few organizations that do not enjoy talking about themselves. Then they translated their ideas into a programme of activity for the summer and autumn of 1963 which provided for a series of parallel actions, run jointly and severally by most of the groups and wings which made up the campaign. It was called *Tell Britain*, and it included projects run by CND, YCND, CUCND, and the Committee of 100, an autumn project, Fallex '63, in which everyone combined, and a comprehensive plan of campaign for the coming General Election. CND produced a brochure outlining the whole project and its approach:

Thus the programme will be the work of the whole of the movement in harness, the tributaries (while retaining total independence and separateness of identity) feeding and strengthening the 'mainstream' of the campaign. There will be no dissociation. No wing will denounce or renounce another. The distinction between 'official' and 'unofficial' will be forgotten. The 'mainstream' will be united for a massive properly articulated push against nuclear policies, and we shall establish ourselves in the public mind as an independent and powerful political force.

But the great difficulty was that Canon Collins and others were firmly opposed to the 'umbrella'. As he tells in his book, *Faith under Fire*, he considered resigning at that time but decided against it. At the next annual conference that summer, he was for the first time opposed as chairman by Michael Mitchel Howard. He outlined in a statement the conditions on which he was willing to stand – that 'CND should abandon its umbrella policy and thereby clear its own public image'; that 'it should concentrate upon putting an intelligent case for nuclear disarmament by Britain, and should do so by every legal means available'; and that 'majority decisions of the elected council and executive, and the self-disciplines asked for, should be respected'. He was elected by a two-thirds majority – but just to show that the AEU was not the only organization which could vote both ways, the conference also accepted by a very large majority the *Tell Britain* programme which was the umbrella in action.

He remained very unhappy and many of his public statements at that time reflected his doubts, uncertainties and hesitancies. In May 1964, just after the Easter March, he changed his mind again and resigned. The statement he issued reiterated his rejection of civil disobedience and of 'non-Tolstoyan anarchy'.

While some of the heretics probably rejoiced to see him go, most campaigners were very sorry. While they often disagreed with his public statements, they accepted with gratitude his commitment to the campaign and they felt that an Easter March without the familiar figure in the cassock would never be the same again. The trouble was, as I once tried to explain to Michael Craft, that John Collins was much too firmly established in his own ways to be able to change, even for so large and ebullient a movement as CND. 'You have to work with people as they are,' I told him, 'and not as you would like them to be.' The basic dilemma was that neither the canon nor the campaign were willing to change.

Olive Gibbs took over as acting chairman and was later elected as chairman, remaining in office for several years. She was in many ways an ideal choice. Her long commitment to CND, her tolerance and good humour, her willingness to stump the country, all these had already made her popular. And while she was a member of the Labour Party, her virulent criticism of it endeared her to the anti-party people, just as her tolerance towards direct action won her friends among the activists.

For a brief period there was a new lease of life in the campaign, but it did not last very long. The changes had come too late and were not strong enough to offset the impact of the Test Ban Treaty (which some people thought heralded everlasting peace) or of the Cuba crisis which spread confusion rather than clarity (had nuclear weapons stopped or nearly started a war?) In 1960 or in 1961, it might have been different. In 1963, it was too late. So, with a dull thud, we hit the General Election of 1964.

It seems to me now that there were three reasons why CND failed both then and earlier not only to achieve any of its main objectives but also to consolidate any new approach to politics.

First, it was not just that the orthodox approach, on an issue of such magnitude, was bound to be cushioned and confined by the establishments. It was much more due to the fact that the attempt to combine a sort of guided democracy with an out-of-hand mass movement was bound to fail. This was not only the fault of the leadership. While they certainly wanted to keep the campaign on their lines, most campaigners wanted it both ways. They wanted to have their cake and eat it, to remain respectable within the establishment and to challenge it too, to operate inside and outside conventional politics, to marry orthodoxy and nonconformism, to remain inside the system and to destroy it, to create a new sort of politics within the confines of the old. It was this dichotomy that killed it.

Second, the radical wing of the movement never succeeded in mounting a sharp enough challenge to swing the campaign abruptly from the old to the new. Though it looked as if they might, in September 1961, their next demonstration at Wethersfield was a dreadful mistake, principally because it moved from the centre of power to the periphery. And because so many sat and paid their fines and went home, the emphasis on personal action never overcame the ingrained habit of relying on a leadership. There were too many Canon Collins, not enough Michael Randles.

Third, it had not only no ideology to sustain it but very little hard political content even to its short-term aims; and what little existed was distrusted and discarded by many in the movement whose interest and concern was ethically based, who saw all politics as rather nasty and dirty. And those who had some sort of politics, often sectarian, hung on to their own. No effective effort was made to provide a meeting point. This would not have been easy. Stuart Hall outlined the problem in *Sanity* (May 1963):

> Can a political shape be imposed upon or arise from a movement which contains within its ranks such garden varieties as anarchists, non-violent revolutionaries, proto-Trotskyists, New Left socialists, soft-shoe communists, constituency Labour Party members, renegade liberals, pacifist old-timers, beatniks and vegetarians, *Peace News*, *Sanity*, *Solidarity*, *Anarchy* and *War and Peace*? By any book, the answer should be 'No.' No single flag, no slogan, no ideology, no king, can command the allegiance of so motley an army of the good.

Some coherence, some centre, he went on, must emerge. But it didn't. Inevitably this limited and constricted it. When tests were resumed or a Berlin crisis loomed up, they lacked the know-how to profit from events and a base from which to operate. Too often the only reaction was a demonstration. And when the Test Ban Treaty created an illusion of partial victory, they had no political bases, let alone an ideology, to carry them on. By the end of 1966, CND gave up the hard struggle to remain something different, adopted membership at last, and became an organization rather than a campaign.

Yet it would be wrong and unfair to suggest that the CNDs achieved little or nothing. They spread throughout Britain and around the world, both among ordinary people and among their leaders, a wide knowledge and awareness of the nature and implications of nuclear arms without which nuclear tests might still be frequent, nuclear powers far more numerous than they are, and nuclear weapons might well, by now, have been used. That alone is no small achievement.

While unilateralism at home and non-alignment abroad were strategies rather than substitutes for an ideology, at least they indicated a breaking loose, a liberation from conventional policies and politics. They blasted open a road which has not yet been closed. The symbol and the style go marching on, nowadays in other hands, but certainly not dead yet.

CND International

The Conference in Basel
It was not very long after its founding that CND got itself involved with similar movements against atomic arms abroad. In the spring of 1958 we were visited in our Fleet Street offices by Theo Pirker, who was secretary of the Kampagne gegen Atomrüstung in Bavaria, centred on Munich.

He had a scheme for a conference of European intellectuals to be held in Switzerland in the summer of 1958. Canon Collins approved the idea that CND should jointly sponsor it with the Kampagne. A few days later I went off to Zurich for a meeting with the chairman of the Kampagne, Hans Werner Richter, a well-known writer, Heinrich Buchbinder from the Swiss CND, and Theo Pirker. A conference was planned in Basel on 5 and 6 July. Lord Russell agreed to sponsor it and a number of other eminent Europeans joined him. Then only a week or so before it was due to take place, the Swiss Government banned it.

Lord Russell wrote an angry letter to the president of the Swiss Confederation, but received no reply.

The Conference in London and Frankfurt
There was only one thing to do – to start again from the beginning. This time we planned to hold the conference partly in London and partly in Frankfurt in January 1959. It opened with a press conference and public meeting at St Pancras Town Hall on Friday, 16 January and met in conference at the Central Hall, Westminster on the following day. Among the main speakers were Lord Russell (who received a standing ovation), Dr Robert Jungk, author of *Brighter than a Thousand Suns*, Hans Werner Richter and Professor Joseph Rotblat. It was agreed there to establish a European Federation against Nuclear Arms linking movements in

West Germany, Switzerland, Sweden, Holland and Britain. The London part of the conference ended on Sunday morning with a service at St Paul's Cathedral, as the canon was in residence that month. This was an unusual occasion as a number of those who attended had probably not been to church for quite a long time.

After the service seventy of the delegates to the conference went off to Gatwick by coach and thence by charter plane to Frankfurt. The costs of travel and all the arrangements in Frankfurt were borne by the city of Frankfurt whose Oberburgomeister, Dr Werner Bockelmann, was a strong opponent of nuclear arms.

The plane arrived in Frankfurt rather late, owing to interminable delays at Gatwick. We were taken to our hotel – the Basiler Hof (where Hitler used to stay when in Frankfurt) and given light refreshments. Then, long after the advertised time, we were taken to the Paulskirche (where the first all-German parliament met in 1848) for the meeting. We would not have been surprised to find the hall empty and everyone gone home, but not so. It was packed and as we entered we found the best orchestra in Frankfurt playing *Finlandia*. James Cameron described this very impressive meeting in the *News Chronicle* when he got home again:

> Then we came into the great chamber of the Paulskirche, the enormous reconstructed hall of St Paul which must be one of the most hugely impressive rooms in Europe – an immense circular stone interior with a vaulted beamed roof like a timber web, stark and lovely, lit with enormous fluorescent chains. It was full to the doors.
>
> All those who deride the nuclear disarmament business, who have been pleased to amuse themselves at some of its admittedly more fantastic aspects, should have been here Sunday night in Germany. Three thousand people filled every inch of this splendid place, while hundreds more were turned away into the freezing white night of the Paulsplatz ...
>
> The most extraordinary thing about all this was that it was formal and indeed official; the entire proceedings were sponsored by Frankfurt's most excellent Lord Mayor and paid for – including the

chartered aircraft from London – out of the rates and trade union contributions. It is hard to imagine anywhere else where a municipal responsibility could be made of what is, after all, a pretty controversial subject, and it says a lot for the dominant position of an energetic Oberburgomeister in a German community.

'It is simply,' said this mayor, Dr Werner Bockelmann, 'that almost all the people here feel as we do.'

Willi Brandt sent a message of support. One of the speakers was Waldemar von Knöringen, a vice-president of the Social Democratic Party. 'You intellectuals have got to get going politically,' he said. 'The SPD is behind this heart and soul. If we weren't we would be betraying ourselves.'

No premonitions of changes to come in the Social Democratic Party stirred the audience that night. It was not much later that it 'betrayed itself', ceasing to support the anti-nuclear movements in Germany, cutting off funds, learning to live with NATO and the bomb.

That was to follow, but that night we left the meeting and went to a reception given by the Oberburgomeister. Then there occurred the most moving of all the happenings on that extraordinary day. Benn Levy spoke. It was his first visit to Germany since before the Nazis. He said to his host ... 'Six million of my people were murdered by Germans ... but any German who opposes nuclear weapons is my friend.'

That was the beginning of the European Federation against Nuclear Arms. It never really lived up to that auspicious birth. It contained only six really functioning organizations: CND in Britain, the Anti-Atoombom Actie in Holland, the Aktionsgruppen mot Svenks Atoombom in Sweden which was later superseded by the Kampanjen mot Atomvapen, and two in Germany, the Kampf dem Atomtod, created and supported by the SPD, and the Kampagne gegen Atomrüstung in Bavaria, more like CND. There were a number of other individuals who attended meetings who had no real organization behind them, like Claude Bourdet from

France where Le Mouvement contre l'Armement Atomique was not set up until several years later, after the end of the Algerian war.

It wrote itself a constitution and some aims. These included opposition to the spread of nuclear arms, support for a multilateral nuclear disarmament, for unilateral initiatives, and for the use of nuclear power for peaceful purposes only. It was also restrictive. No country could have more than two member organizations in the confederation and any new members had to be agreed by a two-thirds majority of the working committee and also be acceptable to any existing member in that country. This was mainly because some members were concerned about direct action organizations. They wanted to keep them out. For this reason it did little recruiting. It was happy as it was.

It opened its operation with a rather grandiose project – an attempt to persuade the Swiss Government to call a meeting of the signatory powers of the Red Cross Convention for the purpose of banning nuclear weapons. An ambitious plan was drawn up for collection of signatures, a drive for funds and subscriptions, to end with another international conference. A great deal of work was done on it in Germany and Switzerland, but little elsewhere. The other organizations were far too busy on their own affairs. The Congress never took place. The Convention is still unaltered.

The London Conference, 1961
By 1960, however, there began to be difficulties between Canon Collins and the Germans. By that time the SPD had altered its policy and was much more timid in supporting the German movements. Since the Kampf dem Atomtod was almost entirely dominated by and dependent on the party, and the Kampagne largely so, Dr Walter Menzel, an MP from Dortmund who represented the Kampf on the committee of the European Federation, acted as a brake on its operations. The trouble started at a meeting of the Committee in Schliersee near Munich in March where Canon Collins reported that in December 1959 he had called together a small meeting in London with members of the

World Council of Peace, including two Russians and Dr Hromadka from Prague to discuss the possibility of organizing an East/West conference on Pugwash lines, but not limited to scientists. Also present were Claude Bourdet, George de Bock from Holland and three people from CND. Canon Collins asked the federation to support such a conference in principle and asked for permission for a further meeting to discuss the invitations.

Dr Menzel was furious. Anti-communism was still rife in West Germany and the SPD was terrified of accusations from the right of communist links. Canon Collins was by then president of the Federation. If he went ahead, the Federation would be linked and, through it, the Kampf and the SPD. The entire proposal was bitterly opposed by Menzel. Hans Werner Richter tactfully tried to postpone it. But an amendment was moved by Bertil Svahnström from Sweden permitting the president to hold further discussions and to report to a sub-committee of the Federation before taking any further action. It was agreed, but only just.

The sub-committee met in Bonn on 4 May and at the same time we met von Knöringen again and tried to convince him of the merits of such an East/West conference. Von Knöringen had moved a long way since that night in the Paulskirche. He was not convinced.

A preparatory conference was held in London from 24 to 26 June. It was attended by nineteen people from Britain, France, Italy, Sweden, Brazil, India, Australia, Yugoslavia, the USA and the USSR. The programme for a conference was agreed: disarmament with special reference to nuclear disarmament; cooperation and coexistence; the prosperity and well being of mankind. Quite a large field!

It was also agreed to invite about 150 to 200 people, that there should be no press statements without general consent, and that representation be balanced between West, East and Third World.

Unfortunately for Dr Menzel and Canon Collins, though no press report of the meeting was sent out, Ilya Ehrenburg who attended was recognized at the airport and the whole project came into the light of day – but as a personal initiative of the canon's.

The European Federation met shortly afterwards on 23 and 24

▲ 9   Bertrand Russell following his wife into Bow Street Court on 12 September 1961, when he was jailed for a week.

▲ 10a The Committee of 100 talks to the man in the Moscow Street, Red Square, July 1962.

◀ 10b The demonstration against tyranny in Greece outside Horse Guards, 9 July 1963.

July in an obscure hotel in Ealing. There, open war broke out. Infuriated because of the press leak, and because invitations to the conference had been sent out on 7 July, before consultations with the Federation, Dr Menzel demanded the resignation of the president.

The battle raged to and fro. John Collins offered two compromises – to hand the conference over to the Federation, which was hardly a compromise as they did not want it anyway; or to continue with the conference and, if it became dangerous for the Federation, to resign as president. Neither of these were acceptable to Dr Menzel, and finally in order to allay German fears, to hold the Federation together, and to rescue his conference, Collins had to resign, temporarily.

Canon Collins continued to have trouble with his conference. He tried to get CND to take it on, but they agreed with so small a majority, seven to five, that he withdrew the request. I suspect that Christian Action also turned it down. So it went forward as a personal initiative and, as such conferences go, was extraordinarily successful.

It was smaller than planned. Only about sixty delegates attended, but they were a reasonably balanced group and included a number of top names, like Ehrenburg, Korniecbuk, Erich Fromm, Linus Pauling, Archbishop Roberts, Professor Gower, Jayaprakash Narayan, Dr Hromadka. The European Federation, unofficially, was there with Dr Heinz Kloppenburg, Heinrich Buchbinder and Bertil Svahnström and, of course, myself. (By then, I was one of the Federation's secretaries.)

What made it outstanding was its timing. The Berlin crisis was at its height. Russia had resumed testing. The United States was expected to at any moment. A small sub-committee was set up to produce a statement and met in an upstairs room. It put forward a number of proposals for the settlement of the Berlin and German problems. These included the establishment of a free city in Berlin, guaranteed by the four states and the UN and with a UN presence; recognition of the existence of two German States; recognition of the boundaries of the two states; re-unification to be a matter for the two German States; no further rearmament for both German

States; no nuclear weapons on their territory; a de-nuclearized zone in central Europe, as proposed by Rapacki.

But the keynote paragraphs of the statement concerned the question of testing:

> We deplore the resumption of nuclear testing and reaffirming our attitude we oppose war, nuclear weapons and all nuclear testing of any kind, in the atmosphere, underground, under water, and in outer space, both as intensifying preparations for nuclear war and as a danger to the health of present and future generations.
>
> We call on all the governments now carrying out or planning nuclear tests to halt them immediately, not to resume such testing and to come to an agreement on a permanent and controlled test ban, separately or as part of general disarmament.

The fact that Soviet delegates of the importance of Ehrenburg and Korniechuk had signed such a statement condemning the action of their own government in resuming tests was something quite new. Since the Russians had agreed to sign, all other delegates from the East also agreed and, so far as I remember, the statement was agreed unanimously. But, so I was told later, it was never published in the USSR.

Canon Collins resumed his functions. The Kampf dem Atomtod died, the Kampagne gegen Atomrüstung dwindled. But while the Federation languished, Europe was humming with anti-atomic activity. The marches had spread across Europe. There was a large and very young CND in Denmark. The new CND had arrived in Sweden. There was one in Norway. A new organization was established in Germany, Ostermarsch der Atomwaffengegners – the Easter March of opponents of atomic weapons. Naturally all these groups had close links with CND in Britain, the mother of all the marches. It became impossible to ignore them and at last, under pressure from Bertil Svahnström and me, we held a meeting in Copenhagen to which all the new CNDs in Scandinavia were invited, together with a representative of the Yugoslav League of Peace.

At that meeting, only the Yugoslav League of Peace was admitted. The question of the German Easter marchers was raised but the constitution blocked them since, officially, both the Kampf and the Kampagne were still alive. It was decided to review the constitution at the next meeting in London in September and to invite the Easter marchers to attend. Great victory for expansion! But before this meeting, there were two more conferences in Accra and Moscow.

The Accra Assembly

When CND adopted the policy of positive neutralism in 1961 it was suggested that an international conference of the many new and old, non-aligned peace movements would be valuable. Nothing happened for two reasons: Canon Collins was involved in his own, personal, East/West conference; and there was no money. Yet an opportunity arose for such a conference after John Collins had visited Kwame Nkrumah to discuss problems of refugees from South Africa in 1961. Before he left I suggested to him that he should ask Nkrumah, who was closely involved in the meetings of non-aligned states, whether his government would be willing to act as host for a conference of non-aligned peace movements and individuals, to be sponsored and organized by CND and the European Federation.

Somewhat to my surprise we received a letter from Nkrumah not long after John returned to London, saying that he was willing to do this. So it came about that on a freezing Boxing Day at the end of 1961 I flew from London Airport to meet Heinrich Buchbinder in Accra. There we had preliminary discussions with Geoffrey Bing (who had been Attorney General and was now an adviser to Nkrumah) and one or two others. There was also some discussion in London. It was agreed, or so I understood, that the Government of Ghana would meet all the costs of the conference including the travelling expenses of delegates, but that control would remain in the hands of Canon Collins, CND and the European Federation. It was to be called the Accra Assembly – 'The World without the Bomb'. A Preparatory Committee was established consisting of Mr E. C. Quaye of the Ghana Council for

Nuclear Disarmament, Professor Ritchie Calder, Mr D. Chaman Lall, an Indian MP, Heinrich Buchbinder and Professor Josué de Castro. It is a pity that this Preparatory Committee never met even once. Apart from a preparatory meeting held in Yugoslavia from 24 to 27 February, which some but not all of the Preparatory Committee attended, the organization of the Assembly was left to the officials in Ghana in consultation with Heinrich Buchbinder and myself.

It was my suggestion that since Ghana was host for the Assembly itself, another non-aligned country should be invited to house the preparatory meeting and the Yugoslavs readily agreed. They provided us with every facility. It was here that the main lines of the conference were laid down and preliminary meetings were held of five commissions. These were on the Reduction of International Tensions; on Methods of Effective Inspection and Control of Disarmament; on the Transformation of Existing Military Nuclear Materials to Peaceful Uses and the Prevention of the Spread of Nuclear Weapons; on Economic Problems involved in and arising through Disarmament; and Examination of Fundamental Problems – hunger, disease, ignorance, poverty and servitude.

In Zagreb, it was agreed to change the whole conception of the conference. This was explained in a statement:

> ... It would be useless for the Assembly to deliberate in the absence of informed groups of majority feeling in the major countries of the world, and particularly in such states as possess nuclear armament or plan to acquire it. There will, therefore, be present at the Assembly a limited number of experts who, though speaking in their personal capacities, will be chosen as representative of the main trend of thought in their respective countries.

It was agreed to invite also as 'experts' a number of representatives from organizations concerned with disarmament and international relations. The experts were not to be invited to subscribe to the documents issued from the conference. These were mainly chaps from the World Council of Peace.

This undoubtedly changed the character of the conference, but it was not necessarily a bad thing. While it was now, more or less, an East/West conference, it was certainly illuminating in some ways. During the course of the Assembly it soon became clear that on a number of issues the 'experts' from the big powers had an identity of view. They included Professor Kozevnikov from the USSR, William Foster and a Rand Corporation man from the USA. In the Commission on the Disarmament Process with which I spent most of my time, they both asked the other to represent their point of view in their absence.

The Assembly met in Accra from 21 to 28 June. It is difficult even now to assess its importance, how far it could be called successful. In many ways it was excellent. Nkrumah opened it with a notable speech and I am still not sure how much of it was written by Geoffrey Bing and how much by Nkrumah. The commissions worked hard and well and produced some admirable reports. There were receptions for delegates and a banquet at the Ambassador Hotel where most delegates were staying.

But behind all this there was a hell of a row. It all began a few days before the Assembly was due to open when Heinrich Buchbinder and I arrived in Accra. When I left London, John Collins was under the impression that as the original sponsor of the Assembly he would chair the plenary sessions and he asked me to ensure that. He himself was not due to arrive in Accra until early in the morning of the day on which it opened.

Shortly after we arrived, we were informed by Geoffrey Bing that in the view of Nkrumah it was not suitable that a conference in Africa should be chaired by a Christian minister. It was OK for John to chair the steering committee which was to be set up but he was unacceptable for the plenary sessions. This placed us in a tremendous quandary. Heinrich was of the opinion that the only thing we could do was to accept the inevitable.

Throughout the Assembly John Collins remained very sore about the way in which he had been demoted. Relations with the Ghanaian officials deteriorated rapidly and he never managed to get to Nkrumah himself. When we got to the point of discussing the future of the Assembly, things got even worse. It was agreed to establish a Continuing Committee with a secretariat in Accra and it was clear that Ghana was going to decide who would sit on it. John Collins and Heinrich Buchbinder were informed that one of them was acceptable, not both. By that time John was so angry that he let Heinrich's name go forward. But while Ghana had apparently decided to keep the Assembly under their control, they seemed also undecided about what and whom they wanted. So they approached both Sean MacBride and Seyid Mohammed El Fasi, Dean of the University of Rabat and a member of the Council of UNESCO, to chair the Continuing Committee. They eventually decided on El Fasi, but forgot to inform Sean of their decision!

The final list of the committee looked very good. There was El Fasi, Sean MacBride, Professor Candido Mendes de Almeida from Brazil, Dr Baffour from Kumasi, Heinrich Buchbinder, Dr Fuad Galal from the UAR, Dr Gikonyo Kiana from Kenya, Diwan Chaman Lall from India, Professor Ivan Supek from Yugoslavia and Dr Tabibi from Afghanistan. I attended its first meeting on the roof of the Ambassador Hotel. After that it only met once, in Sweden, just after the first Bi-Annual Conference of the International Confederation for Disarmament and Peace, established in 1963. It then spent most of its time arguing about whether it should join the Confederation which at least had two advantages over it – it met regularly, and it was active. The Accra Assembly never met again although on one occasion Sean MacBride and Professor Supek travelled all the way to Rabat for a meeting which had been cancelled.

The secretariat lived on in Accra and occasionally circulated papers. The secretary, Frank Boaten, travelled the world and attended ICDP conferences. An American publicist, Julie Medlock, attached herself to the secretariat and also sent out documents, but nothing was done. With the fall of Nkrumah, Frank Boaten was made head of the Ghanaian Foreign Office and the Accra Assembly died. Except for one week in June 1962 it had never really lived.

It was probably naive of us to have thought that it would be possible for us to keep such a conference firmly under our own control. We were entirely dependent on the Ghanaian Government for its financing. We knew too little about Ghanaian politics, let alone African politics. We had no clear idea of what we wanted from the Assembly, in terms of an ongoing organization. Maybe if a group of non-aligned states had been collected jointly to sponsor such an international, a more permanent and viable organization might have been created. As it was, the Accra Assembly lived and died with Nkrumah rule in Ghana.

After the London conference of September 1961, some of those who attended met briefly and discussed the possibility of establishing an International of non-aligned peace movements. At that time, in spite of the eruption of new movements, mainly nuclear disarmament movements, all over the world, it was decided to wait. This was probably partly because those associated with the European Federation were happy with the status quo. At Accra there were many delegates associated with old and new, non-aligned peace movements. They held two meetings, chaired by Dr Homer Jack, Executive Director of the American Committee for a Sane Nuclear Policy, to discuss, once again, the possibility of a new International of organizations for which the Accra Assembly, even if it survived, would not cater. This time there was strong pressure in favour of the project. It was agreed to ask the European Federation to call a conference for the purpose. But before the confederation could meet to consider the request, another large conference took place, this time in Moscow.

The Moscow Conference
This was a big jamboree affair, organized by the World Council of Peace. It was, in a sense, another East/West conference in so far as they made great efforts to persuade people from the peace movements in the West to attend, especially from the new movements. In this they were successful. Lord Russell and Canon Collins agreed to sponsor it. Kingsley Martin and Sydney Silverman attended it. Many of the delegations covered what is known as a 'broad spectrum' of opinion.

It enjoyed very considerable publicity in Britain, thanks to the Labour Party. For many years the party had religiously expelled members who sponsored or attended such conferences, since the World Council of Peace and most of its associated organizations were on the Labour Party list of proscribed organizations. It had also at one time prevented Labour MPs speaking on platforms with members of the Communist Party. However, during the late fifties and early sixties, these nursemaiding activities had declined. CND was never threatened with proscription, even after the Communist Party began to support it in 1960. Canon Collins and a number of other members of the party had cooperated on the 1961 Conference in London. Suddenly, however, they threatened to expel both Lord Russell and Canon John Collins.

It was a ridiculous and for them a dangerous action for it might even have re-united Lord Russell and Canon Collins against the Labour Party. The campaign and the committee cooperated in defying Transport House. The press and most of Britain saw the move as ludicrous. None of the sponsors and none of those intending to go to Moscow withdrew or resigned. Indeed, it probably encouraged a number of new delegates.

The party dithered and dathered. It forgot its threat to expel and accused Lord Russell of failing to pay his membership fee, which he promptly did. Some years later, of course, he tore up his party card at a meeting in Mahatma Gandhi Hall in London.

After this preliminary frolic the Moscow Conference went ahead, and revealed very clearly the existence of a new, widespread, non-aligned peace movement. A Minority Report was prepared by a number of delegates, including Kingsley Martin, Sydney Silverman, Claude Bourdet and many others from other countries. But the issuing of a Minority Statement was not the only subversive activity. Some delegations turned up with leaflets in Russian opposing the manufacture, possession, use and testing of nuclear weapons by all countries. This turned out to be less revolutionary than they hoped. They were courteously permitted to distribute them within the Conference, but not outside in the city of Moscow.

The World Council of Peace, having invited so heterogeneous a collection of people, obviously expected that there would be diversity. Indeed, that may well have been the aim of some within it who were bored with its monolithic approach. But while variety within the Conference was OK, outside in Moscow it was not permitted. Yet some of the delegates from the Committee of 100 and other similar groups and individuals from other countries were determined to raise the banner of dissent not only within the conference hall but outside in the streets of Moscow. Needless to say, the hard core of this group was in the British delegation. They planned a demonstration in Red Square, only a small one, with a banner and leaflets to distribute. Some of the British delegates were hotly opposed to the proposal, ranging from communists to Canon Collins, though the canon played little part in the discussion as he arrived only to make a 'keynote' speech and departed after a meeting with Khrushchev.

The delegates to the Conference, several thousands strong, already bemused with minority reports and leaflets in Russian, most of whom could not understand them, were then treated to the unexpected delight of heated meetings of the British delegation in the corridors and back corners of the conference hall. Kingsley Martin, who led the British delegation, took the chair at these meetings, in so far as it was possible to 'take a chair' in a corridor where there were no chairs. The British communists were outraged, indeed, more outraged than some members of the Praesidium and secretariat of the WCP. Eventually, as usual in such circumstances, it was agreed that if some people wanted to go and demonstrate in Red Square, they would do it. The inevitable was accepted. But also as usual, quite a lot of people went along to see what happened.

Naturally, after all that hoo-ha, the Soviets must have been forewarned of what was to come. The group of demonstrators arrived in Red Square and set up their banner. Almost immediately it was taken from them, and they were left there bannerless. But there were quite a lot of people circulating through the square who were interested in this brief and uncommon occurrence. They gathered around the foreigners and for several hours, with the help of one or two who spoke English, they stood around in groups arguing the toss about nuclear weapons, nuclear tests, disarmament, the cold war. Those who had insisted on their right to demonstrate though they had lost their banner were more than satisfied. Those who went along to watch also enjoyed the occasion. It was, of course, widely publicized around the world, especially in the Western Press, but not in *Pravda*.

The Oxford Conference
There was one other lead-in to the new International. A number of young people from peace movements and CNDs met that summer in a Quaker camp in the United States called Camp Sunnybrook. They came out very firmly in favour of a new International. Daniel Elwyn Jones who was one of the leaders of YCND in Britain was there and came home enthused with the idea. Gerry Hunnius and Dimitri Roussopoulos from the Canadian CND were also there and came through London on their way to Moscow armed with an equal enthusiasm. Gerry Hunnius returned to London and came as an observer to the meeting of the European Federation in London in September which discussed the requests from Accra, from Moscow, from Camp Sunnybrook, and from many other quarters that the Federation should organize a conference to establish a new International.

The London meeting was probably the most representative meeting the Federation had held since its inception in London and Frankfurt. True, the Kampf dem Atomtod was no longer there, and the Kampagne gegen Atomrüstung was dying. But in their place there was Andreas Buro of the German Easter-marchers, the Swedes, the Danes, the Yugoslavs, the French, the Irish, the Swiss, the British, of course, and an observer from Canada. The constitution was changed and the Easter marchers accepted, also the Irish. The proposal that CND should organize a conference to extend the Federation into a real International was accepted with little trouble. It was agreed to hold it in January 1963 in Oxford.

Only the presidents of the Federation were unhappy – I still don't quite know why. Canon Collins, and this was my second major disagreement with him, did not want an umbrella International which would include direct action groups and it was clearly impossible to exclude them. For the States, this would have meant the exclusion of the highly respected and dearly loved A. J. Muste. In many European countries the dominant organizations combined the roles of CND and the Committee of 100. They were indivisible.

But also, Heinrich Buchbinder, who was now a president (a Troika had been established for the presidency, John Collins,

Heinrich Buchbinder and Dr Heinz Kloppenburg from Germany), was really only interested in left political groups, operating on and through left parties and trade unions and he had no use for the new movements, like the Easter marchers. He thought they were politically naive and he would not accept my suggestion that an alliance would provide them with an opportunity for political education. However, the meeting, apart from its presidents, was fully in favour and, reluctantly, they had to agree. I set to work sending out invitations, arranging for accommodation and a place to meet in (Somerville College, Oxford) and the response was excellent.

However, before the Conference met, there was further trouble because the three presidents, without consulting the organizations invited, even those in the Federation, invited the World Council of Peace to send ten observers to the Conference. (In fact, Canon Collins did persuade the Council of CND to agree to an invitation to one observer, but no more.)

The presidents met in London in early December where they agreed to this, against strong objections from me. It is not very easy opposing three presidents altogether. Nevertheless, after the Oxford Conference had taken place and we had weathered all the difficulties, and the new International was born, Canon Collins told me that I had been right in one statement I had made – that the invitation to ten observers from the WCP would cause trouble. It certainly did.

Since the purpose of the new International was to provide an International for independent, non-aligned peace movements, new and old, and since the argument about the WCP observers revolved around that concept, it would be wise at this point to say a little about non-alignment and how it related to the Oxford Conference, to the new International, and to the problem of the WCP observers.

It was never our intention to establish an International of Western peace movements, as a counterpart to the World Council of Peace, which mainly catered for movements in the 'socialist' countries and those in the West cooperating with them and sharing their point of view. It was not to be an anti-communist replica of NATO, challenging the communist bloc. The movements which we invited to join the new International were independent in the sense that they were free to judge each issue, each development, the policies and actions of countries, big and small, and of the blocs, from an independent point of view, free to judge each on its merits. It was this independence of both blocs that had given the new CND movements an image which even the right-wing press had been forced to acknowledge.

For most of us the question of the observers from the WCP was not a matter of refusing to meet or talk with them. It was a matter of tact and tactics. It was going to be difficult enough to mix all these different sorts of peace-makers and pacifists, some of whom were deeply suspicious of each other, without adding as many as ten observers from the WCP. They would have been the largest delegation there (there were, so far as I remember, about eight Americans and seven Italians, but most organizations had sent only one or two people). They were quite happy to talk and meet with the people from the World Council of Peace after they had settled their business. But for the time wasted on interminable arguments and confusion, this might have been possible at Oxford. As it was, they met us eventually in London.

The Oxford Conference was notable for many reasons. It was held during one of those fortunately rare periods of bitter cold in Britain. The roads were icy. There was deep snow around the college and, owing to its lay-out, delegates had to plod from one house to another through the snow. The central heating broke down. British delegates used to the harsh primitiveness of British conditions suffered in comparative silence. The others, from the States, from Asia, from Africa, were voluble in complaining. Luckily, we established a bar, liberally supplied with whisky, which helped them to survive.

The cold outside and inside was countered also by the heat engendered by the invitation to the WCP observers. Owing to many protests, Canon Collins postponed their arrival until after the Conference had discussed the matter.

The row nearly wrecked the Conference. In between its normal sessions, late at night and early in the morning, delegates debated the matter. It didn't help that there was immense confusion about what Canon Collins had said to the WCP, what he had been asked to say, what they had said. The real problem was the way it was handled and the distrust that built up. A. J. Muste tried to get a consensus but on this occasion failed. 'Only five minutes more,' he said after a caucus of the US delegation, 'and I could have done it.' And one reason why more and more delegates opposed the admittance of the ten, was that unfortunately the whole issue came to be seen as deliberately disruptive, as a device to divide the Conference. Many delegates began to believe that CND was out to sabotage the Conference and the new International.

There was a sizeable CND delegation at the Conference, about half a dozen in all, including Canon Collins, Mrs Antoinette Pirie who supported his position, Ritchie Calder, Michael Mitchel Howard, Anthony Greenwood, Stuart Hall, and Daniel Elwyn Jones representing YCND and CUCND.

Daniel insisted on calling a meeting of the CND Delegation. It met and agreed that CND, in council and in conference, was entirely in favour of a non-aligned International. So it was agreed that, at the next plenary session of the Conference, statements should be made by Canon Collins for CND, and by Daniel for YCND, re-affirming the campaign's support for the new International. This was done. It improved the atmosphere.

The observers never reached Oxford. After the Conference a delegation from the new formed Confederation met them at the Russell Hotel in London. It was not a very happy meeting. They had certainly been roughly treated and it was not their fault that their visit had fallen on such stony ground.

But before that meeting took place, in a final, stormy session, the International Confederation for Disarmament and Peace was born. I said at the time that only an International which was desperately needed could have survived so difficult a birth. Kenneth Lee, of the Friends Peace Committee, did much to save the situation. He became chairman of the Continuing Committee, a task which required all his Quaker tolerance and reconciling talents.

ICDP continues to flourish, in spite of the financial problems which beset the non-aligned, whether States or movements. Most of the independent and active peace movements and groups in the world belong to it. Some, who had doubts about it in 1963, are back with it – Dr Kloppenburg is one of its six presidents; Heinrich Buchbinder is a member of its council. Canon Collins stayed out.

Once firmly established on its own feet, the new Confederation cooperated on a number of projects with the World Council of Peace, especially in the Stockholm Conference on Vietnam which we both sponsored with other Internationals. There is a great deal more understanding between us, which is not to suggest that major differences have disappeared. ICDP is freer to act and react to conflict situations, especially where the Soviet Union is involved, as in Czechoslovakia in August 1968. Its Bi-Annual Conference meeting in Llubljana, only two days after the Warsaw Pact Intervention, immediately condemned it. ICDP has continued to operate against Soviet action there. There are also enormous differences in methodology between many of our movements and most of theirs. Our people are the more radical, more activist; they are the orthodox.

The arguments I had with Canon Collins about the Oxford Conference and about the new Confederation wasn't a new difference of opinion. It was just a part of the argument about the sort of movement CND was and the sort of International required. He wanted a small, restricted group, like the European Federation against Nuclear Arms from which activist, direct action groups were excluded. He wanted small, high level East/West conferences rather than two cooperating and competing Internationals, each operating from very different points of view, but able to cooperate in spite of that.

After 1965, the rapid growth of peace movements and groups in response to the escalation of the war in Vietnam, both in the United States and elsewhere, produced an entirely new situation. Only an International able to cooperate with and contribute to a wide variety of organizations (many practising civil disobedience to a far greater extent than the DAC and the Committee of 100) could play a useful role or could survive – as ICDP did.

CND and Greece

In 1963 and 1964 CND and, to a greater extent, the Committee of 100 got involved in Greek politics. While this was one of the fringe activities of the movement, it received a great deal of publicity and, for a time, was extraordinarily effective. However, it also frightened off a number of our supporters for reasons which I have never been able to understand. It was a mixed blessing.

In 1963 it was Grigoris Lambrakis who was largely responsible for the links between the peace movements in Britain and in Greece. He was an independent Member of the Greek Parliament, supporting the Left Party. He was a doctor and had been a great athlete. He was loved throughout Greece and he had built a large independent peace movement in the country which, until then, had only a communist-aligned peace committee. Already he had adopted the CND symbol and it was mainly because he was seeking relations with CND and similar movements that he came as a delegate to the Oxford Conference in January 1963.

Grigoris Lambrakis returned to Britain again for the 1963 Easter March. He marched all the way from Aldermaston, carrying a banner 'ELLAS' and while the anarchists and the solidarity mob were holding their banner pole across Hyde Park Corner to hold up the march, he was laying a wreath on the statue of Byron nearby, for Byron was for him the symbol of British support for Greek independence.

In Greece, the peace movement was something more than an organization seeking peace and disarmament. It was also a campaign for human rights, for the right to demonstrate, to dissent, to speak freely, to vote freely, a campaign for the liberation of hundreds of prisoners in Greek prison camps, some of whom had been there for many years. And the Youth Movement that was set up called itself, first, the Committee of 100 and then, later, the Society for Nuclear Disarmament: Bertrand Russell. Either they knew nothing of the rows in Britain, or they ignored them. But to the Greek king and the Greek right wing, a large, independent peace movement with international links was a real threat. This is why they banned the march from Marathon to Athens which Lambrakis planned for 21 April 1963. It was clear that hundreds of thousands would join the march and some Committee of 100 and CND people had managed to get in for it, though those wearing CND badges had been turned back at the airport and the frontiers.

It was on 20 April, the eve of the march, that the Government acted. Police cordons were put on all the roads to Marathon to stop people getting there. On the morning of 21 April, ten thousand police turned out in Athens to try and prevent people reaching the assembly point for buses. Nearly a thousand were arrested ... the organizers claimed 1,300, the police 900. They were slapped and beaten both in the streets and at police stations. Later they were released without being charged.

But Lambrakis got through the cordons and reached Marathon. Protected by his parliamentary immunity (MPs could not be arrested) he marched on his own four miles from Marathon on the road to Athens, carrying the banner 'ELLAS' that he had taken earlier that year from Aldermaston to London.

That was the first Marathon March. On the following evening, in spite of the ban, 3,500 attended a meeting in a theatre in Athens. One of the speakers was Malcolm Macmillan, formerly Labour MP for the Western Isles, who had long associations with Greece.

The movement continued to grow and, as a result, Grigoris Lambrakis's life was threatened. Only a month after he had marched from Marathon, he went to a meeting in his constituency in Salonika. The hall was surrounded by members of a fascist organization. He asked for police protection. It was refused. As he left the hall after the meeting he was run down by a motorcycle combination and killed.

Immediately, the Centre Party accused the right-wing

▲ 11a Defeated but still there: the CND March at Blackpool in 1961, the year they lost the unilateralist resolution which they had won in 1960.

▼ 11b CND Annual Conference. On the platform: Olive Gibbs, John Collins, Peggy Duff, Richard Robinson (Treasurer), Antoinette Pirie and James Cameron.

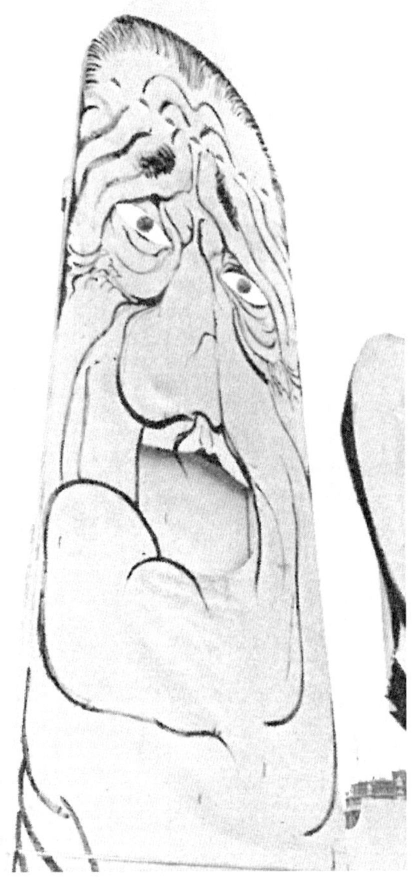

▲ 12a The glorious beginning: Mary Ure in Whitehall advertising the 'Star in our Eyes' show, 1959.

▲ 12b The bitter ending: Gerald Scarfe's twenty-foot-high L.B.J. puppet in Trafalgar Square, 1966.

government of responsibility for his death. Karamanlis, the Prime Minister, was, so they said, 'the moral perpetrator of Lambrakis's murder'. They accused the Government of using fascists to do their dirty work and of allowing the murderers to escape. The arrests were made by private citizens.

On 28 May another march took place in Athens ... but this was not banned. It was the funeral of Grigoris Lambrakis. David Boulton who represented CND said it was the greatest march he ever saw in his life. At least half a million took part. Here is how he described it in *Sanity*:

Athens was brought to a standstill. The building workers went on strike for the day, and everyone just left their desks and their benches. Throughout the morning, groups of people made their way to the cathedral carrying enormous flowered wreaths made up in the CND symbol. During the funeral procession itself, flowers and symbol wreaths were flung into the streets from the houses and shops along the route. Behind the coffin walked a dozen members or so of the Athens Committee of 100, carrying a plain silk banner decorated with the symbol.

The demonstration was a model of non-violence. This was non-violence arrived at by the route of experience rather than by theorizing. The most frequent slogans shouted were 'Long live Lambrakis' and 'No more blood.' When one demonstrator near me shouted what was translated as 'Death to the murderers', he was immediately hushed by those around him. The Greek left knows what violence means. They know that if they choose violence they choose the enemy's weapons. They know that it cannot be their road to victory.

David told me later that as the enormous procession moved out of the centre of Athens into the working-class areas, the police disappeared and left the ordinary people to mourn their dead. Years later, five years later, I went to Athens and was taken to the cemetery to see Lambrakis's grave. At its head was a plain grey stone into which the CND symbol had been cut. Months later I went back again, after the *coup d'état* and went again to the grave.

The stone and symbol were still there, untouched and unchanged, but the plate with his name at the foot of the grave had been broken. I hope that when freedom returns to Greece and I can go back again that stone will still be there with its symbol, and Lambrakis still remembered.

David Boulton came back to London and for a time there seemed nothing that the Committee and CND could do. Then a unique opportunity arose. King Paul and Queen Frederica of Greece were invited to London on a state visit. The King, and even more Queen Frederica, symbolized the repression of the Greek right. Here was a real occasion for demonstration. For the Committee it was easy. Swiftly they planned a march from Trafalgar Square to Buckingham Palace on the day of the arrival of the royal pair, 9 July. Naturally this posed tremendous problems for the police and the Government, for marches to the palace are not permitted, except on formal State occasions, by the Guards.

It was not so easy for CND. It was so much more conservative, so much more law-abiding. It was not a direct question of nuclear arms, but of solidarity with a similar movement which we had helped into being and which was suffering repression, of support for a fine man, sharing our beliefs, who had died for them. This had to be explained to campaigners, to the canon, to Council and Executive. However, it was finally agreed to organize a march on Sunday, 7 July, two days before the king and queen arrived, from Byron's statue at Hyde Park Corner, round the West End to Marble Arch. But it was also agreed to send a small delegation to leave a wreath, in the shape of the symbol, at Buckingham Palace.

The police were very unhappy, especially about the wreath, and as we waited in the park for the start of the march they tried very hard to persuade us to abandon that particular part of the demonstration. But we refused to be dissuaded and as the march went along Piccadilly, David Boulton and Canon Collins left it to cross Green Park with the wreath for delivery. They arrived at the palace and propped up the wreath against the railings. Almost immediately a small man wearing a bowler hat swept it up and took it into the palace. I wondered then and still wonder what they did with it.

The Committee, of course, had fewer inhibitions. All over London the single word 'Tyranny' appeared on walls. There is one still, as I write, on the low wall outside St Pancras Station facing the Town Hall. On the night of the demonstration every effort was made by the police to stop the demonstration reaching the palace. The first part in Trafalgar Square and Whitehall ended in a clash with the police. Then a number of demonstrators, led by George Clark, waving a newspaper and, so it was alleged, shouting 'Follow me', broke through into the park. George and a number of others were arrested, including Peter Moule, then secretary of the Committee, and Terry Chandler. That was one issue which became a *cause célèbre*. But there were eight others arrested – Donald Rooum, *Peace News'* cartoonist, Ronald Ede, Gregory Hill, John Apostolou, Colin Derwin, John and Ronald Ryall, and Richard Fear. That was another *cause célèbre*. George Clark was charged with incitement, Peter Moule and Terry Chandler with conspiracy, and all the others with possessing offensive weapons, namely, pieces of brick. Later those bricks became notorious.

Meanwhile, throughout the rest of the royal visit, demonstrations, more or less organized, continued. Wherever King Paul and his consort appeared there were demonstrators and, on one occasion, outside a theatre there was booing. The ever hostile press reported that the dear queen was booed, but they got the wrong queen.

There were four developments from this display of solidarity with the Greek peace movement and with Lambrakis.

First, there were the cases of George Clark, Peter Moule and Terry Chandler. George was sentenced to eighteen months on his charge of incitement. There were protests even from the national press and the *Daily Herald* pointed out that George had got a much larger sentence for a non-violent crime than some crimes of savage violence at about the same time. CND, in spite of its addiction to legality, was stirred to action. A letter signed by Canon Collins, Arthur Goss, Anthony Greenwood, Jacquetta Hawkes, Laurie Kershaw, Kingsley Martin, Michael Mitchel Howard, Malcolm Purdie and Jeremy Thorpe was sent to the press on 24 September. The issue it raised was certainly a matter of great importance for all organizations concerned with demonstrations:

> The issues raised by the sentence of eighteen months on Mr George Clark at the London Sessions on 10 September affect the personal liberties of us all. Mr Clark was convicted of 'inciting people to commit a nuisance by unlawfully obstructing the highway' during the demonstration at the time of the visit of the king and queen of Greece. The penalty for obstruction, if Mr Clark were proved to have incited people to it, would have been £2; the penalty for 'incitement' is 'at large', that is, it can be any term of weeks, months or years imprisonment that the court decides to inflict. On the basis of this sentence anyone who leads or takes a prominent part in any demonstration is liable to an indefinitely long sentence of imprisonment.

They appealed for funds to defray the costs of George's appeal. On 18 November George Clark won his appeal. The Appeal Court ruled that the jury which convicted him had been improperly directed. Meanwhile, of course, George who had not been released on bail pending the appeal had spent two months in Wormwood Scrubs.

This, for all organizations which run demonstrations, was a vitally important decision. But George's release was also linked, indirectly, with the second of the developments from the Greek demonstrations.

This concerned the charges against Donald Rooum and seven others for possessing offensive weapons, i.e., pieces of brick. In all these cases the only witnesses were policemen.

The first to be tried were Colin Derwin and the two Ryall brothers. They were convicted, found guilty, and fined £5. Their solicitor advised against appeal, on the grounds that the defendants could never win against three police witnesses. Later, Derwin was given a conditional discharge.

Donald Rooum, however, was made of tougher stuff. He was a Yorkshireman. He was tried on 8 August. The police claimed that they had found a piece of brick in his pocket. The only corroboration came from police. Furthermore, Donald produced an expert witness. He proved that although the brick which the police claimed to have found in his pocket was in a highly crumbling condition, there was no trace of brick dust in his pocket.

He was acquitted. *Peace News* openly accused the police officer concerned with framing the prisoner by planting the brick. No action was taken against the paper, but Donald Rooum took legal action against the police officer.

Meanwhile, the rest of the cases proceeded on their way. Richard Fear was tried on 11 September, and acquitted. But on 17 September John Apostolou was convicted and fined £10 with ten guineas costs. The State was obviously at sixes and sevens. It seems likely that John Apostolou suffered for his Greek name.

The law appeared to be in a complete state of 'assiness'. In October, charges against Ronald Ede and Gregory Hill were withdrawn. John Apostolou won his appeal. The sentence was quashed and he was awarded twenty-five guineas costs. On 13 November the State dropped its last defences. Rooum, Hill, Ede and Apostolou were offered nearly £1,600 in compensation and the Home Secretary announced an internal, private, investigation into the arrests.

There were widespread demands from Members of Parliament and from the *Daily Herald* and the *People* for a public inquiry but the Home Secretary refused. Then the news leaked out that Detective-Sergeant Harold Challenor, the senior officer responsible for the arrests, was a patient at Netherne Hospital at Coulsden, Surrey. A little later he was involved in a road accident when he was run down by a lorry. Superintendent Du Rose, who headed the police investigation, reported to the Home Secretary and to the Director of Public Prosecutions. In March 1964 Challenor, together with three other policemen, David Oakey, Frank Battes and Keith Goldsmith, were charged at Marlborough Street Magistrates' Court with conspiracy to pervert the course of justice. During the hearing evidence was presented not only on the planting of the bricks but of physical assault. The hearing was adjourned because Challenor was taken ill in court. A few weeks later all four were committed for trial at the Old Bailey. The Old Bailey trial was postponed because Challenor was still unfit and when, at last, it began, on 4 June, the principal medical officer at Brixton Prison stated that Challenor was suffering from paranoid schizophrenia. Of the other three, Battes was sentenced to three years imprisonment, Oakey and Goldsmith to four years, later reduced on appeal to three years.

Two major inquiries followed. The Chief Constable of Wolverhampton was appointed on 2 July to investigate fresh charges of corruption. The second, a public inquiry, the first to be held under the 1964 Police Act, was concerned with the circumstances in which it was possible for Challenor to remain on duty in spite of his rapidly worsening mental state. Great efforts were made to whitewash the police, but with little success. The release of a number of prisoners who had been arrested and charged by Challenor added to the public unease.

In sentencing the three policemen, Oakey, Battes and Goldsmith, Mr Justice Lawton said: 'Honest police officers are the buttress of society. But dishonest, perjured officers are like an infernal machine ticking away to the destruction of us all.' It is important to stress here that but for the arrest, during the demonstrations against the Greek royal pair, of men of the quality of Donald Rooum, Challenor's sanity might never have been questioned and his excesses might have continued for much longer.

The demonstration against the visit of the Greek royal pair received a great deal of publicity, most of it hostile. The effect on public opinion both within and outside the movement was disastrous, mainly because the queen had been involved. This was an astonishing revelation both for CND and for the committee.

Here was a movement which had challenged the establishment all along the roads from Aldermaston to London; at the Labour Party Conference and at innumerable trade union conferences; on the streets and squares in Central London. But on an issue which involved the deliberate murder of a fine man, dedicated to peace and democratic rights, they dived for cover, because the queen was involved.

Campaign Caravan Workshops, which was operating that summer down in deepest Dorset and wildest Wilts, discovered a new and virulent hostility to the Ban the Bomb movement. CND found that some of its oldest supporters, who had helped it for many years with donations, suddenly disappeared. Michael Howard and I spent an evening on the telephone to try to discover the reason why they had suddenly stopped sending their donations. One and all they gave the same answer: the Greek demonstrations and the queen.

It was partly, of course, that it was difficult to explain to people the importance of support for the Greek peace movement and the strong links between CND and the Committee and those who led the movement, at great risk to themselves, in Greece. Certainly the press did not help. But what was odd was that there was a lot of support for George Clark and the others charged at that time. This was an issue which people understood and to which they responded. But the danger, the threat, to George and the others was minimal compared with the dangers faced by those who led the movements for peace and civil rights in Greece. Eighteen months in prison for George was bad, of course, very bad. But there was no possibility of torture, of the sort of repression and fascist oppression which existed in Greece in 1964 and which was intensified after the *coup d'état*. His life was safe. His liberty was only temporarily threatened. I must confess that the failure of the movement as a whole to react to the murder of Lambrakis and all it implied was something I never forgave it.

While the reactions in Britain to the demonstrations were extremely mixed, in Greece they were wholly good. On 6 August, Hiroshima Day, about a month after the London demonstrations, the Society for Nuclear Disarmament: Bertrand Russell, planned a further demonstration. A number of Britons turned up for the occasion and were turned back at the borders, the airports, and the ports. They included David Boulton who decided the time had come for CND to adopt civil disobedience. He sat down in the airport and had to be carried into the plane which took him back to Britain. But a General Election followed on 2 November, and there was a slight swing to the left, sufficient to put the elder Papandreou into power. It is clear that the world reactions from the demonstrations against King Paul and Queen Frederica had played a considerable part in the swing.

The new government was a centre government. It was certainly not left-wing. Yet in Greece a centrist government was a tremendous achievement and one of the first results was that hundreds of prisoners were released. Some of them had been in prison for ten to twenty years. They were not released unconditionally, but on parole. If trouble started, or the government changed, they could be sent back immediately to their prison camps not merely with new sentences, but with the balance of the old as well. This is what happened in 1967. But in 1964, 1965 and until the *coup d'état*, they were free.

But meanwhile there were other consequences of the change. The driver of the motorcycle combination which had killed Grigoris Lambrakis, and his passenger, who had been held in custody, were actually charged and with them a group of thirty right-wingers, including some police, who were accused of complicity. They were all members of an ultra right-wing, fascist organization in Salonika, the leader of which had been convicted of wartime collaboration with the Nazis. Later, the film *Z* told the story of Lambrakis's murder and of the trial of his murderers. Later still, in May 1971, Christos Sartsetakis, the magistrate who challenged the secret service to ensure that justice was done, was himself arrested and charged with planning bomb explosions against the Junta.

Another sequel was that in 1965 and 1966 the Marathon Marches actually happened. They were enormous. In 1965 it was estimated that half a million took part. In 1966 it was as large, though the police prevented it passing through the centre of Athens and tried to prevent buses leaving for Marathon. On the last six kilometres, the march filled one side of a big dual carriageway. The other side of the carriageway was filled with an equal number of supporters who had come out from the city to join the march. Both years, the CND symbol was everywhere – on flags, on pennants, on banners, on badges, on brooches, even on eye-glasses. In 1966 a number of Labour MPs took part – Reg Freeson, Stan Orme, Russ and Anne Kerr and many others from Britain.

'Please be careful,' the Foreign Office told Stan Orme. 'We are trying to sell the Greek Government a nuclear reactor.'

I went to Athens on the eve of the *coup d'état*, in the early summer of 1967. By that time I had left CND and was working for the International Confederation. Before I arrived there the march from Marathon had been banned, but I received a cable saying 'Please come', so I went, pausing in Rome for an ecstatic demonstration against the war in Vietnam in a Piazza. Once again in Greece there was a political crisis beating up. The king had succeeded in destroying the centre government. There was to be a General Election. The king was trying, with the right, to avoid a Papandreou victory in the election. Shortly after my arrival I went to what turned out to be probably the last demonstration in Athens, at the university. There were hundreds of police around the University Square, uniformed and plainclothed. The only demonstration since then took place recently when they buried the elder Papandreou.

I have never before or since been in a city in which there was such a sense of fear, of ominous expectation of the worst to come. Saigon has something of the same atmosphere but there the worst has come. In Athens in April 1967 it was still to come, but everyone knew it. Everyone on the left knew that somehow, sometime, the king or the right or the army, or all three together, would combine to maintain the status quo, to put out the lights, to stifle democracy in Greece. It wasn't a question of 'Yes, they will' or 'No, they won't'. It was a question of when.

People were frightened. Fear is not something to be ashamed of in a country like Greece. Fear is a badge of courage for people who go on doing what they feel they must, in spite of the danger, in spite of their fear.

There was no march. First it was banned by the Government, and the ban was accepted when the election was announced because according to the constitution there can be no demonstrations during an election period. They fought for the constitution and would not challenge it. So, instead, we walked up to the Hill of Pyx, where Pericles argued with the Athenians, and read a statement about freedom and peace in Greece and in

Vietnam. It was typical of our Greek friends that at that stage of their history they were as concerned about the rights of the people of Vietnam as their own.

Then there was a public meeting at which the leaders of the foreign delegations spoke about peace, about Greece, about Vietnam. Tariq Ali brought a message from Bertrand Russell and with his usual ebullience promised that Russell would come for the postponed march after the election which they hoped to hold but never did. Thich Nhat Hanh, the Buddhist monk, talked about Vietnam. I spoke about Lambrakis, about the links between Greece and Britain, the links between Greece and Vietnam.

When the meeting was over, as we went out into the street, the police were waiting and watching in squads all around the hall. There is something about police where they represent a fascist ideology that chills the marrow of one's bones. I have seen them in Northern Ireland, I have seen them in France, in Italy. I have read or heard of them in the States. I have seen them in Japan. This is not to say that in this guise and under that flag they don't exist in many other countries, east and west. But they were never so grey-faced, so threatening as I saw them that night in Athens.

I left Athens on the Tuesday, two days before the *coup d'état.*

In the autumn of 1967 I went back, carefully hidden in a group of eighty travel agents. I traipsed around Athens and went to Crete, and drove around the Peloponnesus, and stayed in the most luxurious hotel I have ever known in Vouliagmeni up the coast from Athens and, briefly, in between, spent a few hours seeing the few friends I had come to see.

There is very little one can do about it. Resign from the Labour Party, as I did, on the issue of their failure to denounce the Junta, for their persistent support for the United States in Vietnam. One can send occasional letters by devious means. One can go to an occasional demonstration.

That is why I am sure that whatever we did in CND and in the Committee, which did much more, we were right to do it. Peace is not a negative state of existence, an absence of arms, nuclear and conventional. It is more than the practice of nonviolence or the absence of war. Peace and the right to liberty and the pursuit of happiness, as Thomas Jefferson wrote into the American Declaration of Independence, which Ho Chi Minh rewrote into the Vietnamese Declaration of Independence, are indivisible. The Greeks (and the Vietnamese, and the Czechs) have just as much right to choose their own government, reject their own king, to stay out of prison camps, to be free from torture whatever side they may live of an arbitrary line drawn at Yalta or agreed between Churchill and Stalin.

The Greeks are condemned for the reasons which Nkrumah outlined in his speech at the Accra Assembly, quoting the attitude of the great powers:

> It is true that we revolutionized our social systems. It is true that some of us executed our kings and emperors in the name of liberty, but this is a luxury to which we were entitled and to which you are not. You must bear all your present misfortunes because otherwise you will upset the balance of power on which we depend for our safety.

What's Left . . . ?

What's Left ... ?

... of the humanitarian causes? They're still there. Lots of people continue to give money for cancer research, for mental health, for disasters – floods and earthquakes, for starving Biafrans or long-suffering Vietnamese. Lots of top people will sign appeals and letters to *The Times.* The stage army of the good is still on the march. This is just as well because most government aid either has strings attached or is for guns.

Look at the curious aid system in South Vietnam. The United States sends in lots of luxury and semi-luxury goods which are bought by the Vietnamese bourgeoisie in the cities at high prices. The proceeds plus import taxes and customs duties, plus an artificially low rate of exchange for the dollar, balances the South Vietnamese budget, seventy per cent of which is used for the war. So most of the aid pays for the war and thereby increases the miseries of the peasants who cannot afford and don't want motor scooters anyway.

Unfortunately, it is much easier to collect money for aid to suffering than it is to force through political decisions which would eradicate the suffering. Charity is free, but political change is severely rationed. Indeed, it could be said that to a certain extent charity syphons off the pressures on governments. It provides a respectable, non-political means to react to man's inhumanity to man. It is difficult to deny, for instance, that much of the voluntary aid in South Vietnam becomes, intrinsically, a part of the American presence, of the intervention – and a number of the people involved, like Don Luce of International Voluntary Services, have resigned for that reason.

In Britain, the law which insists that charities must be nonpolitical reinforces the dichotomy. The irony of the situation could be clearly seen during the Biafran war. Thousands of goodhearted Britons gave money to send food for starving women and children while at the same time the British government was sending arms to the Federal Government which were used to create more starvation and suffering. Yet if organizations like Oxfam publicly criticized government policies or ran campaigns against them they would lose their charitable status.

I do not question for one moment that aid should ignore differences of race, nationality or creed. Discrimination of that sort is a form of proselytizing. But it is totally illogical that organizations which provide aid for human suffering created by governments should be prohibited from condemning the policies which cause that suffering and from seeking to change them. Charity should not be blind-folded, like Justice – but she certainly needs a sword!

What's left ...
... of St Pancras and Camden? The Council goes on meeting ten times a year in that grim and undistinguished rectangular block opposite the Victorian excesses of St Pancras station and, no doubt, committees continue to meet nightly. Recently I met one of the Chief Officers whom I had not seen since the Conservatives took over control. 'How goes it?' I asked. 'Much the same,' he replied. 'Things have changed very little.' True, very few people in the borough will have noticed much difference, for the powers of a local council are so circumscribed by the policies of the national government, and the policies of national governments, whether Labour or Tory, are so nearly identical that it really doesn't make mnch difference who's in or who's out at the Town Hall.

If democracy is supposed to allow people to participate in government and in decision making, there is really very little of it left in Britain. Here is a good example – in one St Pancras election Labour was returned with a large majority on a swing far greater than the national swing, on a promise to get rid of a hated differential rent scheme. Then they discovered that it simply wasn't possible to get rid of the scheme except by reducing a great many rents and that would mean a surcharge, even though a majority of the local people had voted against the scheme. So councillors have become rather inexperienced social workers in the areas they represent and public relations officers for their parties. They have no real powers and neither have the people they represent.

Would it be possible to recreate some degree of local autonomy? To give people some real say in what goes on in their areas? To do that, what matters is not the process of election, which means very little when there is no real choice, but the right of people to veto, when roused. If local communities had the right, like villages in North Vietnam, to recall their elected committees and sack them, that would be a very healthy revolution at least at the local level. And that is probably the best place to start, for the hope of starting any sort of revolution at the top is very dim indeed.

What's left ...
... of the Left? That's a very thorny question. Flying around the world as I do nowadays it seems to me when I come back to Britain that there's less Left here in Britain than anywhere else in the world.

So far as the Left in the Labour Party is concerned I don't want to be unkind to my many old friends with whose dilemmas I heartily sympathize, but one must start by recognizing the unpalatable fact that even in the past the Left rarely mustered any spectacular victories.

In the twenties they failed to stop the party and the TUC selling out on the General Strike. In the thirties they failed to stop the Labour Government selling out in 1931, and later in Spain. In the forties they failed to stop the Labour Government cooling off on socialism – though Aneurin Bevan successfully rescued nationalization of steel by threatening to resign – and they failed to keep Ernie Bevin out of the cold war. In the fifties the Bevanites failed to win a single significant policy victory. In the sixties – well, enough of that!

Yet it seems to me that the position now in the seventies is far worse than it has ever been. At least in those earlier days the Left sometimes looked capable of winning. In the thirties Cripps, Nye and George Strauss succeeded in changing the constitution so that constituency party representatives got onto the NEC and for a brief period Lansbury was actually the leader of the party, though Ernie Bevin soon put paid to that. In the forties, as I said, they won on steel. In the fifties, at least as long as Nye was there, there was a credible alternative leadership. But not now. Who would bother to change Wilson, even after the shambles of the 1970 election, for Callaghan, or George Brown, or Roy Jenkins? And there is no one among the genuine Left who even pretends to be an alternative or who has any chance.

Secondly, the divorce between the movement and the Parliamentary Labour Party has become a chasm and is now so complete that conference is an utter mockery and the NEC is powerless. Yet both the conference and the congress of the TUC go on passing resolutions as if they were still valid, though they know very well that the Parliamentary Party will ignore them. And the Left goes on planning left-wing resolutions though they must know that even if they were passed they would be worthless. So conferences remain a brief and unimportant source of embarrassment for ministers and ex-ministers but so many of the Left have gone that even now they can always get the standing ovation they need for their public images.

The NEC remains dominated by the right and even if it wasn't it would be just as impotent. So recently, the *Tribune* group have been trying to unseat ministers whom in the fifties they got elected on to it. But the disease cannot be cured by electing a new NEC, for the new would be just as hamstrung as the old. Indeed there has been a considerable swing to the left in the leadership of the unions but it hasn't made much difference – yet. And lately, the right (Denis Healey) has even started to win seats in the Constituency section of the NEC, long a Left stronghold.

Thirdly, since the real stumbling block is the Parliamentary Labour Party, the only organization which really has the power to veto government or opposition policies, and since all candidates are chosen by local parties, one simple way out would be to elect new candidates, new MPs. The Bevanites thought of that one. The rejection of some lip-serving MPs would be an excellent tonic for democracy in Britain. But this is not so easy as it sounds. It has been tried in a number of places but has rarely worked. During the twenty years and more in which I worked in and around the Labour Party very few sitting MPs were rejected and when they were it was usually for old age, alcoholism or illness – though S. O. Davies showed the Party in Merthyr that old age was tougher than they thought!

The last reason is crucial – it was the Left which was running the government from 1964 to 1970. Harold Wilson resigned with Aneurin Bevan in 1951. Nearly all the old stars of the Bevanite movement were leading ministers. The new parliamentary Left are mainly the boys from the old Bevanite Second XI and maybe it is partly their links with and loyalty to the old First XI which helps to make them so ineffective. These are the people who in the early fifties manned the *Tribune* brains trusts, moved the resolutions for the Left at conferences, won the seats on the NEC. To the young who cannot remember the early fifties they may look pretty dreadful, but to those of us who are old enough to remember, they look ghastly. And although there are good men and women there, a new credibility gap has been created. How can we be sure that even if the new Left were elected to the leadership they would be any better than the old?

Hardly any of them talk any longer of fundamental changes in society. They no longer have revolutionary aims. Most of them can hardly be called radicals. They are good 'liberals' all and I have begun to understand why the great 'liberals' in the United States get presented with pigs' heads, for there is nothing so dangerous for the Left as good 'liberals'. In America, they escalated the war in Vietnam and would still be supporting it if the US had won. In Britain, the old Bevanite Left collaborated in British support for the war, even if the front runners were hardened cold warriors like Michael Stewart, George Brown and Denis Healey.

Raymond Barrillon, writing in *Le Monde* about the French Communist Party and its reactions to the student and workers risings in May and June 1968, recognized that the party had lost the revolutionary aims it still claimed to possess. 'The originality of the communist course', he wrote, 'is that it has combined going off with the train while remaining on the platform.' But the Labour

Party in Britain and the social democratic parties in Europe no longer even pretend to be catching the train. They are too busy repainting the station and refurbishing the waiting-rooms.

The disease is an epidemic which has swept through western Europe. The aim is to run capitalism a little more efficiently, a little more humanely, than the conservatives. It is a sort of softshoe capitalism. In Britain the Left no longer talks of winning the commanding heights of the economy, which was Nye's aim. They have even tried to survive by throwing away the hard-won rights of workers and unions, gained under the scourge of unemployment and repression in the days when Aneurin Bevan was walking the Welsh valleys dreaming of power to put things right, and Harold Wilson was being photographed in knickerbockers outside 10 Downing Street.

Certainly the final changes in the party and its aims were rooted in the desire to win power, after almost a decade in opposition, and to hold it. No one would quarrel with the contention that a party must win power to implement its aims. But the principles inspiring its aims should have dictated its decisions in power and, on the contrary, they have been forgotten. It is not only that they have abandoned any attempt radically to alter society in Britain; what is worse is that they have accepted the values of a system which according to their history and traditions they should be challenging. It is sad now to remember the optimism of 1945 when, after all the long drawn out horrors of the thirties and the war, after the culminating terror of the atomic bombs on Hiroshima and Nagasaki, there was a new world coming up. The new world never grew up.

Recently I met two old friends in St Pancras Labour Party whom I had not seen for a long time – working-class people from a solid working-class area of the borough. It was during those days just before the June 1970 election when the polls had convinced us all that Labour would win.

'We go on working in the party,' they told me, 'but we don't have any faith in it. We think that the Labour Party has now become the Tory Party and soon the Tory Party will disappear. Then, sometime in the future, a new socialist party will emerge.' 'I hope you may be right,' I told them, 'I hope I live to see it.' A few weeks later, the Tories won the election.

What's left ...
... of CND? It started, or rather they started, for there were many of them, in the late fifties in response to the escalation in nuclear testing and in the quantity and quality of nuclear weapons. They were fed by crises that threatened us with nuclear annihilation, from Berlin to Cuba. The campaigns spread across the world partly because fall-out does not discriminate between countries and partly because in the new small world in which we live campaigns tend to proliferate as rapidly as weapons and wars. Where are they now? Quite a lot of them are dead – in Canada, in Scandinavia, in Australia. Others have widened their aims to new concerns – in the United States, in Germany, in France. CND persists in Britain – but the CNDs no longer dominate the peace movements or the Left.

You could blame it on frustration. They won mass support for what looked like a simple, single issue and, in the absence of any real progress except in general awareness of the nuclear danger and one partial test ban treaty, most of them declined or died. That is the simple answer, but not the only answer. The trouble is and was that the simple moral issue to which the campaigns clung as the source of all evil was a symptom rather than a cause. The invention and development of nuclear weapons coincided with and was fed by a similar escalation in the cold war. But it was the cold war which enlarged the danger and made the weapons so threatening. The two were indivisibly linked. CND in Britain partly recognized this when it extended its aims from 'Ban the British Bomb' to 'Ban the Blocs', but not wholly, for the main reason for the change was ethical. There was little political recognition that the bombs were the children of the blocs, that the blocs were the offspring of the cold war, and that the cold war was sustained and nourished by political systems, especially in the West, but also in the East. It is not surprising, therefore, that frustration erupted. There were too many people in CND who disliked and distrusted politics and too few with either the will or the capacity to transform the movement into a different and more political entity.

So they remained, especially in Britain, issue-orientated campaigns, concerned only with nuclear disarmament. CND agreed to oppose chemical and biological weapons because, like nuclear weapons, they are indiscriminate. But for anything else it did it insisted on providing a link with the issue of nuclear war. So they excused their involvement in protest against the war in Vietnam by the danger of a nuclear world war in Indo-China – as if, but for that, it would have been acceptable.

It is not surprising that other issues ousted the CNDs from their dominant position in the peace movements and on the Left. In Britain, and even more abroad, the war in Vietnam superseded the Bomb in public interest and concern. Here, because the methods of the US army are so dreadful, the protest was basically rooted in a moral revulsion, similar in quality to that which had brought thousands out on to the Aldermaston marches. But there was one fundamental difference.

Many of the students and academics who came into the protest movements against the war realized that it was the American system which had to be challenged. They recognized the war not as a single issue, an unfortunate aberration, but as an extreme example of American ruthlessness in seeking to maintain and increase its military and economic domination of much of the world. And they did not underestimate their task. 'We may stop the seventh war from now,' wrote Carl Oglesby, one of the early Presidents of Students for a Democratic Society. There has developed in the United States a sharp confrontation between the State and dissenters, especially the young. This could be pre-revolutionary, for they certainly aim to change the system; or it could be pre-fascist, if the reactions of the 'silent majority' grow more repressive, authoritarian, and violent. But at least they avoided CND's great mistake – that it was a simple matter of a short, brisk campaign.

There have been similar, though slightly different, developments in Western Europe. Many of the young people who inspired and organized the Vietnam campaigns in the mid-sixties moved from a passionate opposition to the war to an examination of the societies which created and condoned the war. They extended their field of operations to much wider issues. In a sense, they responded to Castro's call for the creation of more and more Vietnams, but the liberation they sought was not in the Third World but in the highly developed industrialized societies of the affluent West.

France is a good example. Le Comité National pour le Vietnam, an intensely militant and largely young organization, disappeared during the 'events' of May and June 1968 and was never seen again. They moved from revolution in Vietnam to revolution at home. The students and teachers got themselves involved in long, far-ranging discussions about education and the functions of a university or school. The young workers of Citroen and Renault at Boulogne-Billancourt and Flins talked and argued about management and participation, *co-gestion* and *auto-gestion*. The journalists and technicians in ORTF, in radio and television, stayed out on strike far longer than anyone else at grave risk to their jobs in a vain attempt to achieve impartiality on the air – in a country where the mass media are supposed to be free. Wages, hours of work, holidays, were not the important issues, though the CGT and the Communist Party tried to make them so.

The biggest tragedy is that the one experiment which seemed to offer most hope of progress and one in which again the young played a large part – in Czechoslovakia – was smothered. The attempted reformation there was the most important and the most far-reaching of all the developments in industrialized countries. There was the same ebullience and a much closer alliance between students, intellectuals and workers. Many older people who had criticized the long hair and outlandish dress of the young changed their minds when they saw them sitting in front of the Russian tanks. The Unions supported the student strikes and the factories backed the opposition of writers and journalists to censorship. In strangling the Czechoslovak reformation at birth, or during early childhood, the Soviet Union and its allies are certainly as guilty as the United States of crimes against liberation, for they succeeded in repressing the Czechs and Slovaks while Johnson and Nixon have not yet won in Vietnam, nor in the United States.

For most of the students, the old left parties, the social democrats and the communists, offer no attractions, though there are one or two exceptions, as in Chile. The degeneration of social democracy, the ossification of most communist parties, has killed all faith in progress that way. Elections all too often offer unspeakable choices between men of the same colour and quality. But neither have peace and disarmament returned to the centre of the stage. It is not that people are against peace or that they oppose disarmament. They are seen as something a long way away, unrealistic in present circumstances. They continue to have authority, but little audience. The trouble, I think, lies in this. At the end of the fifties people saw co-existence and *détente* as alternatives to nuclear annihilation. At the end of the sixties, people (and especially the young) see them as alternatives to revolution and change. In 1960 when Khrushchev sabotaged the Paris Summit Meeting (either because of the U2 overflights, or because he lost support for co-existence in Moscow), we were devastated. This was seen as a catastrophe which brought war closer. Nowadays when the two big super-powers meet, many dive for cover. They see such meetings as a collaboration at the expense of the Third World, of small countries, like Greece and Czechoslovakia, and of individuals repressed both in the East and in the West.

Disarmament has degenerated into controlled rearmament which perpetuates the hegemonies of the two Great Powers. The Non-Proliferation Treaty did nothing to restrict their stockpiles of nuclear weapons and, more recently, faithful Britain has been assisting the United States in continuing the use of chemical weapons in Vietnam by tabling a treaty at Geneva which concerns only biological weapons and by excluding CS gas from its interpretation of the 1925 Geneva Protocol. Co-existence between the USSR and the US continues to increase. There remains the over-riding danger that such co-existence could leave one or both free to act against China, against revolution and liberation in the Third World or within their own spheres of influence.

What can the campaigns do? They can wrap themselves up in

their single issues and in the purity of their pacifist concerns, ignoring the essential links between repression and arms, between imperialisms and the arms race, between liberation, revolution, and peace. If so, they will, no doubt, survive and do good work, mounting small campaigns on single issues in Ruislip, Porton or Nancecuke. But, in my view, this is a form of escapism, like peace research. If we want to be an integral part of a world movement seeking a dual liberation – of the oppressed of the Third World, and of the repressed of the developed world, we have to relate to that, for wars will cease and disarmament will become a practical possibility only in the context of these two liberations. But as long as the dual repressions continue, new movements will arise and it may be possible that radical change will come, not through orthodox organizations with carefully worked out programmes and ideologies, but from a mass refusal to conform, even by the technocrats who are the new proletariat of industrialized societies. It was, after all, a mass refusal by Vietnamese peasants to conform that eventually led more Americans than ever before to question the nature of their own society.

Such movements may be very uncomfortable to live with. Their rhetoric may offend our sensibilities, their anarchism our sense of order, and they will not always be non-violent. But while it may be sad for the CNDs to see their black and white symbol which originally meant nuclear disarmament moving out of their hands as the symbol of new protests and with other marchers, it is still concerned with the death of man and the safety of the unborn child.

When the 7,000 people arrested in Washington during the protests against the war in Vietnam stood in the RFK Stadium into which they were herded in the form of a giant CND symbol, where were the thousands who sat in Trafalgar Square ten years earlier? When the men of the 101st Airborne Division of the US Army carved out a gigantic CND symbol on the scarred soil of Vietnam with a bulldozer, where were the hundreds of thousands who marched from Aldermaston?

'No man,' wrote John Donne, 'is an island.' That goes for CNDs too.

Index